9/14/75

St. Louis Community College

Library

5801 Wilson Avenue
St. Louis, Missouri 63110

THE STRUCTURE OF *Leaves of Grass*

THE STRUCTURE OF
Leaves of Grass

by Thomas Edward Crawley

UNIVERSITY OF TEXAS PRESS · AUSTIN & LONDON

International Standard Book Number 0–292–70086–5
Library of Congress Catalog Number 78–139519
© 1970 by Thomas Edward Crawley
Printed by The University of Texas Printing Division, Austin
Bound by Universal Bookbindery, Inc., San Antonio

TO
ROBERTA ARMISTEAD CRAWLEY
*for never having said,
"I suffer'd, I was there."*

PREFACE

At one point in "Song of Myself" the friendly poet takes his reader aside with these words, "This hour I tell things in confidence, / I might not tell everyone, but I will tell you." With each friendly reader I take such a Whitmanian liberty at the very start. I believe that anyone who finds anything of value in this study will be interested in the confidences shared here.

In 1954, during graduate-school days at the University of North Carolina, it was my good fortune to enroll in a Whitman seminar conducted by Professor Floyd Stovall. The inception of this study was a paper prepared for that seminar. At Professor Stovall's suggestion that paper was expanded and supplemented during the following year, and the book as it now stands, except for revisions of a routine and technical nature and for the incorporation of relevant scholarship of the last ten years, was completed and the manuscript submitted to him, chapter by chapter, in the late spring and early summer of 1955. Upon my departure from Chapel Hill in July of 1955 I suffered this product of twelve stimulating and intellectually eventful months to be laid aside and have just returned to it after the swift passage of a little more than a decade.

I am cheered to find that my study has stood this very limited test of time. The large body of Whitman scholarship produced during the last ten years has necessitated no major changes and has in many instances strengthened particular aspects of my approach and interpretation. For this strengthening I am grateful.

The essay with which this study originated was entitled "A Structural Analysis of *Leaves of Grass*." That essay, after a few additions and revisions, has become Chapter IV, as it appears in the following pages, and has provided the nucleus for Chapter III, "The Christ-Symbol in *Leaves of Grass*." With apologies to Whitman, it must be admitted that in the process of composition Poe's technique of first establishing in mind the climax or highest point of interest and then building toward it was unconsciously utilized. As the title implies, "A Structural Analysis of *Leaves of Grass*" is the *crux*, or as Whitman might say the *crest*, of this entire study. "The Christ-Symbol in *Leaves of Grass*" in its present form was the second chapter written; however, it should be remembered that the essence of this chapter was an important part of the original essay, indeed it was the key to the entire concept of structure, just as it is in this expanded interpretation.

The awareness of an effective unifying principle at work in *Leaves of Grass* and of the ripeness of its fruition in 1881 led naturally to unanswered questions regarding its origin and operation. The resultant examination of the first seven editions of *Leaves of Grass* supplied illuminating hints, if not always conclusive answers. The facts and interpretations derived from this examination are the substance of Chapter V, "The Evolution of *Leaves of Grass*," the third chapter written. The organization of this complex chapter was largely determined by its direct, natal relationship to "A Structural Analysis of *Leaves of Grass*," and a grasp of its full significance is dependent upon an acquaintance with that preceding chapter.

Chapter II, "Whitman's Organic Principle and Poet-Prophet," the fourth chapter written, is primarily introductory in function and makes no pretense to originality or inclusiveness. It is an attempt to restate certain fundamentals of Whitman's poetic theory and practice in terms particularly applicable to the immediate problems of this study. Finally, Chapter I, "Introduction," is something of a reminiscence of the thought and experience precipitating such critical analysis.

In preparing for and executing this project I have focused my attention upon primary materials, for the following reasons. Even the casual student of American literature is aware of the difficulty involved in extricating *Leaves of Grass* from its biographical and sociological entanglements, real or fancied, and in observing it in that reasonable isolation which every serious work of art deserves. The unique nature of the work itself, no less than the unique nature of Walt Whitman the man, invites this particular kind of entanglement and abuse. I have been unable to discover a single analysis of *Leaves of Grass* or of its growth that has consistently focused upon the work itself and excluded all except the most objective biographical fact and interpretation, as such criticism should do. Granted, there is an obvious and significant relationship between the Walt of *Leaves of Grass* and Walter Whitman the man; nevertheless, deliberately or unwittingly to confuse the two in either biography or criticism results in an injustice to both, as the present state of Whitman scholarship abundantly proves. To my knowledge there is no so-called study of the structure or growth of the book that does not prove to be primarily a study of the complications or growth of the man. Without denying the importance of biographical and psychological considerations in the criticism of *Leaves of Grass* in particular, this study is the result of an attempt to subordinate them at all times to considerations of the poem itself. Such an attempt is long overdue and has, I believe, proved rewarding.

Although the work that follows has been carefully documented, I would like to comment briefly and generally on a few important works relating to Chapters III, IV, and V, the major chapters of this study. First of all, I would like to acknowledge my indebtedness to Basil de Selincourt's *Walt Whitman: A Critical Study* and to Floyd Stovall's "Main Drifts in Whitman's Poetry." These two works have been invaluable in their suggestiveness. The former asserts that there is a unifying principle or spirit in *Leaves of Grass,* but does not attempt to define it or to trace it throughout the work. I have attempted to do both. In addition, Selincourt's remarks regarding relationships between "poem clusters," though brief and sometimes superficial, suggested a technique which has paid off handsomely. Stovall's essay has proved stimulating in pointing up a thought progression in *Leaves of Grass* strikingly parallel to major chronological developments in both the man and the successive editions of the book. Irving C. Story's "The Structural Pattern of *Leaves of Grass,*" did not become available to me until a year after Chapter IV was completed. Although the article is comparatively brief, I have found in it parallels which prove reassuring.

There are three early studies touching on the problem reviewed in Chapter V, "The Evolution of *Leaves of Grass.*" The first is Oscar Lovell Triggs's "The Growth of *Leaves of Grass.*" This short essay is inadequate; Triggs knew all the editions thoroughly, but he does not discuss them in detail and offers little critical comment. Short discussions by C. J. Furness in *Walt Whitman's Workshop* and by W. S. Kennedy in *The Fight of a Book for the World* do little more than indicate the need for an extensive investigation of the various editions. Killis Campbell's "The Evolution of Whitman as Artist," as the title implies, places emphasis on the nature of the poet's development rather than on the book itself. Sculley Bradley's "The Problem of a Variorum Edition of Whitman's *Leaves of Grass*" has proved helpful in anticipating the difficulties involved in such a work. Finally, the most interesting discussion of the evolution of the book is Frederik Schyberg's chapter "*Leaves of Grass,* 1855–89" in his biography of Whitman. My discussion of the matter was written prior to my reading of this book and none of my findings or conclusions have been altered as a result of that reading. Schyberg interprets his findings (which, as far as they go, are similar to those in this study) in biographical terms with somewhat different results. The precise psychological complications which I have attempted to minimize were evidently his meat and drink—the determining factors in his original and interesting observation. The two studies, Schyberg's and my own, offer a striking contrast in point of view and approach.

Any expression of gratitude on my part should begin with an acknowledgment of the many unnamed friends and associates who have through their wisdom sharpened my insights or through their kindness lightened my labors.

In expressing my indebtedness to Professor Stovall I hardly know where to start. My fellow graduate students would have me begin with a tribute to his brilliance and good sense in the lecture hall and seminar room; my wife, with a tribute to his warmth and understanding as a friend. My own inclination is to turn to a passage from his beloved Emerson. "The office of the scholar is to cheer, to raise, and to guide men by showing them facts amidst appearances." This office, both private and public, Professor Stovall has performed "justly, skillfully, and magnanimously." As for this book in particular, his was the inspiration, the patience, and the guidance that made it possible. If in any small way it cheers or raises or guides, it is to the extent that I have approached the ideal which he projected; where it fails in these offices, that failure I gladly accept, grateful for the experience of having tried.

I am similarly indebted to Professor Carroll Hollis, who has been altogether gracious in advising and aiding me during these final months of revision and proofreading. I am most appreciative of the quick encouragement he gave when it was sorely needed and of his continuing interest and helpfulness.

I am deeply grateful to the president and Board of Trustees of Hampden-Sydney College for making available to me the time and funds necessary for the completion of this project and to the Board of Christian Education of the Presbyterian Church in the United States for a generous research grant.

Above all I am grateful for the patience, understanding, and tireless help of my wife, to whom this book is dedicated with admiration and affection.

THOMAS EDWARD CRAWLEY

CONTENTS

THE STRUCTURE OF *Leaves of Grass*

CHAPTER I

Introduction

This study of the structure of *Leaves of Grass* is the result of two significant personal experiences: first, that of reading Whitman's poem carefully, but somewhat at random, viewing *Leaves of Grass* as little more than a handy one-volume edition of the collected lyrics of the poet, related, yes, and grouped broadly, according to subject matter, but in no particularly significant way; second, that of reading *Leaves of Grass* as a unified work, as something more than a series of lyrics, as a single poetic achievement, lyrical, and yet in its totality not without an epic quality and direction. The second reading was a revelation. "Then felt I like some watcher of the skies, when a new planet swims into his ken." *Leaves of Grass* suddenly took on new magnitude and purport. A sense of the oneness of the whole gave new force and beauty to the component parts, and in many instances transformed seemingly trivial lyrics into exciting, meaningful poetry. Many lyrics loved before were dearer now. I recalled some of the poet's own admonitions: "If there is anything whatever in *Leaves of Grass*—anything that sets it apart as a fact of importance—that thing must be its totality— its massings."[1] "But I hold to something more . . . —claim a full, not a partial, judgement upon my work—I am not to be known as a piece of something but as a totality."[2] "You can detach poems from the book and wonder why they were written. But if you see them in their place in the book you know why I wrote them."[3] "The words of my book nothing, the drift of it everything."[4] "The book needs each of its parts to keep its perfect unity. Above everything else it stands for unity. Take it to pieces—even with a gentle hand—and it is no longer the same product."[5] Late in life when questioned about the Rossetti selection of his poems, which he was reluctant to permit, he stated, "I never gave my assent to any abbreviated edition which I didn't live to regret."[6] In one of his notorious reviews of his own work, preparing the way for the 1860 edition, he wrote: "Indeed, Leaves of Grass has not yet been really published at all. Walt Whitman . . . has lazily loafed on . . . evidently building not so much with reference to any part itself, considered alone, but more with reference to the ensemble, always bearing in mind the combination of the whole to justify the parts when finished."[7] What he was pleased to do was accomplished in the 1881 edition. In a note written in August

[1] Horace Traubel, *With Walt Whitman in Camden*, II, 373.

[2] *Ibid.*, I, 272.

[3] *Ibid.*, p. 105.

[4] Walt Whitman, "Shut Not Your Doors," *Leaves of Grass: The Complete Writings of Walt Whitman*, ed. Richard Maurice Bucke, Thomas B. Harned, and Horace Traubel, I, 14. (Unless otherwise specified, all references to Whitman's works are to this edition.)

[5] Traubel, *With Walt Whitman in Camden*, I, 282.

[6] *Ibid.*, III, 299–308 (Whitman-Rossetti correspondence regarding selection); II, 359.

[7] Walt Whitman, *A Child's Reminiscence*, ed. Thomas O. Mabbott and Rollo G. Silver, pp. 19–20.

of that year he announces, "Am putting the last touches on the printer's copy of my new volume of *Leaves of Grass*—the completed book at last."[8] As we shall see later, this announcement became an enduring conviction. He was skeptical of permitting even annexes in the subsequent editions. On July 5, 1887, he questioned Traubel, "I have been thinking a good deal about Sands at Seventy . . . I want to know whether you feel that they will be out of place in *Leaves of Grass*—not integral—too distinctly different in character to connect with the study?" He had already put the question to Bucke and anticipated advice on the matter from Harned.[9]

That the structure of *Leaves of Grass* was perfected would be a position hardly tenable. A complete crystallization would not be in keeping with the expansive spirit of the work, its lyrical and emotional content, or the style of its author. Whitman's reluctance to make any such unqualified assertion would seem to be indicated in "A Backward Glance O'er Travel'd Roads": "The word I myself put primarily for the description of them as they stand at last, is the word *suggestiveness*. I round and finish little, if anything; and could not, consistently with my scheme. The reader will always have his or her part to do, just as I have had mine."[10] Whitman, I believe, wanted distinct design and direction in his work without loss of fluidity. Critics have varied widely in their reactions to such claims. Santayana is an extremist in the camp of doubters. Speaking of the hodgepodge nature of *Leaves of Grass*, he says, "This abundance of detail without organization, this wealth of perception without intelligence and of imagination without taste, makes the singularity of Whitman's genius."[11] At times Canby seems to be of this group—one of its moderates. He admits that a certain unity is provided by the presence of Walt the Kosmos throughout the book, but charges that Whitman failed in his repeated attempts

---

[8] *Specimen Days*, V, 17.
[9] Traubel, *With Walt Whitman in Camden*, I, 423.
[10] "A Backward Glance O'er Travel'd Roads," III, 58.
[11] George Santayana, *Interpretations of Poetry and Religion*, p. 180.

to achieve a symphonic unity—"a message as a whole, that would be simpler than the diverse lessons of its parts."[12] He is very close to the position of Santayana when he says, "no one but a Whitman specialist ever reads the 'Leaves' from cover to cover. No one should."[13] Mumford is a worthy representative of a second group of critics—those who are sympathetic with Whitman's claims of totality, but retain some reservations regarding the effectiveness of his practice of his principle of "suggestiveness." Notice how Mumford takes the essence of Whitman's claim and gives it a mildly negative phrasing: "What he meant to create is implied in all his poems; the whole of it was never, perhaps, expressed."[14] Finally, there are the believers, considerable in number even after we exclude the "hot little prophets." Selincourt says, "The student of Milton who reads one book of *Paradise Lost* is in a better position to gauge the value and significance of the whole poem than the student of Whitman who judges him by chosen morsels—even though the choice be well and wisely made."[15] Continuing in this vein, he recognizes challenging difficulties, "To admit an apparent chaos is to claim that the unity of the work if it exists is elusive and profound."[16] James Thomson agrees: "To quote him piecemeal is to give buckets of brine, or at most wavelets, as representative of the ocean. For his nature has an oceanic amplitude and depth, its powers and glory are in its immensity; nothing less than a shoreless horizon-ring can contain enough to give a true idea thereof."[17] Myers makes an interesting observation: "The unity of thought in the twelve significant poems of 1855, added to their original lack of titles, suggests that they might have been woven into one long epic, if Whitman had not

[12] Henry Seidel Canby, *Walt Whitman: An American*, p. 337.
[13] *Ibid.*, p. 338.
[14] Lewis Mumford, *The Golden Day*, pp. 135–136.
[15] Basil de Selincourt, *Walt Whitman: A Critical Study*, p. 122.
[16] *Ibid.*, p. 123.
[17] James Thomson, *Walt Whitman: The Man and the Poet*, p. 29.

been converted to Poe's theory that long poems are not suited
to modern needs."[18]

Myers is referring to a reminiscence in "A Backward Glance
O'er Travel'd Roads": "But I was repaid in Poe's prose by the
idea that (at any rate for our occasion, our day) there can be
no such thing as a long poem. The same thought had been
haunting my mind before, but Poe's argument, though short,
work'd the sum and proved it to me."[19] This argument, which
finds its fullest expression at the beginning of "The Poetic
Principle," not only levels charges of absurdity against modern
American attempts at the epic, but points to *Paradise Lost* as
nothing more than a series of minor poems. Looking further
into the past, Poe says that there is good reason to believe that
the *Iliad*, while epic in intention, is nonetheless basically a
series of lyrics.[20] There is evidence that Whitman was not over-
stating the case when he said that similar considerations had
been *haunting* his mind. Among his notes we find the following
jottings: "*Leaves of Grass* must be called *not* objective but
altogether subjective—. . . . Yet the great Greek poems, also
the Teutonic poems, also Shakespeare and all the great masters
have been objective, epic—they have described characters,
events, wars, heroes, etc."[21] "Subjective or lyric, objective or
epic, as for instance the Iliad is notably objective but *Leaves
of Grass* are profoundly subjective."[22] "Of the many critical
theories about the construction of the *Niebelungen* the most
plausible is that the ballads or versions floating about, were
collected . . . and fused into one connected Epic . . . united upon
the thread of one man's plot."[23]

---

[18] H. A. Myers, "Whitman's Conception of the Spiritual Democracy, 1855–
56," *AL* 6 (November 1934), 251.

[19] "A Backward Glance O'er Travel'd Roads," III, 56.

[20] Edgar Allan Poe, *The Complete Poems and Stories of Edgar Allan Poe
with Selections from His Critical Writings*, ed. Arthur Hobson Quinn and Edward H. O'Neill, II, 1021–1022.

[21] "Notes and Fragments," IX, 43.

[22] *Ibid.*, p. 228.

[23] *Ibid.*, p. 187.

When we relate these notations to a second group, we begin
to understand Whitman's dilemma:

> America needs her own poems in her own body and spirit dif-
> ferent from all hitherto—freer—more muscular, comprehending
> more and unspeakably grander. . . . *Caution*—Not to blaart con-
> stantly for *Native American* models, literature, etc., and bluster
> out "nothing foreign." The best way to promulge native Amer-
> ican models and literatures is to supply such forcible and superb
> native American models that they will, by their own volition,
> move to the head of all and put foreign models in the second
> class.[24]

> Sustenance for the great geniuses of the world is always plenty
> and the main ingredients of it are perhaps always the same. Yet
> nothing ever happened to former heroes, sages, and poets so in-
> spiring to them, so fit to shine resplendent, light upon them and
> make them original creators of works newer, nobler, grander, as
> the events of the last eighty years. I mean the advent of America.[25]

Whitman's position was a difficult one. He was a lyric poet
who felt called to sing new songs, subjective and democratic,
yet not without grand and heroic qualities worthy of the New
World and the Modern Man. In other words, he must remain a
lyrist and yet give expression to an epic intent. In notes which
were prepared for an introduction to an American edition of
Leaves of Grass and which were written sometime between 1860
and 1867, Whitman seems to feel that his problem has been
satisfactorily solved:

> The theory of the poem involves both the expression of the hottest,
> wildest passion, bravest, sturdiest character, not however illus-
> trated after any of the well known types, the identities of the great
> bards old or modern. Nor Prometheus is here, nor Agamemnon,
> nor Aeneas, nor Hamlet, nor Iago, nor Antony, nor any of Dante's

[24] *Ibid.*, pp. 29–30.
[25] *Ibid.*, p. 106.

scenes or persons, nor ballad of lord or lady, nor Lucretian philosophy, nor any special system of philosophy, nor striking lyric
achievement, nor Childe Harold, nor any epic tale with beginning,
climax and termination. Yet something of perhaps similar purpose, very definite, compact (and curiously digesting and including all the list we have just named), very simple even and
applying directly to the reader at first hand, is the main result
(and purpose) of this book, namely to suggest the substance and
form of a large, sane, perfect Human Being or character for an
American man and for woman. While other things are in the
book, studies, digressions of various sorts, this is undoubtedly
its essential purpose and its key, so that in the poem taken as a
whole unquestionably appears a great Person, entirely modern,
at least as great as anything in the Homeric or Shakespearean
character, a person with the free courage of Achilles, the craft of
Ulysses, the attributes even of the Greek deities. Majesty, passion,
temper, amativeness, Romeo, Lear, Antony, immense self-esteem,
but after democratic forms, measureless love, the old eternal elements of first-class humanity. Yet worked over, cast in a new
mould, and here chanted or anyhow put down and stated with
invariable reference to the United States and the occasions of
today and the future.[26]

It is fundamental to an appreciation of the problem facing
Whitman in giving unity and direction to his work to remember
that he was a lyric poet; although *Leaves of Grass* is epic in
proportion and purpose, it is still a collection of lyrics; though
it is in a sense an epiclike account of the growth of a hero and
his nation, there is no narrative element knitting its parts together. This is a fact so obvious that it is easily forgot. He
chose to identify man and nation in terms of emotional and
spiritual experience. It is the subtle, elusive manner in which
he does this without the aid of clearly defined episodes and
narrative thread that gives *Leaves of Grass* that essentially

[26] Clifton Joseph Furness, *Walt Whitman's Workshop*, pp. 136–137.

emotional and spiritual quality which transcends time and renders it ageless. Whitman's ability to cast lyrical expression in an epic mold is unique in the history of English and American poetry. David Daiches has pointed out this particular contribution with eloquence.[27] As we shall see later, that very expansiveness of personality, spirit, and technique which offends the impatient reader is the key to this resourceful fusion of types. The skill with which Whitman maintains his perilous balance is attested by the way in which the work embraces the reader and encourages him to identify himself with the hero or central figure of the argument. Any attempt to force the free, spontaneous lyricism of *Leaves* into a rigid design would do violence to the masterpiece; on the other hand, a failure to recognize a oneness of the whole, to sense an elusive, unifying principle, would do even greater violence. It is to the task of determining this unifying principle that this study has set itself.

The need for such a study is a real one when no less a critic than Malcolm Cowley can make such observations as these: "It is a short book, this first edition of *Leaves of Grass*; it contains only twelve poems, including 'Song of Myself,' but they summarize or suggest all his later achievements; and for other poets they are better than those achievements, because in this first book Whitman was a great explorer, whereas later he was at best a methodical exploiter and at worst a mere expounder by rote of his own discoveries." Cowley goes on to explain Whitman's genius by inviting us to recall a universal experience, that experience when "for a moment, at most for a day, our eyes were opened by some extreme emotion, usually love or fear of imminent death, and suddenly the homely objects around us took on new shapes, became filled with life and wonder; everything was intensely itself, yet we were part of it. With Whitman the momentary experience seems to have lasted for months or years, until he had written the finest long poem ('Song of Myself') of his century. He also, for a wonder, wrote

[27] David Daiches, "Walt Whitman: Impressionist Prophet," in *Leaves of Grass One Hundred Years After*, ed. Milton Hindus, pp. 109–122.

great poems in his later periods; but 'Song of Myself' is his miracle."[28] Certainly there is good reason for Cowley's admiration for "Song of Myself," just as there is some suggestion of insight in his experience of the emotional eye opening. However, his failure to see any significant development in *Leaves of Grass*, other than a few great poems, after the 1855 edition, and his attempt to account for its poetic achievements in terms of a momentary emotional state sustained for years are two absurdities which tend to strengthen one another. Granted, the 1855 *Leaves of Grass*, which Cowley has edited with skill and care, was a milestone in American prosody; it was, however, the mere promise of the fruits of 1881.[29] If all that Whitman had to sustain him in his work was an extended emotional experience, then the 1881 achievement would have been "for a wonder" indeed. That achievement was born of great purpose and plan. With Whitman's own guidance something of the nature of these can be discerned.

[28] Malcolm Cowley, "Walt Whitman: The Miracle," *New Republic*, March 18, 1946, pp. 385–388.
[29] *Walt Whitman's* LEAVES OF GRASS: *The First (1855) Edition*, ed. Malcolm Cowley.

CHAPTER II

Whitman's Organic Principle
and Poet-Prophet

If there is a unifying principle which has produced a significant structural pattern in *Leaves of Grass*, rendering it epiclike, an analysis of that principle and its workings should be initiated with a consideration of Whitman's own attitude toward the process of poetic composition. A glance at any one of the prefaces, *Democratic Vistas*, *November Boughs*, and any of a large number of poems (including such significant ones as "A Song of the Rolling Earth" or "Song of the Answerer") demonstrates at once Whitman's constant concern with the theory of poetic composition, both in his prose and in his poetry. Allen says, "His written words do not anywhere show a clear distinction in his own mind between his thought and his manner of expressing it."[1] This fact is not to be lamented. Whether the failure is an unconscious one on Whitman's part or another example of his cunning, it indicates his complete identification with the organic theory of expression and, of course, explains its presence as a major theme in *Leaves of Grass* itself. Just when Whitman began pondering this theory is difficult to determine; however, its influence upon his thought was quite evident as early as March 1851, when he lectured before the Brooklyn Art Union.[2] At any rate, no small part of his efforts throughout his poetic career went into his absorption and adaptation of this theory. Looking back over the results with satisfaction, he observed, "Indeed, and anyhow, to put it specifically, has not the time arrived when . . . there must imperatively come a readjustment of the whole theory and nature of poetry?"[3] As an initiator of this adjustment Whitman was careful not to found a school or to formulate a static theory. "To speak in literature with the perfect rectitude and insouciance of the movement of animals and the unimpeachableness of the sentiment of trees in woods and grass by the roadside is the flawless triumph of art."[4] He taught freedom and naturalness at all costs. Nevertheless, reluctant though he was to specify techniques, the very fact of his rebellion against conventional practices brought forth statements, running throughout the entire body of his writings and conversation, which enable us to detect a theory of poetry in many respects unusually definite and dynamic.[5]

There are two important aspects of this theory which are of significance to this study: Whitman's particular concept of organic art and the almost unique way in which he relates this

[1] Gay Wilson Allen, *American Prosody*, p. 217.
[2] Gay Wilson Allen, *The Solitary Singer*, p. 110.
[3] "A Backward Glance O'er Travel'd Roads," III, 51.
[4] "Preface, 1855," V, 170–171.
[5] Gamaliel Bradford, "Portraits of American Authors: II. Walt Whitman," *Bookman* 42 (December 1915), 534.

to the nature and role of his poet-prophet.[6] This poet-prophet is central in his thinking as a theorist and emerges, of course, as the hero of *Leaves of Grass*.

THE ORGANIC PRINCIPLE[7]

In his "1876 Preface" Whitman affirms, "As I have lived in fresh lands . . . and in a revolutionary age, future-founding, I have felt to identify the points of that age, these lands, in my recitatives, altogether in my own way. Thus my form has strictly grown from my purports and facts, and is the analogy of them."[8] He was not loath to "lock horns," to use his own phrase, with those who think the question of art, so-called, the greatest thing.

I have not seen without learning something therefrom, how, with hardly an exception, the poets of this age devote themselves, always mainly, sometimes altogether, to fine rhyme, spicy verbalism, the fabric and cut of the garment, jewelry, *concetti*, style, art. Today these adjuncts are certainly the effort, beyond all else. Yet the lesson of Nature undoubtedly is, to proceed with single purpose toward the result necessitated, and for which the time has arrived, utterly regardless of the outputs of shape, appearance or criticism, which are always left to settle themselves. I have not only not bothered much about style, form, art, etc., but confess

---

[6] For a brief review of other aspects of Whitman's theory see Richard P. Adams, "Whitman: A Brief Revaluation," *Tulane Studies in English* 5 (1955), 111–149.

[7] General treatments of the subject are as follows: W. S. Kennedy, "The Style of Leaves of Grass," *Reminiscences of Walt Whitman*, pp. 149–190; Basil de Selincourt, *Walt Whitman: A Critical Study*, pp. 73–83; Norman Foerster, *American Criticism*, pp. 157–222; F. O. Matthiessen, *American Renaissance*, pp. 517–625; Gay Wilson Allen, *Walt Whitman Handbook*, pp. 292–302, 375–437; Richard H. Fogle, "Organic Form in American Criticism: 1840–1870," *The Development of American Literary Criticism*, ed. Floyd Stovall, pp. 75–111. There are two helpful studies of the subject which are not concerned with Whitman but give excellent background material: Emerson Grant Sutcliffe, "Emerson's Theory of Literary Expression," *University of Illinois Studies in Language and Literature* 8 (1923), 9–143; Fred W. Lorch, "Thoreau and the Organic Principle of Poetry," *PMLA* 53 (March 1938), 286–302.

[8] "Preface, 1876," V, 203.

more or less apathy . . . toward them throughout, asking of them
nothing but negative advantages—that they should never impede
me, and never under any circumstances, or for their own purposes
only, assume any mastery over me.[9]

While these pronouncements are significant because representative of Whitman's general attitude, they are of particular interest because of the pivotal phrase "the lesson of Nature."
Whitman the organicist always looked to Nature as the great
teacher. This accounts for his enthusiasm for and serious study
of primitive literatures. He speaks of *Leaves of Grass* as

a conference amid Nature, and in the spirit of Nature's genesis
and primal sanity. A conference of our two Souls exclusively, as
if the rest of the world, with its mocking misconceptions, were for
a while left and escaped from. . . . In short, the book will not
serve as books serve. But may be—as the rude air, the salt sea, the
fire, the woods, and the rocky ground—sharp, full of danger, full
of contradictions and offense. These elements, silent and old, stand
or move and out of them curiously comes everything. I too
(though a resident and singer of cities) came from them, and can
boast, as I now do, that in their presence, before giving them here,
I have sternly tried each passage of the following chants.[10]

This does not deny Whitman's indebtedness to the intellectual atmosphere of the mid-nineteenth century. Through Coleridge, Carlyle, and Emerson he had become acquainted with
the organicism of the German romanticists. It was with their
assistance that he came to see the significance of natural objects
and phenomena as symbols of spiritual truth. His declaration

I accept Reality and dare not question it,
Materialism first and last imbuing.

finds its transcendental justification in the passage

Strange and hard that paradox true I give,

9 "An Old Man's Rejoinder," VI, 284–285.
10 Clifton Joseph Furness, *Walt Whitman's Workshop*, p. 130.

Objects gross and the unseen soul are one.[11]

A recurring question in Whitman's poetry and prose is once phrased this way: "Do you suppose nature has nothing under those beautiful, terrible, irrational forms?"[12] Although Whitman could claim no great scientific knowledge, he was hospitable toward the natural science of his day.[13] "There shall be love between the poet and the man of demonstrable science," he declared.[14] His concept of evolution during his formative years was pre-Darwinian, and the natural science that he knew viewed the world not as a mechanism, but as a living, growing organism.[15] Thus with the man of science "walking one side of" him and the transcendentalist "close-walking the other side of" him, Whitman came to see the "lesson of Nature" as that of growth from within, her concrete expression the emanation of spirit.

When the full-grown poet came,
Out spake pleased Nature (the round impassive globe,
    with all its shows of day and night,) saying,
    He is mine;
But out spake too the Soul of man, proud, jealous
    and unreconciled, *Nay, he is mine alone*;
—Then the full-grown poet stood between the two,
    and took each by the hand;
And to-day and ever so stands, as blender, uniter,
    tightly holding hands,
Which he will never release until he reconciles
    the two,
And wholly and joyously blends them.[16]

The full-grown poet does much more than imitate the objects of nature; he sees "into the life of things." It is this ability to

[11] "Song of Myself," I, 61; "A Song for Occupations," I, 263.
[12] "Notes and Fragments," IX, 162.
[13] Newton Arvin, *Whitman*, p. 166.
[14] "Preface, 1855," V, 173.
[15] Allen, *Walt Whitman Handbook*, p. 264.
[16] "When the Full-Grown Poet Came," III, 18.

lay hold of, or rather to become an unobstructed channel for, the "spirit of Nature" that proves his creativity.[17]

> I permit to speak at every hazard,
> Nature without check with original energy.[18]

The poetic quality is not marshalled in rhyme or uniformity or abstract addresses to things nor in melancholy complaints or good precepts, but is the life of these and much else and is in the soul. The profit of rhyme is that it drops the seeds of a sweeter and more luxuriant rhyme, and of uniformity that it conveys itself into its own roots in the ground out of sight. The rhyme and uniformity of perfect poems show the free growth of metrical laws and bud from them as unerringly and loosely as lilacs or roses on a bush, and take shapes as compact as the shapes of chestnuts and oranges and melons and pears, and shed the perfume impalpable to form. The fluency and ornaments of the finest poems or music or orations or recitations are not independent, but dependent.[19]

These are the particular thoughts that prompt Whitman to talk of "returning mainly to the antique feeling."[20] They account for his fondness for the adjectives *bardic, primitive, elemental*—for his qualified praise of the poems of Goethe: "They appear to me as great as the antique in all respects except one. That is the antique poems were *growths*—they were never studied from antiques."[21]

When Whitman uses one of his favorite expressions, that a poem must "tally nature," he has this concept of *growth* in mind.[22] "The form of the perfect poem, like that of a perfect animal or tree, is a free organic growth in which each part is in proportion and harmonious with the whole design."[23] Just as

---

[17] "Preface, 1855," V, 171.
[18] "Song of Myself," I, 33.
[19] "Preface, 1855," V, 166.
[20] "Poetry To-Day in America," V, 216.
[21] "Notes and Fragments," IX, 112.
[22] "Democratic Vistas," *Collect*, V, 134.
[23] Floyd Stovall, *Walt Whitman*, p. xxv.

the plant springs from the seed and takes shape after its kind, so the great poem springs from the germinal idea or emotion and takes shape after its kind. There are as many potential shapes as there are seeds or germinal ideas. A poem should be "adorned as the goodly tree is, by the efflorescence of its own branches, not by garlands hung on."[24] Just how common and basic such analogies are with Whitman is suggested by his repeated use of the grass-symbol alone. Van Wyck Brooks speaks of Whitman himself as "a great vegetable of a man, all of a piece in roots, flavor, substantiality, and succulence, well-ripened in the common sunshine."[25] But to return to the *growth* analogy, obviously it is used to demonstrate the principle that the form of a great poem is the result of a shaping from within, not from without—that it is organic, not mechanical.[26] The outer form depends upon the inner life. Coleridge provided Whitman with what has remained probably the clearest prose statement of this concept.

> The form is mechanic, when on any given material we impress a pre-determined form, not necessarily arising out of the properties of the material; . . . The organic form, on the other hand, is innate; it shapes, as it develops, itself from within, and the fulness of its development is one and the same with the perfection of its outward form. Nature, the prime genial artist, inexhaustible in diverse powers, is equally inexhaustible in forms;—each exterior is the physiognomy of the being within,—its true image reflected and thrown out from the concave mirror.[27]

As long as Whitman kept with predetermined forms, his themes remained conventional and his expression weak and ineffectual.[28] His characteristic freshness and vitality of expres-

---

[24] "Walt Whitman and Oratory," VIII, 260.

[25] Van Wyck Brooks, *America's Coming of Age*, p. 112.

[26] Foerster, *American Criticism*, p. 171.

[27] Samuel Taylor Coleridge, *The Literary Remains of Samuel Taylor Coleridge*, ed. Henry Nelson Coleridge, II, 67–68.

[28] Killis Campbell, "The Evolution of Whitman as an Artist," *AL* 6 (November 1934), 254–255.

sion did not appear until he rebelled against forcing his ideas into preestablished molds, until he said to himself with confidence, "Walt you contain enough, why don't you let it out then?"[29] Notebooks dating as early as 1847 and pointing toward *Leaves of Grass* demonstrate that this admonition can be taken literally, for the ideas and spirit were there struggling for poetic expression.[30] It was not until Whitman had thought long that he accepted himself as a part of Nature, containing the truth and the way no less than she, already filled with her "substantial" words "that print cannot touch."[31] Here, for Whitman, was the fountainhead of song. "All beauty comes from beautiful blood and a beautiful brain. . . . Who troubles himself about his ornaments or fluency is lost."[32] But, as we shall see, the way was not an easy one; looking back over it, Whitman spoke of Taine's words as solace to his "frequent bruises and sulky vanity": "All original art . . . is self-regulated, and no original art can be regulated from without; it carries its own counterpoise, and does not receive it from elsewhere—lives on its own blood."[33] Fred Newton Scott gives an accurate, objective picture of Whitman's torturous process of composition and concludes, "Whether one likes his art or not . . . that he held before himself a high and difficult ideal and strove with all the powers of his genius to attain it, is as certain as anything in literary history."[34] The essence of this strife was keeping the way clear for Nature to speak—to stop short of revising his revisions *too much*, of *polishing*. I suspect that there is something other than egotism in Whitman's words to Traubel, "I don't hold it to be principally important to develope special technical flavors. . . . I keep as far away from the mere machinery of composition *as I can*."[35]

[29] "Song of Myself," I, 65.
[30] Henry Seidel Canby, *Walt Whitman: An American*, pp. 87–99.
[31] "A Song of the Rolling Earth," I, 268, 273.
[32] "Preface, 1855," V, 166.
[33] "A Backward Glance O'er Travel'd Roads," III, 64.
[34] Fred Newton Scott, "A Note on Whitman's Prosody," *JEGP* 7 (1908), 141.
[35] Horace Traubel, *With Walt Whitman in Camden*, II, 287.

Whitman's belief that true poetry can spring only from within enters into his conception of his proper relationship to his reader. His intention was not so much to create a poem for his reader as to lead him to create for himself. "I have never so much cared to feed the esthetic or intellectual palates—but if I could arouse from its slumbers that eligibility in every Soul for its own true exercise! if I could only wield that lever!"[36] Whitman had learned the lessons of Nature well; he claimed for his own poems that quality of *suggestiveness* which had endeared her objects to him. Thus we see that his saturation with the organic concept of growth from within is the key to his famous passages on *suggestiveness* and to his desire for and ability to establish a unique relationship with his reader, a matter to be discussed at length later. Ideally, then, his poem "Poets to Come" is addressed to every reader:

> I am a man who, sauntering along without fully
>   stopping, turns a casual look upon you and
>   then averts his face,
> Leaving it to you to prove and define it,
> Expecting the main things from you.[37]

Whitman's exclamation "if I could only wield that lever!" indicates his awareness of the difficulty of realizing such an ideal. Small wonder that at times he lashed out at those who sought the easier way.

The fatal defects our American singers labor under are sub-ordination of spirit . . . and in excess that modern esthetic con-tagion a queer friend of mine calls the *beauty disease.* "The im-moderate taste for beauty and art," says Charles Baudelaire, "leads men into monstrous excesses. In minds imbued with a frantic greed for the beautiful, all the balances of truth and jus-

---

[36] "Some Laggards Yet," VII, 26.
[37] "Poets to Come," I, 15.

tice disappear. There is a lust, a disease of the art faculties, which eats up the moral like a cancer."

[And Whitman adds:]

Of course, by our plentiful verse-makers there is plenty of service perform'd of a kind. . . . We see, in every polite circle a class of accomplished, good-natured persons, fully eligible for certain problems, times and duties—to mix eggnog, to mend broken spectacles, to decide whether the stew'd eels shall precede the sherry or the sherry the stew'd eels . . . and generally to contribute and gracefully adapt their flexibilities and talents, in those ranges, to the world's service. But for real crises, great needs and pulls, moral or physical, they might as well never have been born.[38]

We can make allowances for overstatement and still conclude that Coleridge's organic theory of art is Whitman's practiced ideal. Our examination of the poetry will, I believe, confirm this point of view. Certainly it is inherent in all of his literary criticism. For example, in praise of Dante he says, "The points of the *Inferno* are hasting on, great vigor, a lean and muscular ruggedness, no superfluous flesh. . . . Mark the simplicity of Dante, like the Bible's. . . . One simple trail of idea, epical, makes the poem—all else resolutely ignored. This alone shows the master . . . a great study for diffuse moderns."[39]

While it is beyond our immediate intention to try to define the degree of success with which Whitman practiced his theory, the significance of this chapter depends upon its demonstration of the fact that his whole attitude and approach to his poetry was permeated by such a theory. That it was his cherished ideal has already been established; let us look briefly for an indication of its dynamic presence in Whitman the practitioner. Whitman's point of departure for the application of such a theory was to discard the predetermined metrical patterns of conventional verse and to write in the unit of clause or sentence,

[38] "Poetry To-Day in America," V, 217–218.
[39] "Notes and Fragments," IX, 92–93.

according to the dictates of his "purports and facts." The fact that these units defy the usual methods of scansion does not relegate them to the realm of prose or speech. To look upon their rhythm as prosaic or accidental, as Amy Lowell has done, is to miss the broad poetic sweep of all that Whitman wrote.[40] Matthiessen recognizes this when he writes, "But Whitman's desire to give up borrowed cadences altogether came from his crude re-living of the primitive evolution of poetry."[41] Whitman, in his usual manner, turns to nature for an analogy, the ocean.[42] His selection evokes the picture of a naked youth, his bare feet beating the "hard sand" of a Long Island beach, to the simultaneous rhythm of Homer or Shakespeare and the sea; or of a pensive young man at the side of his ferry-pilot friend, looking down upon the ebb and flow of New York's harbor and her teeming humanity.[43] In these pictures from *Specimen Days* lie the seeds of the rhythms of *Leaves of Grass*. The experiences they recall were unconsciously written into the fabric of Whitman's poetry as surely as they were consciously written into the body of *Leaves of Grass* in "Out of the Cradle Endlessly Rocking" and "Crossing Brooklyn Ferry." Whitman's poetry communicates rhythmically only when read with broad freedom of movement and with a sense of the rolling line. The attitude of the young man in the surf is the perfect attitude for a satisfactory reading of *Leaves of Grass*. When read thus, its elemental movements are poetic in the greatest sense.

Whitman's majestic rhythms are the elemental rhythms learned from the wind and the sea. But the creator of these poetic rhythms was a man, and the central theme to which they are set is the life and experience of man. A second element in the rhythm of *Leaves of Grass*, then, is the rhythm of man himself, uninhibited and free. But it is not the surface rhythm of speech; it is the deeper rhythm, sometimes faltering, often

[40] Amy Lowell, "Walt Whitman and the New Poetry," *Yale Review* 16 (1926–1927), 502–519.
[41] Matthiessen, *American Renaissance*, p. 564.
[42] Traubel, *With Walt Whitman in Camden*, I, 414–415.
[43] *Specimen Days*, IV, 16–17.

subtle, which the great poet detects in the movement of his own body and mind and more universally in the ebb and flow of all human life. It is significant that on the deserted beach and on bustling Broadway alike, long before *Leaves of Grass* had been written, Whitman found exciting rhythmical accompaniments for that poetry which to him was the greatest poetry, the poetry of Homer, and Shakespeare, and the Bible.[44]

Sculley Bradley's "The Fundamental Metrical Principle in Whitman's Poetry," a major contribution to Whitman scholarship, makes an extended discussion of the subject for our purposes superfluous.[45] Bradley accepts Whitman's own analogy as the most satisfactory clew to his prosody. "The rhyme and uniformity of perfect poems show the free growth of metrical laws and bud from them as unerringly and loosely as lilacs or roses on a bush, and take shapes as compact as the shapes of chestnuts and oranges and melons and pears, and shed the perfume impalpable to form."[46] He comments, "The poet was not expressing a completely new and original ideal, although he acted upon it perhaps more fully than any previous artist had done."[47] After a brilliant analysis of individual lines and entire poems, Bradley concludes:

> It would be foolhardy to declare, since we have no direct evidence, that Whitman had rationalized the formal tendencies which I have illustrated, and that he had organized them into a prosody which he consciously followed. It has been said that he avoided, for wise reasons, the concrete declaration of his specific practices. Yet if such formal perfection as I have shown came merely by the exercise of artistic instinct during years of revision and re-

[44] *Ibid.*, p. 20.

[45] Sculley Bradley, "The Fundamental Metrical Principle in Whitman's Poetry," *AL* 10 (January 1939), 437–459. Three other valuable contributions are Scott, "A Note on Whitman's Prosody," *JEGP* 7 (1908), 134–153; Ruth Mary Weeks, "Phrasal Prosody," *English Journal* 10 (January 1921), 11–19; John Erskine, "A Note on Whitman's Prosody," *SP* 20 (July 1923), 336–344.

[46] For a fuller quotation of this passage see page 17 of this study.

[47] Bradley, "The Fundamental Metrical Principle in Whitman's Poetry," p. 440.

writing, then surely that instinct was the mark of a profound artistic genius. . . . Whether instinctively or consciously, the poet achieved the aspiration revealed in his prefaces: to shape his words to the exact surface and movement of the spirit in nature or in truth.[48]

In relation to our study the pertinence of the following observations derived from Bradley's objective study is obvious: (1) Whitman, in his efforts to originate a metrical principle answering his particular needs, reverted to "the most *primitive* [the italics are mine] and persistent characteristics of English poetic rhythm [those of Old English verse in which quantity was felt as the duration of time between stresses, the intervals being relatively fixed throughout a given work, but accommodating a widely variable number of unstressed syllables]."[49] (2) Although the organic theory influenced Whitman profoundly in his development of his rhythmical lines, its influence is perhaps even more strikingly demonstrated by the long odic sections which he substituted for more conventional and traditional stanzas.[50] (3) Whitman's use of nature analogies in explaining his artistic devices is accurate and indicative of the "organic" theory which he practiced but never called by name.[51] (4) Whitman's favorite stanzas are pyramidal in form, and, when utilized in sequence, produce an effect best described in terms of sea-movement.[52] (5) The reading of Whitman's lines "requires a greater degree of participation on the part of the reader than does the reading of syllabic verse."[53]

Bradley concludes his essay as follows:

All of this would have little point but for the genius by which he was able to transmute his special sense of rhythm into phrases which, as Symonds said, "should exactly suit the matter or the

---

[48] *Ibid.*, p. 458.
[49] *Ibid.*, pp. 438, 442.
[50] *Ibid.*, p. 447.
[51] *Ibid.*, p. 441.
[52] *Ibid.*, pp. 449–451.
[53] *Ibid.*, p. 446.

emotion to be expressed. The countless clear and perfect phrases
he invented . . . are hung, like golden medals of consummate
workmanship . . . in rich clusters over every poem he produced.
And, what he aimed at above all, these phrases are redolent of
the very spirit of the emotions they suggest, communicate the
breadth and largeness of the natural things they indicate, embody
the essence of realities in living words which palpitate and burn
forever."[54]

Reduced to its simplest terms, then, Whitman's organic concept led him to discard conventional verse and stanza patterns
and to create new, yet old, forms to tally his "purports and
facts." The tremendous sweep of his concept is suggested in his
criticisms of the Bible:

All the poems of Orientalism, with the Old and New Testaments at the centre, tend to deep and wide . . . psychological development—with little, or nothing at all, of the mere esthetic,
the principal verse-requirement of our day. . . . Compared with
the famed epics of Greece, and the lesser ones since, the spinal
supports of the Bible are simple and meagre. All its history, biography, narratives, etc., are as beads, strung on and indicating
the eternal thread of the Deific purpose and power. Yet with only
deepest faith for impetus, and such Deific purpose for palpable
or impalpable theme, it often transcends the masterpieces of
Hellas and all masterpieces. The metaphors daring beyond account, the lawless soul, extravagant by our standards, the glow
of love and friendship, the fervent kiss—nothing in argument
or logic, but unsurpass'd in proverbs, in religious ecstacy, in
suggestions of common mortality and death, man's great equal-
izers—the spirit everything, the ceremonies and forms of the
church nothing, faith limitless, its immense sensuousness im-
mensely spiritual. . . . No true bard will ever contravene the
Bible. If the time ever comes when iconoclasm does its extreme
in one direction against the Books of the Bible in its present form,
the collection must still survive in another, and dominate just

[54] Ibid., p. 459; John Addington Symonds, *Walt Whitman: A Study*, p. 150.

as much as hitherto, or more than hitherto, through its divine
and primal poetic structure. To me, that is the living and definite
element-principle of the work, evolving everything else. . . . Even
to our Nineteenth Century here are the fountainheads of song.[55]

These critical comments make clear the didacticism inherent in Whitman's concept of organic art—a noble didacticism.
"The greatest poet does not moralize or make applications of
morals . . . he knows the soul . . . never acknowledging any lessons but its own."[56] Whitman warns us, "No one will get at
my verses who insists upon viewing them as a literary performance, or attempt at such performance, or as aiming mainly
toward art or aestheticism."[57] Had Whitman been more of a
humorist, he would have been capable of Shaw's remark, "When
he [the academic artist] declares that art should not be didactic, all the people who have nothing to teach and all the people
who don't want to learn agree with him emphatically."[58] It is
interesting that in the climactic stanza of "Song of Myself"
at the moment that Whitman assumes the Christ-stature he also
becomes the great teacher and significantly, I think, closes the
section with two of the least aesthetic lines he ever wrote:

Eleves, I salute you! come forward!
Continue your annotations, continue your questionings.[59]

In hailing the poet as teacher, we have come full circle in our
consideration of Whitman's organic theory. At the beginning
of our discussion Nature was teacher; now the poet has learned
her lesson complete, becoming teacher in his own turn, and
folks expect of him "more than the beauty and dignity which
always attach to dumb real objects . . . they expect him to indicate the path between reality and their souls."[60] Whitman's

[55] "The Bible as Poetry," VI, 104–106, 109.
[56] "Preface, 1855," V, 170.
[57] "A Backward Glance O'er Travel'd Roads," III, 65.
[58] George Bernard Shaw, "Epistle Dedicatory," *Man and Superman, The
Collected Works of Bernard Shaw*, X, xxxvii–xxxviii.
[59] "Song of Myself," I, 88.
[60] "Preface, 1855," V, 165.

concept of the Poet-Prophet is the *natural outgrowth*, one might almost say the fulfillment, of his ideal of organic art.

> I know I am solid and sound,
> To me the converging objects of the universe
>   perpetually flow,
> All are written to me, and I must get what the
>   writing means.[61]

THE POET-PROPHET

Whitman felt that the greatness of a poet depends largely upon three essentials: his capacities for seeing, for accepting, and for sharing. The word *prophet* and its derivatives were such important words to Whitman that more than once he comments on their exact significance. Having likened Carlyle to the prophet Isaiah, he explains: "The word prophecy is much misused; it seems narrowed to prediction merely. That is not the main sense of the Hebrew word translated 'prophet'; it means one whose mind bubbles up and pours forth as a fountain, from inner, divine spontaneities revealing God. Prediction is a very minor part of prophecy. The great matter is to reveal and outpour the God-like suggestions pressing for birth in the soul. This is briefly the doctrine of the Friends or Quakers."[62] When the purity of the word *prophet*, as Whitman used it, is preserved, its identification with his concept of the *true poet* is inevitable. Prophecy and poetry alike are "the expression of a sound mind speaking after the ideal—and not after the apparent."[63] Like Wordsworth, he believed that seeing "into the life of things" was the first and cardinal requisite if the poet was to qualify for his proper function. No amount of decorative skill or brilliance could atone if this were lacking. Oscar Wilde, whom he liked personally, troubled him as a poet. "He has extraordinary brilliancy of genius," he observed, "with perhaps rather too little root in eternal soils."[64]

61 "Song of Myself," I, 57.
62 *Specimen Days*, IV, 307.
63 *Ibid.*, V, 13 (footnote, quote from Emerson).
64 Traubel, *With Walt Whitman in Camden*, II, 279.

A second essential of the poet-prophet is that he accept the terms of life—that he have the cheerful faith to partake freely of his own time and place. It is an act of faith to affirm that "The United States themselves are essentially the greatest poem," that "Here at last is something in the doings of man that corresponds with the broadcast doings of the day and night."[65] "What is authorship in itself if you cart it away from the main stream of life?" Whitman asks. "It is starved, starved: it is a dead limb off the tree—it is the unquickened seed in the ground."[66] The vision of the ideal comes first, as we have seen, but it cannot exist in a vacuum; it must be brought to bear upon life. This is the lesson from the greatest of all singers, the Hebrew prophets: they speak for a land and for a people.

This brings us to a third and final essential: the poet-prophet must share his experience with all mankind. Whitman combines the three elements when he says, "The poets are the divine mediums—through them come the spirits and the materials to all the people, men and women."[67] Furness says of Whitman, "Art for anything less than humanity's sake was inconceivable to him."[68] One of the unique qualities of the poet-prophet of *Leaves of Grass* is that he reaches out to all mankind longingly; his messages are at once vigorous and gentle; confident in his strength, he stands and knocks, but does not force entrance. His poems are

> Buds to be unfolded on the old terms,
> If you bring the warmth of the sun to them they will open and
>   bring form, color, perfume to you,
> If you become the aliment and the wet they will become flowers,
>   fruits, tall branches and trees.[69]

With these three basic elements in mind, let us examine Whitman's poet-prophet in more detail.

[65] "Preface, 1855," V, 161.
[66] Traubel, *With Walt Whitman in Camden*, II, 167.
[67] "Notes and Fragments," IX, 127.
[68] Furness, *Walt Whitman's Workshop*, p. 11.
[69] "Roots and Leaves Themselves Alone," I, 150.

The main sources of Whitman's conception are not far to seek. Emerson's essay "The Poet" and Carlyle's *Heroes and Hero Worship* and *Sartor Resartus* are generally acknowledged to have been significant in aiding Whitman in formulating his concept of the long-awaited prophet of spiritual democracy. They aided him in visualizing the mission of such a poet and were sources of inspiration throughout his life. It may be well to review briefly Whitman's relationship to these men and to set forth some of the doctrines of each which find parallels in *Leaves of Grass*.

The problem of the Emerson-Whitman relationship is not as confusing as it may seem at first glance.[70] Trowbridge has preserved for us Whitman's famous acknowledgment, "I was simmering, simmering, simmering; Emerson brought me to a boil," and states that Whitman first read the *Essays* in 1854.[71] This date became somewhat controversial when Kennedy quoted a letter from Whitman, dated February 25, 1887, saying that he had not read Emerson before starting *Leaves of Grass*.[72] Gohdes reviews the matter and concludes, correctly it seems to me, "That he [Whitman] lied about the date of his first acquaintance with Emerson's works cannot be doubted.[73] Certainly, all the evidence tends to discredit Whitman's letter of 1887. In 1855 Whitman eagerly sent a copy of his first *Leaves* to Emerson and in 1856 was not loath to call him "master." It is true that Whitman was inclined to minimize this relationship for a time after 1856, understandably so, in view of attacks on his originality and of Emerson's so-called cooling off. The younger poet's final pronouncement on the latter circumstance was philosophical, stating that Emerson was silenced but not changed.[74]

[70] John B. Moore, "The Master of Whitman," *SP* 23 (January 1926), 77–89; Clarence Gohdes, "Whitman and Emerson," *Sewanee Review* 37 (January–March 1929), 79–93.

[71] John Townsend Trowbridge, *My Own Story: With Recollections of Noted Persons*, p. 367.

[72] Kennedy, *Reminiscences of Walt Whitman*, pp. 76–77.

[73] Gohdes, "Whitman and Emerson," p. 92.

[74] Traubel, *With Walt Whitman in Camden*, I, 111.

As to the former, attackers on his originality did not flourish for long, for though he may have started from Emerson, his results are far, far different.[75] Whitman always claimed for Emerson unshared glory among the American poets.[76] In 1888, in answer to Traubel's questions, he stated sanely, "Master he was, for me, then. But I got my roots stronger in the earth—master would not do anymore." Laughing mildly, he prophesied that his last word about Emerson would "be loyal, . . . after all impatiences, loyal, loyal."[77] It is no reflection on Whitman (except for the minor matter of the lie), then, to accept Trowbridge's date for the reading of the *Essays*, or, remembering that Emerson was very much "in the air," to push Whitman's first enchantment, through lectures and periodicals, as far back as the late 1840's.[78] As a glance at the index to *With Walt Whitman in Camden* will show, Emerson was never long out of Whitman's mind, conscious or unconscious, or without his love and respect. Those Emersonian ideas that particularly concern us here are most effectively and fully expressed in his essay "The Poet."[79]

Emerson begins his essay with an attack on those shallow poets who follow the doctrine of beauty and never perceive the "instant dependence of form upon soul."[80] They do not possess the beautiful soul essential to the poet-prophet. They are unfit, not representative, as the poet, who stands among partial men for the complete man, is representative.[81] "The birth of a poet is the principal event in chronology. Man, never so often deceived, still watches for the arrival of a brother who can hold

[75] Matthiessen, *American Renaissance*, p. 522; Allen, *The Solitary Singer*, pp. 155–156.

[76] Traubel, *With Walt Whitman in Camden*, III, 390; on one occasion Whitman put Bryant in first place, Emerson in second (II, 533).

[77] *Ibid.*, II, 69.

[78] Moore, "The Master of Whitman," p. 81.

[79] Ralph Waldo Emerson, *The Complete Works of Ralph Waldo Emerson*, III, 3–42.

[80] *Ibid.*, p. 3.

[81] *Ibid.*, p. 5.

him steady to a truth until he has made it his own."[82] That brother, the poet-prophet, comes not with a mastery of neat meters, but with a mastery of those meter-making thoughts that produce great poems.[83] He knows the secret of the world, "that Being passes into Appearance and Unity into Variety." The universe is the externalization of the soul.[84] To him "bare lists of words are found suggestive," and things ugly and distorted are transformed as he reattaches them to nature and the whole.[85] "Though thou should'st walk the world over, thou shalt not be able to find a condition inopportune or ignoble.[86] . . . America is a poem in our eyes; its ample geography dazzles the imagination, and it will not wait long for meters." The ideal poet for effecting this must surpass Milton, who is too literary, and Homer, who is too literal and historical.[87] Finally, "The religions of the world are the ejaculations of a few imaginative men."[88] "Time and nature yield us many gifts, but not yet the timely man, the new religion, the reconciler, whom all things wait. . . . We have yet had no genius in America, with tyrannous eye, which knew the value of our incomparable materials, and saw, in the barbarism and materialism of the times, another carnival of the same gods whose picture he so much admires in Homer."[89]

Whitman's literary relationship with Carlyle is free of such personal and emotional complications as color his relationship with Emerson. In spite of the fact that Carlyle was antidemocratic and anti-American and that *Democratic Vistas* was in large part an answer to *Shooting Niagara*, Whitman recognized him as "more significant than any modern man" and freely

[82] *Ibid.*, p. 11.
[83] *Ibid.*, p. 9.
[84] *Ibid.*, p. 14.
[85] *Ibid.*, pp. 17–18.
[86] *Ibid.*, p. 42.
[87] *Ibid.*, p. 38.
[88] *Ibid.*, p. 34.
[89] *Ibid.*, p. 37.

acknowledged his influence.[90] "Carlyle is always grist to my mill, no matter what form he comes in or where he comes from."[91] Carlyle may have been antidemocratic, but he was also antifeudal, and for that he had Whitman's love.

> Who cares that he wrote about Dr. Francia, and "Shooting Niagara"—and the "Nigger Question"—and didn't at all admire our United States? (I doubt if he ever thought or said half as bad words about us as we deserve.) How he splashes like leviathan in the seas of modern literature and politics! . . . Accordingly, though he was no chartist or radical, I consider Carlyle's by far the most indignant comment or protest anent the fruits of feudalism to-day in Great Britain—the increasing poverty and degradation of the homeless, landless twenty million, while a few thousands, or rather a few hundreds, possess the entire soil, the money, and the fat berths.[92]

During his formative years, Whitman was well acquainted with the work of Carlyle. As early as 1846 he wrote reviews of *Heroes and Hero Worship* and *Sartor Resartus* for the *Brooklyn Daily Eagle*.[93] In these works Carlyle's ideas of the poet-prophet are clearly outlined.[94] First of all, it is sincerity and depth of vision that make a poet. It is his thought that is important, and it should be spoken out plainly, in finer music than mere rhyme and jingle.[95] The poetic hero is of common stock, an unrefined child of nature, a worker who despises riches and knows the common lot.[96] He is the loving and brotherly son of

---

[90] Traubel, *With Walt Whitman in Camden*, II, 300; Gregory Paine, "The Literary Relations of Whitman and Carlyle with Especial Reference to Their Contrasting Views on Democracy," *SP* 36 (July 1939), 550–563.

[91] Traubel, *With Walt Whitman in Camden*, III, 19.

[92] *Specimen Days*, IV, 307–308.

[93] Walt Whitman, *The Gathering of the Forces*, ed. Cleveland Rodgers and John Black, 290–291.

[94] Fred Manning Smith, "Whitman's Poet-Prophet and Carlyle's Hero," *PMLA* 55 (December 1940), 1146–1164; Smith, "Whitman's Debt to Carlyle's *Sartor Resartus*," *MLQ* 3 (March 1942), 51–65.

[95] Thomas Carlyle, *Heroes and Hero Worship, The Works of Thomas Carlyle*, V, 83–84.

[96] *Ibid.*, pp. 63, 67, 69, 71–72.

man who becomes the spokesman, the voice of his age.[97] Carlyle says of Dante, "In this Dante . . . ten silent centuries . . . found a voice. . . . It is a great thing for a nation that it get an articulate voice; that it produce a man who will speak forth melodiously what the heart of it means."[98] This voice is the voice of authority, the voice of the great believer, not the cynic, for it springs from the heart of the mystical experience.[99] Finally, there is Carlyle's rebuke of Voltaire for his attacks on Christianity: "Perhaps the clothes of our religion are worn out and new clothes are needed—Wilt thou help us to embody the divine spirit of that Religion in a New Mythus?"[100]

The numerous parallels to these thoughts of Emerson and Carlyle found in Whitman's work will become obvious during the course of this study. Though the treatment of the two men has been of necessity brief and incomplete, the basic ideas relating to the poet-prophet in *Leaves of Grass* have been touched upon. It would seem that Emerson contributed primarily to the cosmic and spiritual elements in Whitman's creation; Carlyle, to the humane and social. Upon this background in superimposed triadic design of seer, accepter, and sharer, these further details are sketched in.

1. *The Poet-Prophet Must See*

Whitman's affection for Emerson and his acceptance of him as the greatest of all American poets has been noted. His few expressions of doubt evidently grew out of those transient moods of loneliness that must come to all profound and dedicated artists, for he doubts Emerson because of his delight in "verbal polish" and "quaint conceits" and on that basis rather unjustly suspects him of appreciating Waller and Lovelace more fully than the Hebrew prophets or Homer.[101] How like profound and dedicated Milton when, resentful of the popu-

[97] *Ibid.*, pp. 25, 53–54, 93–95.
[98] *Ibid.*, pp. 93, 114.
[99] Carlyle, *Sartor Resartus*, I, 40–41.
[100] *Ibid.*, p. 154.
[101] "Notes Left Over," V, 269.

larity of this same Lovelace and his kin, he asks in his loneliness:

> Were it not better done as others use,
> To sport with Amaryllis in the shade,
> Or with the tangles of Neaera's hair?
> [Lycidas, 67–69]

Whitman sees the same conditions surrounding him and being no less cosmic in his poetic ambitions is disturbed by shallow singers who seem to shrink from "the sturdy and universal."[102] Obviously, Emerson was not of these, but he was not as completely divorced from them as his lonely disciple would have him be. Whitman's consolation is not unlike that which spurred Milton on: "To such, or the luckiest of them, as we see, the audiences are limitless and profitable; but they cease presently. While this day, or any day, to workmen portraying interior or spiritual life, the audiences are limited, and often laggard—but they last forever."[103] It was the struggle with this kind of doubt and questioning, it would seem, that finally made Whitman strong in his belief in the cosmic personality he was writing into his *Leaves of Grass*, a new breed of poet who did not "deign to defend God or the perfection of things or liberty or the exquisite beauty and reality of the soul."[104]

Whitman's poet-prophet shares the true mystic's "yearning to get beyond the evaluation of finite existence and to apprehend the perfection of everything in its place."[105] He seeks that divine thread running through all humanity which can restore men to the open air and the sunlight to move again as the gods. Bucke thought that he saw in Whitman's mystic experience on a "transparent summer morning" the very moment when poet became prophet.[106] Swinburne was the first of many to see in

---

[102] "Poetry To-Day in America," V, 215–216.

[103] "Democratic Vistas," *Collect*, V, 120.

[104] "Preface, 1855," V, 183.

[105] H. A. Myers, "Whitman's Conception of the Spiritual Democracy, 1855–56," *AL* 6 (November 1934), 243.

[106] Horace Traubel, Richard Maurice Bucke, and Thomas Harned, *In Re Walt Whitman*, p. 329–347.

Whitman a parallel to the "elemental and eternal" qualities of Blake's mysticism, a parallel which Thomson qualifies by observing that while "Blake never grasps or cares for the common world of reality, Whitman never loosens his embrace of it."[107] This attachment to materials is a vital part of the poet-prophet's cosmic nature. Whitman's lines "My foothold is tenon'd and mortis'd in granite, . . . And I know the amplitude of time" mark a new variation of the mystic theme.[108]

Just how this variation came to be is suggested in *Democratic Vistas*. "America demands a poetry that is bold, modern, all-surrounding and Kosmical. . . . It must in no respect ignore science or the modern."[109] True, the prophet must always seek the "One" in the palpable many, but the lesson of the modern is that science aids rather than hinders. The poet-prophet of *Leaves of Grass* is confirmed in his mysticism by new revelations of the unshakable laws of science.[110] He feels as Wordsworth felt that the true poet instinctively rejoices in the truths that the man of science seeks as "remote and unknown" benefactors. The poet-prophet, therefore, could never be startled or unsettled by scientific discovery; rather he waits patiently, confident of being affirmed.

After the noble inventors, after the scientists,
   the chemist, the geologist, ethnologist,
Finally shall come the poet worthy that name,
The true son of God shall come singing his songs.[111]

The greatness of the poet-prophet grows out of his ability to "see into the life of things." He welcomes the illuminating, advancing sunrise of modern science. Old superstitions and intrigues retreat with the shadows, and the new cosmic poet can be born.

[107] Algernon Charles Swinburne, *William Blake*, p. 300; James Thomson, *Walt Whitman, the Man and the Poet*, p. 29; Allen, *Walt Whitman Handbook*, pp. 241–254.

[108] "Song of Myself," I, 57.

[109] "Democratic Vistas," *Collect*, V, 128.

[110] Foerster, *American Criticism*, pp. 200–205.

[111] "Passage to India," II, 190–191.

2. *The Poet-Prophet Must Accept*

Science confirms the vision of the true poet and encourages him to come to terms with a new world. This new world, imperfect, yet rich and dynamic, stirs the prophetic soul.

> A newer garden of creation, no primal solitude,
> Dense, joyous, modern, populous millions, cities
>   and farms,
> With iron interlaced, composite, tied, many in one,
> By all the world contributed—freedom's law's and
>   thrift's society,
> The crown and teeming paradise, so far, of time's
>   accumulations,
> To justify the past.[112]

It is this America, culmination of the past, that Whitman has in mind when he says, "It almost seems as if a poetry with cosmic and dynamic features of magnitude and limitlessness suitable to the human soul, were never possible before."[113] Here the greater vision of the modern man can be brought to bear on the greater materials of the new garden provided for it, "perceive what is permanent in the flux of things, and explain the law of its development."[114] Whitman marked the following passage in an article from *Graham's Magazine*, "The mountains, rivers, forests and the elements that gird them round about would be only blank conditions of matter if the mind did not fling its own divinity around them." His marginal comment was, "This I think is one of the most indicative sentences I ever read."[115] "The direct trial of him who would be the greatest poet is to-day. If he does not flood himself with the immediate age as with vast oceanic tides—if he be not himself the age transfigur'd, and if to him is not open'd the eternity which gives similitude to all periods and locations and processes

---

[112] "The Prairie States," II, 177.
[113] "A Backward Glance O'er Travel'd Roads," III, 49.
[114] Stovall, *Walt Whitman*, p. xxv.
[115] "Notes and Fragments," IX, 53.

. . . —let him merge in the general run, and await his development."[116]

The mystic can come to terms with his world of time and place only by realizing it as a part of the divine scheme. In more practical terms, the mystic can accept the finite only in terms of the future, of its latent perfectibility. He assumes stature as a poet-prophet in proportion to his ability to give substance and power to his vision of the beckoning ideal. "In short, as, though it may not be realized, it is strictly true, that a few first-class poets, philosophs, and authors, have substantially settled and given status to the entire religion, education, law, sociology, etc., of the hitherto civilized world, by tingeing and often creating the atmosphere out of which they have arisen, such also must stamp, and more than ever stamp, the interior and real democratic construction of this American continent, today, and days to come."[117]

Inherent in this concept of the poet-prophet is his complete identification with his land. "Long, long are the processes of the development of a nationality. Only to the rapt vision does the seen become the prophecy of the unseen."[118] But the poet-prophet is patient, at times even stoical.[119] He never attacks a convention merely for the sake of reform; he attacks only those conventions which stand in the way of his vision of reality.[120] Whitman never doubted the future of America, provided she could find her prophetic voice.

I count with such absolute certainty on the great future of the United States—different from, though founded on, the past—that I have always invoked that future, and surrounded myself with it, before or while singing my songs. . . . Of men or states, few realize how much they live in the future. That rising like pinnacles, gives its main significance to all you and I are doing

---

[116] "Preface, 1855," V, 181.

[117] "Democratic Vistas," *Collect*, V, 56–57.

[118] "Poetry To-Day in America," V, 225.

[119] C. E. Pulos, "Whitman and Epictetus: The Stoical Element in *Leaves of Grass*," *JEGP* 55 (January 1956), 75–84.

[120] Myers, "Whitman's Conception of the Spiritual Democracy," p. 252.

today. Without it, there were little meaning in lands or poems—
little purport in human lives. All ages, all Nations and States,
have been such prophecies. But where any former ones with
prophecy so broad, so clear, as our times, our lands—as those of
the West?[121]

With the poet-prophet to guide and sustain, these states will become great and continuous, "will expand to the amplitude of
their destiny, and become illustrations and culminating parts
of the cosmos and of civilization."[122]

You who celebrate bygones,
Who have explored the outward, the surfaces of the
    races, the life that has exhibited itself,
Who have treated of man as of the creature of
    politics, aggregates, rulers and priests,
I, habitan of the Alleghanies, treating of him as
    he is in himself in his own rights,
Pressing the pulse of the life that has seldom
    exhibited itself, (the great pride of man in himself,)
Chanter of Personality, outlining what is yet to be,
I project the history of the future.[123]

This is the calling of the true poet. He challenges his nation
with the chants of the unseen ideal inherent in the seen, regardless of the apparent imperfections of his time or the immediate
possibilities of their correction. He accepts the things around
him as "a necessary preliminary to the ultimate reality."[124]

Here first the duties of to-day, the lessons of the
    concrete,
Wealth, order, travel, shelter, products, plenty;
As of the building of some varied, vast, perpetual
    edifice,

---

[121] "Preface, 1876," V, 200.
[122] "Poetry To-Day in America," V, 227 (footnote).
[123] "To a Historian," I, 4.
[124] Vernon Louis Parrington, *Main Currents in American Thought,* III, 83.

Whence arise inevitable in time, the towering roofs,
  the lamps,
The solid-planted spires tall shooting to the stars.[125]

3. The Poet-Prophet Must Share

The implication of all that has been said about the poet-prophet is that he alone is qualified to be the great national leader. It is the completeness of his vision, his grasp of first principles, that qualifies him. Whitman shared Emerson's skepticism of reformers—his distrust of the partial, particular nature of their interests.[126] True and lasting reformation can come only through the development of spiritual and heroic individuals; therefore, the great national leader is less interested in the superficialities of political and social systems than in the potentialities of each individual man. "The literature, songs, esthetics, etc., of a country are of importance principally because they furnish the materials and suggestions of personality for the women and men of that country, and enforce them in a thousand effective ways."[127] The largeness of the individual determines the largeness of the nation. The poet-prophet must work through each man and woman; he must become a factor in the evolution of the human being. This conviction is the source of Whitman's particular brand of didacticism.

> The true question to ask respecting a book is *Has it helped any human soul?* This is the hint, statement, not only of the great literatus, his book, but of every great artist. It may be that all works of art are to be first tried by their art qualities, their image-forming talent, and their dramatic, pictorial, plot-constructing, euphonious and other talents. Then, when ever claiming to be first-class works, they are to be strictly and sternly tried by their foundation in, and radiation, in the highest sense, and always indirectly, of the ethic principles, and eligibility to free. arouse, dilate.[128]

125 "The United States to Old World Critics," III, 312–313.
126 "I Hear It Was Charged against Me," I, 154.
127 "Democratic Vistas," *Collect*, V, 95.
128 *Ibid.*, p. 139.

This is the moral "aidancy" which Foerster points out as a major element in Whitman's theory of poetry.[129] It is one of the characteristics of the great literatures of India, Palestine, Greece, and of the works of Dante and Shakespeare, that made Whitman view them as great landmarks in the history of mankind.[130]

Though many have questioned Whitman's genuine artistry, few have failed to recognize his ability to establish an intimate contact with his reader. He attached importance to this quality during his early years as an editor. In an editorial for the *Brooklyn Eagle* he writes, "There is a curious kind of sympathy . . . that arises in the mind of the newspaper conductor with the public he serves. He gets to love them."[131] This declaration, along with later editorials attacking "morality by legislation," suggests a new warmth and tolerance somewhat foreign to the author of *Franklin Evans* and marks, I believe, a decided advance toward the broad morality and humanity of the poet of *Leaves of Grass*.

Stevenson says of *Leaves of Grass*: "However wild, however contradictory, it may be, in parts, this at least may be said for his book, as it may be said of the Christian Gospels, that no one will read it, however respectable, but he gets a knock upon his conscience; no one, however fallen, but he finds a kindly and supporting welcome."[132] This is accepting and sharing in the largest and most selfless sense. It was the lack of such a capacity in Thoreau that concerned Whitman. "He couldn't put his life into any other life—realize why one man was so and another man was not so: was impatient with the people on the street."[133]

[129] Foerster, *American Criticism*, pp. 181–182.

[130] "Notes Left Over," V, 292.

[131] Emory Holloway, *Whitman: An Interpretation*, p. 6 (quotes Whitman editorial from the *Brooklyn Eagle*). There is an interesting discussion of the influence of Whitman the editor on the development of Whitman the poet in *The Uncollected Poetry and Prose of Walt Whitman*, ed. Emory Holloway, I, lxxvi–lxxvii, lxxx–lxxxi.

[132] Robert Louis Stevenson, *The Essay on Walt Whitman by Robert Louis Stevenson: With a Little Journey to the Home of Whitman by Elbert Hubbard*, p. 70.

[133] Traubel, *With Walt Whitman in Camden*, I, 212.

All that the poet-prophet of *Leaves of Grass* possesses, he places at the disposal of one fellow being as readily as another.

> Behold I do not give lectures or a little charity,
> When I give I give myself.[134]

> This is the meal equally set, this the meat for
>   natural hunger,
> It is for the wicked just the same as the righteous,
>   I make appointments with all,
> I will not have a single person slighted or left away,
> The kept-woman, sponger, thief, are hereby invited,
> The heavy-lipp'd slave is invited, the veneralee
>   is invited;
> There shall be no difference between them and the
>   rest.

> This is the press of a bashful hand, this is the
>   float and odor of hair,
> This the touch of my lips to yours, this the murmur
>   of yearning,
> This the far-off depth and height reflecting my own
>   face,
> This the thoughtful merge of myself, and the outlet
>   again.[135]

All that he finds significant in life he would bring to bear on his reader, to reappear through him and shed an equal blessing.

> Stop this day and night with me and you shall possess
>   the origin of all poems,
> You shall possess the good of the earth and sun,
>   (there are millions of suns left,)
> You shall no longer take things at second or third
>   hand, nor look through the eyes of the dead, nor
>   feed on the spectres in books,

134 "Song of Myself," I, 89.
135 *Ibid.*, p. 55.

You shall not look through my eyes either, nor take
   things from me,
You shall listen to all sides and filter them for
   yourself.[136]

The seer, the accepter, the sharer—but the greatest of these
is the sharer. For sharing is the proof of the love of man for his
comrade, the living principle binding all men together, the base
of all metaphysics.[137]

To avoid any possibility of being thought "on the verge of the
usual mistake" of Whitman scholarship, it may be well to recall
that this has been a discussion of Whitman's theory of poetry,
not of Whitman the man. There is no more inclination here to
argue that Whitman the man was a prophet than to argue that
he was an organism. And whether the latter be true and the
former false, or vice versa, is of no concern in this study. The
two basic elements in an artist's theory of poetry have been
pointed out, and nothing more. In discussing these, his organicism and his didacticism, the intention has been to show that
the latter grew logically out of the former and is an integral
part of a noble theory of art. As the attempt has been made to
define Whitman's particular kind of organicism, so has it been
made to define his particular kind of didacticism—just as the
nature-teacher analogy clarifies the former, so the poet-prophet
analogy clarifies the latter.

In the light of Whitman's penetrating restatements of the
organic theory of composition and of his earnest belief in the
prophetic function of the poet, it would seem heresy to attempt
to arrive at the true nature of the structure of *Leaves of Grass*
from the superficial point of view of external form, metrics, or
literary style. On the other hand, resort to the natural alterna-
tive, an approach through subject matter alone, is thwarted by
the magnitude and variety which achieve a large part of their
cumulative effect from the very fact that in Whitman's hands

---

[136] *Ibid.*, p. 35.
[137] "The Base of All Metaphysics," I, 146–147.

they defy compression and order. Out of a consideration of these facts has developed the conviction that the unifying element, the key to the structural pattern of *Leaves of Grass*, is its unique religious *spirit*, defined and sustained throughout by Whitman's use of his carefully drawn, Christ-like poet-prophet. This is in keeping with all that Whitman has written either on, or vaguely related to, the subject.[138] More important than that, as the result of such an approach, the work as a whole, as well as its individual poems, takes on new vitality and significance.

The pervading religiosity in *Leaves of Grass* is unique in its two-dimensional nature. It is at once cosmic and personal, and as such it draws upon the best of two worlds. In its cosmic concern it is peculiarly ancient and mystical in spirit; in its personal concern it is peculiarly modern and democratic.

It is easy for modern man to miss the full significance of Whitman's cosmic concern. Through the agency of modern science the average man has become familiar with the world in which he lives; he no longer finds it sacred in the ancient sense. To him it is an "old top-knot" in a sense that would appall Whitman. He is awed, if at all, not by it, but by his own expanding scientific knowledge of it. His cosmic curiosity may be immense,

---

[138] Quotations from Whitman: "The chief trait of any given poet is always the spirit he brings to the observation of humanity and nature—the mood out of which he contemplates his subjects. What kind of temper, and what amount of faith, reports these things?" (Walt Whitman, *Walt Whitman's Backward Glances*, ed. Sculley Bradley and John Stevenson, p. 17); "In giving the preceding introduction we have not had so much in view to advocate or praise the book, . . . as to prepare the reader . . . for its novel form, and more novel and most free, sturdy, and all-tolerating spirit" (Furness, *Walt Whitman's Workshop*, p. 152); "Still if this [apparent contradiction in Emerson's work] be so in spirit as well as form it were a fatal defect" ("Notes and Fragments Left Over by Walt Whitman," IX, 160); "It is not that he gives his country great poems; it is that he gives his country the spirit which makes the greatest poems and the greatest material for poems" (Notes and Fragments, 30–31); "The originality must be of the spirit . . ." (Notes and Fragments, 37); "I chose the fundamentals for *Leaves of Grass*—heart, spirit . . ." (Traubel, *With Walt Whitman in Camden*, II, 373). In addition there is a significant passage which, if not written by Whitman, was approved by him: "Its form will be unprecedentedly beautiful to all who know its spirit, and to those who do not, it is a matter of no consequence" (Richard Maurice Bucke, *Walt Whitman*, p. 187).

but it is in no sense a religious curiosity. Whitman would consider this tragic. He is modern in his enthusiastic embrace of all that science has to offer, but for him it in no way divests nature of its ancient sacredness. Having praised the great "Savans" of the modern world, he declares that the true poet of that world "must vocalize the vastness and splendor and reality with which Scientism has invested Man and the Universe." He can no longer indulge in "children's tales," "mere amorousness," and "superficial rhyme." Rather, his poems must be "revivified by this tremendous innovation, the Kosmic Spirit." And then he comes to the crux of the matter:

> Only, (for me, at any rate, in all my Prose and Poetry,) joyfully accepting Modern Science, and loyally following it without the slightest hesitation, there remains ever recognized still a higher flight, a higher fact, the Eternal Soul of Man, (of all Else too,) the Spiritual, the Religious—which it is to be the greatest office of Scientism . . . and of future Poetry also, to . . . launch forth in renewed Faith and Scope a hundred fold. To me, the worlds of Religiousness, of the conception of the Divine, and of the Ideal, though mainly latent, are just as absolute in Humanity and the Universe as the world of Chemistry, or anything in the objective worlds. . . . To me, the crown of Savantism is to be, that it surely opens the way for a more splendid Theology, and for ampler and diviner Songs. No year, nor even century, will settle this. There is a phase of the Real, lurking behind the Real, which it is all for.[139]

In many such passages Whitman points to the cosmic concerns of his poet-prophet; he is "religious man" in the most ancient sense. In his view of the sacredness of the cosmos, he harks back to revelations characteristic of the distant religious past of humanity. In doing so he challenges in a powerful way the nonreligious view of the universe encouraged by modern science and modern urban life. The poet-prophet would reassert primitive man's feeling for the sanctity of nature, doing

[139] "Preface, 1876," V, 201–202.

so in the cheerful faith that advancing science would give new scope and meaning to that sanctity.

The significance of Whitman's stress upon this particular dimension of religious experience is pointed up by Mircea Eliade's observation that "the wholly desacralized cosmos is a recent discovery in the history of the human spirit." It is modern man, Eliade says, who has desacralized the world and assumed a profane existence. Even the Christianity of the modern world has lost the cosmic values it once possessed; religious experience is no longer open to the cosmos. The latter "has become opaque, inert, mute; it transmits no message, it holds no cipher."[140]

Eliade's picture of archaic "religious man," as opposed to this nonreligious product of the modern world, echoes Whitman at every point:

> For religious man, nature is never only "natural"; it is always fraught with a religious value. . . . the world is impregnated with sacredness. . . . The gods . . . manifested the different modalities of the sacred in the very structure of the world and of cosmic phenomena. . . . This divine work always preserves its quality of transparency, that is, it spontaneously reveals the many aspects of the sacred. . . . The cosmos as a whole is an organism at once *real, living,* and *sacred*; it simultaneously reveals the modalities of being and of sacrality. . . . Every cosmic fragment is transparent; its own mode of existence shows a particular structure of being, and hence of the sacred. We should never forget that, for religious man, sacrality is a full manifestation of being. . . . the cosmos "lives" and "speaks." . . . there is an absolute reality, *the sacred*, which transcends this world but manifests itself in this world, thereby sanctifying it and making it real.[141]

Eliade is, of course, referring to the "religious man" who sprang from and gave voice to those primitive and oriental cultures which Whitman explored with enthusiasm and from which he

---

[140] Mircea Eliade, *The Sacred and the Profane*, pp. 13, 178–179.
[141] *Ibid.*, pp. 116–117, 138, 165, 202.

derived both inspiration and religious insight. No less than Whitman, he is drawing from the great myths of the ancient world, myths revitalized in modern terms in *Leaves of Grass*, helping define the cosmic elements in its religiosity.

But this ancient and mystical spirit, manifest in the poet-prophet's cosmic concern, is fused with a modern and democratic spirit, manifest in his personal concern. It is the naturalness and thoroughness of this fusion which more than anything else define the unique religious spirit of all of *Leaves of Grass*. Nothing short of a detailed analysis of Whitman's development of the Christ-figure, which is the substance of the next chapter, can convey the full significance of this two-dimensional religiosity as a unifying element, particularly the full significance of its personal concern. One immediate manifestation of the latter, however, is the unique poet-reader relationship, which is sustained throughout the volume. T. J. Rountree sees this as a device for both democratizing and unifying the new poetry. His comment on "Song of Myself" applies to *Leaves* as a whole. " 'Song of Myself' reveals Whitman's urgency for the reader to be reciprocal, and the poet's allowance for this reciprocity gives a unifying effect to the poem. This unity of reciprocity, I think, is a new and valid one."[142]

This second aspect of the pervading spirit in *Leaves*, this desire of the poet to involve the reader in a very special way, is no less religious in nature than the first. To the responsive reader a reaction in some sense religious is inescapable. The reasons for it are invariably subjective, as Whitman would have them be. First, there is the unmistakable tone of authority and prophecy which finds little, if any, rivalry outside the Bible. Second, there is the sense on the part of the reader of being personally and affectionately addressed—an awareness of being compelled to believe or reject, similar to that evoked by the Bible, with the same inability to remain outside the work or indifferent to it, the same sense of universality of message.

[142] T. J. Rountree, "Whitman's Indirect Expression and Its Application to 'Song of Myself,'" *PMLA* 73 (December 1958), 552.

Third, there is an awareness of some powerful single element that makes the work embrace the reader as it does and compels him to identify himself with the hero or central figure of the argument. Finally, the fact that the reader finds himself repeatedly relating the poems to his own religious experience and beliefs confirms the opinion that the spirit is primarily religious.

Whitman's use of religious literature, the Bible in particular, more than anything else accounts for his ability as a poet to involve his reader in this unique way, to challenge his values and commitments, to overcome attitudes of detachment or indifference. Whitman wanted to accomplish this more than anything else, and he wanted to accomplish it with the masses of the American people. Over and over again he says that such a response on the part of a poet's people is the true test of great poetry. While Whitman himself was widely read in the mystical and religious literatures of the Orient, his American audience was not. His own predilection for the Bible as poetry and for Christ as a hero—and even more important, the biblical orientation of the American people, the fact that they were grounded in this tradition as in nothing else and were for the most part spiritually committed to it—led him naturally to draw primarily upon biblical materials. This in no way implies orthodoxy on Whitman's part. Indeed, his lever, his best hope, for evoking a personal response from his American reader, is his persistent unorthodoxy, the subtle and ingenious way in which he moves biblical traditions and figures into the realm of myth and gives them new dimensions of meaning for men caught up in the American democratic experiment. The biblical elements in *Leaves* are used as devices for forceful communication, a communication of what Whitman felt to be new and shocking concepts of man and his relationship to his fellows and to God. For Whitman they were not ends, but beginnings. They were means for probing into and evoking response from the minds and hearts of his American readers.

By this time it should be apparent that Whitman's concept of the artistic responsibility of the poet as he is inspired and taught by nature and must share this inspiration and enlightenment with his brothers "tallies" the religious responsibility of the prophet, felt in terms of his cosmic concern and his personal concern. Just as there is the fusion of the cosmic and the personal on both poetic and religious levels, there is the natural and thorough fusion of the offices of poet and prophet. The poet-prophet, then, is thoroughly modern in his sense of social responsibility, felt toward himself and his fellows; he is thoroughly primitive in his sense of cosmic responsibility, felt toward a cosmos that is living and sacred, not the mere accumulation of material reserves and physical energies which man must somehow merely conserve.

It has been rewarding to discover that the utilization of this concept of *religious spirit*, defined in terms of the Christ-like poet-prophet, as a unifying device in determining the structural pattern of *Leaves of Grass* finds ample confirmation in the form of both internal and external evidence of an objective nature. It might be well to state here that this does not imply that the device arrived at in this study is necessarily that employed consciously by the creative artist at work. From the standpoint of the critic, such a device is justified if it proves illuminating and helpful, provided, of course, that it is one which would appear to be in no way offensive to Whitman or derogatory to any part of his message. That, it has been suggested, is the situation here.

Whitman was such a remarkably original worker and *Leaves of Grass* is such a tremendously complex work that the degree of success or failure of any attempt to define its structure is largely determined by the validity of the approach and the writer's ability to sustain it. This first staggering problem may well be the crucial one. Miller recognizes this and in "Exploration of a Structure" begins his study with an interesting series of conjectures.[143] His conclusion—that a purely *metaphorical* approach is not the answer—is sensible. In the skillful use of

---

[143] James E. Miller, Jr., *A Critical Guide to Leaves of Grass*, pp. 168–173.

metaphor there is applied to the poem an external device which illuminates and reveals, but does not, and by its very nature cannot, define, or as Miller says "discover or prove." After indicating the problem Miller proceeds with a rather conventional twofold approach which is biographical in that he divides the poet's development into three distinct periods and "non-organic" in that he works from a pattern of ideas which *in method of presentation at least* seems somewhat arbitrary and external.[144] The problem is difficult; it is to get inside the poem somehow and work from within outward. Is this possible? The nearest thing to an answer here is to say that this is what this study attempts to do. Its particular approach seems best described in terms of *spirit*.

[144] *Ibid.*, pp. 175–187.

CHAPTER III

The Christ-Symbol in
Leaves of Grass

Before the mass of internal and external evidence which suggests that the pervading spirit of *Leaves of Grass* is religious and that the Christ-symbol is the most significant symbol in the book as a whole is presented, it should be reemphasized that this study is not concerned with the identification of Whitman himself with the Christ-like prophet; rather it is concerned with Whitman's concept and use of that figure as a literary device in *Leaves of Grass.* Such a clarifying statement is imperative in view of the habitual confusion of the two, encouraged by the extreme enthusiasm of many of Whitman's early admirers no less than by the suspicions of later writers.[1]

[1] Some early enthusiasts who lost sight of Whitman's concept in *Leaves of*

Whitman himself gives the best answer to the first group, the enthusiasts, when he writes to Mrs. Gilchrist, "You must not construct such an unauthorized and imaginary figure and call it Walt Whitman, and so devotedly invest your loving nature in it. The actual Walt Whitman is a very plain personage and entirely unworthy such devotion."[2] Granted, Whitman here is speaking under very particular circumstances, those of discouraging a woman whose romantic love is not desired; nevertheless, by this very token, it is one of the few times that we have a statement from Whitman in which he is clearly speaking of his actual self, completely detached from his book. There is little evidence that he ever made extravagant claims for Whitman the actual person. He did make and permit to be made such claims for the ideal poet-prophet in *Leaves of Grass*. That is quite a different matter. Among the early admirers, Donaldson and Edward Carpenter show some signs of understanding this fact. The former writes, "Whitman with the pen was one man—Whitman in private life was another."[3] In Carpenter's portrait of Whitman, the actual man is less idealized than elsewhere, though it is true that Carpenter saw in him an advanced stage of human development.[4] Paul Elmer More was one of the first persons to point out the unintentional disservice done by the early zealots; however, he insists that Whitman, with his own words, can overcome this.[5] Allen has rather well sug-

---

Grass and did it a disservice by making extravagant claims for Whitman the man as prophet or even the modern Christ: William Douglas O'Connor, *The Good Gray Poet: A Vindication;* Richard Maurice Bucke, *Walt Whitman,* pp. 180–181, 187; William Sloane Kennedy, *The Fight of a Book for the World,* p. 38 (quotes Mrs. Gilchrist. See footnote 2, below) ; *The Complete Writings of Walt Whitman,* I, lxxviii, lxxxvi–lxxxvii; John Burroughs, *Whitman: A Study,* pp. 18, 19; Thomas B. Harned, "The Poet of Immortality," in *In Re Walt Whitman,* ed. Horace Traubel, Richard Maurice Bucke, and Thomas Harned, p. 361. The main attackers of Whitman as a poser: John Jay Chapman, "Walt Whitman," *Emerson and Other Essays,* pp. 111–128; Harvey O'Higgins, "Alias Walt Whitman," *Harper's Magazine* (May 1929), 698–707; Esther Shephard, *Walt Whitman's Pose,* pp. 140–151, 392–393.

[2] Clara Barrus, *Whitman and Burroughs: Comrades,* p. 158.

[3] Thomas Donaldson, *Walt Whitman the Man,* p. 8.

[4] Edward Carpenter, *Days With Walt Whitman.*

[5] Paul Elmer More, "Walt Whitman," *Shelburne Essays,* pp. 180–181.

gested the sane approach to the matter when he writes of the "carpenter" legend, "It appears that Whitman became a carpenter for purely economical reasons, and that he dropped the work within two or three years because it bored him."[6] Canby defends Whitman against the later group, the detractors of the poet as a poser. He insists that Whitman's poses (which have been exaggerated in the first place) were not so much poses as an expression of the desire on his part to fulfill his role of dedication. "And the American that he created in his poems, out of what his eyes saw and his ears heard, was meant from the beginning to be the symbol of a faith and a dream. . . . Walt Whitman apart from the *Leaves* is of little importance."[7] Briggs takes a similar stand, "Only his ideal self was intentionally inscribed there [in *Leaves of Grass*]."[8] If during his lifetime Whitman attempted to realize in part this ideal, as he surely did, that does not justify the appellation "poser" in the derogatory sense in which Mrs. Shephard uses it.

A disentanglement of this whole noisy controversy can be found in Frederic I. Carpenter's sensible essay "Walt Whitman's Eidolon." Carpenter says:

> All these "facts" are true. It is quite possible to interpret Whitman as a charlatan. If you are a strict realist, this is the only possible explanation. If you are a moralist of the old school, it is the only satisfactory one. But it is also possible to interpret "Walt Whitman's pose" idealistically. The poet "Walt" of the *Leaves of Grass* was the "eidolon" which Walter Whitman imagined for himself and which he strove to realize, first in his poetry and next in his actual life. This ideal "Walt" was a personification of that democratic dream which Emerson had earlier described abstractly. And this "eidolon"—this "body lurking there within thy body"—was, in the ancient language of idealism, the real Walt Whitman—"the real I myself."

But this simple idealistic explanation is complicated by the

[6] Gay Wilson Allen, *The Solitary Singer*, pp. 116–117.
[7] Henry Seidel Canby, *Walt Whitman: An American*, pp. 159–161, 187.
[8] Arthur E. Briggs, *Walt Whitman, Thinker and Artist*, p. 21.

fact that the actual Walter Whitman struggled not only to realize the ideal "Walt" in his poetry but also to actualize him in his own flesh. . . . He was always bothered by stubborn discrepancies between his early, actual self and his later, ideal self. And, mistakenly, he sought to hide these discrepancies not only from the eyes of the literary public but also from the eyes of his closest friends. Therefore, the ideal Walt Whitman of the poetry has become merged with the composite Walter-Walt of actuality, until the valid imaginative "eidolon" has become suspect, because of the apparent duplicity and confusion of the actual person.

In imagination utterly, and partly in actual fact, Walter Whitman became the ideal Walt. . . . He realized his ideal wholly in his poetry. And he partly succeeded in incarnating his ideal in the flesh.[9]

It is Carpenter's "imaginative 'eidolon,' " the ideal realized in the poetry, Christ-like, and functioning as a unifying poetic device in *Leaves of Grass*, with which we are concerned in this chapter. That this "eidolon" was inherent in all of Whitman's thought and practice as a creative artist is of major importance to our study; whether or not he realized it in actual life, rather beside the point.

The first external evidence which supports the concept of *Leaves of Grass* as being primarily religious in spirit is found in the influence of Emerson's and Carlyle's portraits of the poet-prophet, an influence which has already been analyzed.[10] The second and more significant external evidence is found in Whitman's own prose, notebooks, and recorded conversation. In

[9] Frederic I. Carpenter, "Walt Whitman's Eidolon," *College English* 3 (March 1942), 537–540. In general, important recent criticism has taken a tolerant attitude toward Whitman in regard to his so-called poses. See Newton Arvin, *Whitman*, p. 32; Canby, *Walt Whitman*, pp. 83, 101; Leslie A. Fiedler, "Images of Walt Whitman," *Leaves of Grass One Hundred Years After*, ed. Milton Hindus, pp. 55–73; Floyd Stovall, "Walt Whitman: The Man and the Myth," *The South Atlantic Quarterly* 54, No. 4 (October 1955), 538–551; Gay Wilson Allen, *Walt Whitman: Man, Poet, and Legend*, pp. 3–25, 101–154.

[10] See pages 29–33 of this study.

them are more than one hundred passages suggesting the religious spirit of his poetry, over fifty of which are significant.[11] Of these latter passages, which are scattered throughout his prose, many are climactic or compendious when seen in context.

There are those passages which insist that great poetry is always religious. "The altitude of literature and poetry has always been religious—and always will be."[12] "The highest poetic expression demands a certain element of the religious—indeed, should be transfused with it."[13] "In a very profound sense *religion is the poetry of humanity*."[14] "Then we may attain a poetry worthy the immortal soul of man, and which, while absorbing materials, . . . will, above all, have . . . a freeing, fluidizing, expanding, religious character, exulting with science, fructifying the moral elements, and stimulating aspirations and meditations on the unknown."[15] "In its highest aspect, and striking its grandest average, essential poetry expresses and goes along with essential Religion—has been and is more the adjunct, and more serviceable to that true religion than all the priests and creeds and churches that now exist or have ever existed."[16]

Even more important are the many passages in which Whitman refers to the religious element in *Leaves* and associates it with the spirit of democratic America and his development of the national theme. Here are a few examples. "Ever since what might be called thought, or the budding of thought, fairly began in my mind, I had had the desire to attempt some worthy record of that entire faith and acceptance ('to justify the ways of God to man' is Milton's well-known and ambitious phrase) which is the foundation of moral America."[17] "I claim everything for religion: after the claims of my religion are satis-

---

[11] See the prose references in the section, "On Religion" in the Appendix.
[12] "Democratic Vistas," *Collect*, V, 136.
[13] Horace Traubel, *With Walt Whitman in Camden*, I, 163.
[14] "Five Thousand Poems," VI, 183.
[15] "Democratic Vistas," *Collect*, V, 138.
[16] "Good-Bye My Fancy," VII, 68–69.
[17] "A Backward Glance O'er Travel'd Roads," III, 63.

fied nothing is left for anything else: yet I have been called irreligious—an infidel (God help me!): as if I could have written a word of the *Leaves* without its religious root-ground."[18]

Not that half only, individualism, which isolates. There is another half, which is adhesiveness or love, that fuses, ties and aggregates, making the races comrades, and fraternizing all. Both are to be vitalized by religion (sole worthiest element of man or state), breathing into the proud, material tissues, the breath of life. For I say at the core of democracy, finally, is the religious element. All religions, old and new, are there. Nor may the scheme step forth, clothed in resplendent beauty and command, till these, bearing the best, the latest fruit, the spiritual, shall fully appear.[19]

When I commenced, years ago, elaborating the plan of my poems, and continued turning over that plan, and shifting it in my mind through many years . . . experimenting much, and writing and abandoning much, one deep purpose underlay the others, and has underlain it and its execution ever since—and that has been the religious purpose. . . . This basic purpose has never been departed from in the composition of my verses. . . . And a poet of America (I said) must fill himself with such thoughts, and chant his best out of them. . . . As there can be, in my opinion, no sane and complete personality, nor any grand and electric nationality, without the stock element of religion imbuing all the other elements, . . . so there can be no poetry worthy the name without that element behind all.[20]

Turning to *Leaves of Grass* for internal evidence of an objective nature in the sense that the religious purport is directly expressed, we find more than twenty passages, over ten of which are significant.[21]

[18] Traubel, *With Walt Whitman in Camden*, I, 10.
[19] "Democratic Vistas," *Collect*, V, 80.
[20] "Preface, 1872," V, 189–190.
[21] See the poetry references in the section "On Religion" in the Appendix.

I too, following many and follow'd by many, inaugurate
a religion,

.   .   .   .

I say the whole earth and all the stars in the sky
are for religion's sake.

I say no man has ever yet been half devout enough,
None has ever yet adored or worship'd half enough,
None has begun to think how divine he himself is,
and how certain the future is.

I say that the real and permanent grandeur of these
States must be their religion,
Otherwise there is no real and permanent grandeur;
(Nor character nor life worthy the name without
religion,
Nor land nor man nor woman without religion.) [22]

.   .   .   .

Know you, solely to drop in the earth the germs
of a greater religion,
The following chants each for its kind I sing.

.   .   .   .

For you to share with me two greatnesses, and a
third one rising inclusive and more resplendent,
The greatness of Love and Democracy, and the
greatness of Religion. [23]

We consider bibles and religions divine—I do not
say they are not divine;
I say they have all grown out of you, and may
grow out of you still,
It is not they who give the life, it is you who
give the life,
Leaves are no more shed from the trees, or trees
from the earth, than they are shed out of you. [24]

[22] "Starting from Paumanok," I, 21–22.
[23] *Ibid.*, p. 23.
[24] "A Song for Occupations," I, 262.

Ah more than any priest O soul we too believe in
   God,
But with the mystery of God we dare not dally.[25]

Thee in thy all-supplying, all-enclosing worship—
      thee in no single bible, saviour, merely,
Thy saviours countless, latent within thyself,
      thy bibles incessant within thyself, equal
   to any, divine as any.[26]

At this point another important advance in theory can be
made by further defining the religious spirit of *Leaves of Grass*
as basically Hebraic, more especially, Christ-like. The primary
reason and justification for such a concept must be found in the
thematic development, spirit, "drift," if you will, of the work
as a whole. That this can be found is demonstrated in the discussion of the over-all structure of *Leaves* in Chapter IV. But,
in addition, here again we find ample external and internal objective evidence.

There are more than seventy passages in Whitman's prose
(over thirty of which are significant) indicating his preference
for Hebraic poetry.[27] The major document here is his essay,
"The Bible as Poetry," undoubtedly the most favorable and
enthusiastic criticism he ever wrote, with the possible exception
of a few reviews of his own work.[28] In addition to passages already quoted from the essay, he has this to say:[29]

But will there ever be a time or place—ever a student, however
modern, of the grand art, to whom those compositions [the Old
and New Testaments] will not afford profounder lessons than
all else of their kind in the garnerage of the past? . . .

   Strange but true, that the principal factor in cohering the
nations, eras, and paradoxes of the globe, by giving them a com-

[25] "Passage to India," II, 194.
[26] "Thou Mother with Thy Equal Brood," II, 240.
[27] See the prose reference in the section "On the Bible" in the Appendix.
[28] "The Bible as Poetry," VI, 104–109.
[29] See pp. 25–26 of this study.

mon platform of two or three ideas, a commonalty of origin, and by projecting cosmic brotherhood, the dream of all hope, all time, . . . is to be identified and resolved back into a collection of old poetic lore, which, more than any other one thing else, has been the axis of civilization and history through thousands of years—and except for which this America of ours, with its polity and essentials, could not now be existing.[30]

This passage is especially relevant to this study, as it points to the Bible as poetry, that "old poetic lore" which is the chief source of our concept of brotherhood and of the entire American democratic experiment. It helps explain the particular phraseology he uses in stating his great ambition: "The great construction of the New Bible, not to be diverted from the principal object and the main life work . . . ought to be ready in 1859 . . . founding a new American religion."[31] The call he hoped to answer was once phrased this way, "We need somebody or something whose utterances are like the old Hebrew prophet's."[32]

The truth of the Bible, as Whitman saw it, was Wordsworth's profound poetic truth, at once exalting men and binding them together. "The books of the Bible stand for the final superiority of devout emotions over the rest, and of religious adoration, and ultimate absolute justice, more powerful than haughtiest kings, or millionaires, or majorities."[33] "Theological inferences . . . may be demolished by the scientific and historical inquiries of our times, but the collect of the Bible, as a traditional poem various in its sources and times, still remains the most, in the highest sense, instructive, suggestive, even artistic memorial of the East."[34] "What is in the Bible had better not be paraphrased. The Bible is indescribably perfect—putting it in

---

[30] "The Bible as Poetry," VI, 104, 109.
[31] "Notes and Fragments," IX, 6.
[32] Clifton Joseph Furness, *Walt Whitman's Workshop*, p. 67.
[33] "America's National Literature," VII, 6.
[34] Ellen Frances Frey, *Catalogue of the Walt Whitman Collection in the Duke Library*, Entry No. 40, p. 28.

rhyme, would that improve it or not?"[35] After notes on various religions, he concludes, "Hebrew—the most ethereal and elevated spiritually—this seems to be what subordinates all the rest—the soul rising in vagueness."[36] Finally, in notes for an introduction to an English edition of *Leaves of Grass*, he writes of himself, "The interior and foundation quality of the man is Hebraic, Biblical, Mystic."[37]

There are less than ten uses of the word *bible* in *Leaves of Grass* itself; however, striking biblical echoes and allusions abound in both the poetry and the prose.[38] Gay Wilson Allen has pointed out a total of 197 of these, 37 of which are repetitious.[39]

When we remember that the "God in man" idea is the dominant theme in *Leaves of Grass*, we realize that Whitman's strong attraction to the personality of Christ as the fruition of Hebraic religion and thought is inevitable. There are more than forty direct references to Christ (over twenty of which are significant) in Whitman's prose.[40] These references, of course, do not include the numerous passages indicative of the Christ spirit or idea in general, which are a part of everything he wrote. Whitman sees, as the climactic element in the Hebrew religion, its focus upon "the sublime idea of a coming man or Saviour, a perfect individual."[41] It is in this sense, primarily, that we have referred to his attitude as Hebraic. He parts company with the Hebrews when they refuse to recognize the significance of the New Testament as the fulfillment of this "sublime idea." This fact is clearly indicated in an annotated clipping on "The Unity of the Bible," from the *American Messenger*, an article which takes the typical Protestant point of view that running throughout the entire Bible, Old and New

[35] "Notes and Fragments," IX, 97.
[36] *Ibid.*, p. 55.
[37] Furness, *Walt Whitman's Workshop*, p. 154.
[38] See the poetry references in the section "On the Bible" in the Appendix.
[39] Gay Wilson Allen, "Biblical Echoes in Whitman's Works," *AL* 6 (November 1934), 302–315.
[40] See the prose references in the section "On Christ" in the Appendix.
[41] "Notes and Fragments," IX, 104.

Testaments alike, is one unifying idea, "in a word, Jesus Christ, the Saviour. . . . Jesus Christ the key-note of the whole."[42] It is particularly significant to our study that Whitman attached a note suggesting his desire to impart a similar unity to *Leaves of Grass.* In another note he observes, "The real owners and heirs of the Hebrew Bible, rejecting the New Testament and what it stands for, still wait for the climax of the poem."[43] An interesting aspect of this statement is the easy, natural manner in which Whitman is able to view the significance of the Bible in purely poetic terms, evidently oblivious of any theological considerations; the sin of the Hebrews here is against a poem, not against an ancient faith.

Whitman always refers to Christ in terms of affection and admiration. He is "the holy and just Nazarene"; his story, "the unsurpassedly simple, loving, perfect idyls of the life and death of Christ, in the New Testament."[44] "For us these beacons burn through all the nights. Unknown Egyptians, graving hieroglyphs; . . . Hebrew prophet, with spirituality, as in flashes of lightning; . . . Christ, with bent head, brooding love and peace, like a dove."[45]

> One word can pour such a flood through the soul—Today I will mention Christ's before all other names. . . . Out of Christ are divine words—out of this savior. Some words are fresh-smelling, like lilies, roses, to the soul, blooming without failure.—The name of Christ—all words that have arisen from the life and death of Christ, the divine son, who went about speaking perfect words, no patois—whose life was perfect,—the touch of whose hands and feet was miracles—who was crucified—his flesh laid in a shroud, in the grave.[46]

"And after none of them or their achievement does my stomach

---

[42] Frey, *Catalogue of the Walt Whitman Collection,* Entry No. 25, p. 46.

[43] "Notes and Fragments," IX, 100.

[44] "Sun-Down Papers," No. 8, *The Uncollected Poetry and Prose of Walt Whitman,* ed. Emory Holloway, I, 40 (referred to hereafter as *Uncollected Poetry and Prose*).

[45] "Democratic Vistas," *Collect,* V, 118.

[46] Walt Whitman *An American Primer,* ed. Horace Traubel, pp. 18–19.

say enough and satisfied.—Except Christ; he alone brings the
perfumed bread, ever vivifying me, ever fresh and plenty, ever
welcome and to spare."[47] There are frequent expressions of
great sympathy: "O, Crucified! . . . ever gentle to her that gave
thee birth—thy dreary death-agonies alone—so it seemed to
thee—outdid the pangs of that gazer on the dead."[48] Finally,
there is the touching scene of Whitman and the dying soldier:

> He ask'd me to read him a chapter in the New Testament. I com-
> plied, and ask'd him what I should read. He said, "Make your
> own choice." I open'd at the close of one of the first books of the
> evangelists, and read the chapters describing the latter hours of
> Christ, and the scenes at the crucifixion. The poor, wasted young
> man ask'd me to read the following chapter also, how Christ rose
> again. I read very slowly, for Oscar was feeble. It pleased him
> very much, yet the tears were in his eyes. He ask'd me if I en-
> joy'd religion. I said, "Perhaps not, my dear, in the way you
> mean, and yet, maybe, it is the same." He said, "It is my chief
> reliance." He talk'd of death, and said he did not fear it.[49]

The first of Whitman's poems (not included in *Leaves*) to show
pronounced indications of a new and original style, "Blood-
Money," centers around the betrayal of the "beautiful god,
Jesus" and concludes:

> Witness of anguish, brother of slaves,
> Not with thy price closed the price of thine image:
> And still Iscariot plies his trade.[50]

Again, Allen's highly objective study, "Biblical Echoes in
Whitman's Works," is an important supplement to the findings
presented here. Among his brief conclusions are these:

> The study indicates the strong appeal that the life of Christ had
> for him. . . . My catalogue of his allusions indicates that he drew

---

[47] *Uncollected Poetry and Prose*, II, 83.
[48] "Notes and Fragments," IX, 147–148.
[49] *Specimen Days*, IV, 67–68.
[50] "Blood-Money," VI, 90–91.

most of his biblical inspiration from the New Testament, and still more specifically from the crucifixion scenes of the Christ-drama. . . . The role which he strove to play was modeled far more on the example of Christ than on the prophets of the Old Testament. . . . Nearly three times as many "specific allusions" are found in Whitman's early and juvenile writings as in his later poetry and prose. . . . Thus as Whitman's mind and art matured, the biblical influence became deeper, more abstract, and more difficult to identify precisely.[51]

It has been the purpose of this discussion thus far to establish the fact that, despite Whitman's distaste for formal theology and his complete freedom from religious dogma, religion was of major importance to him and in his mind was always associated primarily, consciously or unconsciously, with the concepts of the Hebrew Bible, more especially with the humane doctrines of Christ, freed, of course, from the supernatural elements stressed by orthodox Christianity. That these became points of reference for all of his religious thinking may have been the unconscious result of environment or of his particular intellectual, emotional, and spiritual timbre. On the other hand, as has already been suggested, such a point of reference may have been consciously established as a result of his awareness of its value in communicating with nineteenth-century Americans, a people for the most part familiar with and unescapably influenced by the Christian religion, regardless of individual predilections. The latter possibility is suggested by his rather surprising editorial comments on a proposed American translation of the Bible. His reservations (stated in 1859) regarding such a project grew out of two considerations: (1) his awareness of the probable loss of the communicative and associational values of the old phraseology, and (2) his awareness of the danger that a break with the old forms might shake the faith of the masses.[52]

---

[51] Allen, "Biblical Echoes in Whitman's Works," pp. 302–303.

[52] Walt Whitman, *I Sit and Look Out*, ed. Emory Holloway and Vernolian Schwartz, pp. 80–82.

Whitman's belief in the didactic function of poetry necessitated his vital concern with communication; his technique of suggestive, indirect, symbolic expression necessitated his concern with the associational values of words, phrases, and ideas. At any rate, it cannot be denied that *Leaves of Grass* sprang out of a rich biblical milieu from which it derived form, color, and vigor. Other religious writings could have offered similar materials; however, Whitman relied on the Hebrew Scriptures as his main point of reference and source of suggestive details, for obvious reasons. Allen's suggestion that by the time of his maturity they had been thoroughly assimilated and had become an integral part of all his thought and expression is an important one. There are comparatively few verbal echoes of the New Testament in *Leaves of Grass*; the experience and the expression are Whitman's own. Nevertheless, one cannot miss the New Testament spirit and scene inherent in such lines as "And brought water and fill'd a tub for his sweated body and bruis'd feet"; "I sat studying at the feet of the great master, . . . O that the great masters might return and study me"; or "Whoever degrades another degrades me, . . . whatever is done or said returns at last to me."[53] The most unmistakable evidence of the significance of the Christ-symbol in *Leaves of Grass* is the subtle, unobtrusive, indirect manner in which it asserts itself throughout the entire work, emerging here and there for a moment "only to wheel and hurry back in the darkness." It is the functioning of this particular symbol in conjunction with the minor ones which, more than anything else, establishes the *spirit* of *Leaves of Grass* and provides the key to its unity and its cumulative effect.

Any thoughtful reading of *Leaves of Grass* is likely to be accompanied by an awareness of the Christ-symbol above all others; it is repeatedly suggested throughout the work, particularly in the climactic passages. A careful search has turned up more than a hundred passages which suggest the Christ

[53] "Song of Myself," I, 44; "Starting from Paumanok," I, 18; "Song of Myself," I, 62.

idea.[54] These range from highly significant passages, such as the climactic one in "Song of Myself," where the poet identifies himself and all men with the crucified Christ,

> That I could forget the mockers and insults!
> That I could forget the trickling tears and the
>   blows of the bludgeons and hammers!
> That I could look with a separate look on my own
>   crucifixion and bloody crowning![55]

to comparatively minor, seemingly unconscious allusions. Among the major allusions are those passages, following the climax in "Song of Myself," which depict the poet's ministry; for example:

> Behold, I do not give lectures or a little charity,
> When I give I give myself.
>
> .   .   .   .
>
> I do not ask who you are, that is not important to me,
> You can do nothing and be nothing but what I will
>   infold you.[56]

The passage in the "Song of the Open Road" where he calls his disciples and instructs them in such matters as their necessary denial of material possessions is another:

> My call is the call of battle, I nourish active
>   rebellion,
> He going with me must go well arm'd,
> He going with me goes often with spare diet,
>   poverty, angry enemies, desertions.[57]

There is the suggestion of baptism in "Out of the Cradle Endlessly Rocking":

> But edging near as privately for me rustling at
>   my feet,

---

[54] See the poetry references in the section "On Christ" in the Appendix.
[55] "Song of Myself," I, 87–88.
[56] *Ibid.*, p. 89.
[57] "Song of the Open Road," I, 59.

Creeping thence steadily up to my ears and laving
   me softly all over,
Death, death, death, death, death.[58]

"Prayer of Columbus" records his Gethsemane:

My terminus near,
The clouds already closing in upon me,
The voyage balk'd, the course disputed, lost,
I yield my ships to Thee.[59]

In addition, there are the complete poems "To Him That Was
Crucified" and "Chanting the Square Deific."[60]

Passages somewhat more limited in implication but nonetheless significant are scattered throughout other poems. There are
those describing the poet-prophet himself and his own mystical
experiences:

No dainty dolce affettuoso I,
Bearded, sun-burnt, gray-neck'd, forbidding, I have
   arrived,
To be wrestled with as I pass for the solid prizes of
   the universe,
For such I afford whoever can persevere to win them.[61]

Swiftly arose and spread around me the peace and
   knowledge that pass all the argument of the earth,
And I know that the hand of God is the promise of my own,
And I know that the spirit of God is the brother of
   my own,

. . . .

And that a kelson of the creation is love, . . .[62]

Surrounded, copest, frontest God, yieldest, the
   aim attain'd,

[58] "Out of the Cradle Endlessly Rocking," II, 13.
[59] "Prayer of Columbus," II, 200.
[60] "To Him That Was Crucified," II, 159; "Chanting the Square Deific," II, 222–225.
[61] "Starting from Paumanok," I, 29.
[62] "Song of Myself," I, 38.

As fill'd with friendship, love complete, the Elder
   Brother found,
The Younger melts in fondness in his arms.[63]

Other passages describe scenes or actions reminiscent of Christ's experiences:

To any one dying, thither I speed and twist the knob
   of the door,
Turn the bed-clothes toward the foot of the bed,
Let the physician and the priest go home.

I seize the descending man and raise him with
   resistless will,
O despairer, here is my neck,
By God, you shall not go down! hang your whole
   weight upon me.[64]

Finally, there are passages indicating attitudes and relationships characteristic of the poet-prophet:

I do not despise you priests, all time, the world over,
My faith is the greatest of faiths and the least
   of faiths,
Enclosing worship ancient and modern and all between
   ancient and modern,
Believing I shall come again upon the earth after
   five thousand years . . .[65]

I hear it was charged against me that I sought to
   destroy institutions,
But really I am neither for nor against institutions,

.   .   .   .

Only I will establish . . .

.   .   .   .

The institution of the dear love of comrades.[66]

---

[63] "Passage to India," II, 196.
[64] "Song of Myself," I, 90.
[65] *Ibid.*, p. 95.
[66] "I Hear It Was Charged against Me," I, 154.

The way is suspicious, the result uncertain, perhaps
    destructive,
You would have to give up all else, I alone would
    expect to be your sole and exclusive standard,

. . . .

The whole past theory of your life and all conformity
    to the lives around you would have to be abandon'd,

. . . .

For I am the new husband and I am the comrade.[67]

Throughout *Leaves of Grass* the reader is continually faced
with some minor allusion, hardly significant in itself, but con-
tributing meaningfully to a powerful cumulative effect. Bringing a few of these together in an uninterrupted list demonstrates this: "Well-begotten, and raised by a perfect mother."[68]
". . . By a mechanic's wife with her babe at her nipple inter-
ceding for every person born."[69] "Afar down I see the first huge
Nothing, I know I was even there."[70] "I teach straying from
me, yet who can stray from me? . . . My words itch at your ears
till you understand them."[71] "When you read these I that was
visible am become invisible; . . . Be it as if I were with you."[72]
"And underneath Christ the divine I see, The dear love of man
for his comrade, . . ."[73] "From wounds made to free you whence
you were prison'd, . . . press forth red drops, . . . stain every song
I sing."[74] ". . . I never knew you, Yet I think I could not refuse
this moment to die for you, if that would save you."[75] "I see
Christ eating the bread of his last supper in the midst of youths
and old persons . . ."[76] "The Lord is not dead, he is risen again

---

[67] "Whoever You Are Holding Me Now in Hand," I, 140–141.
[68] "Starting from Paumanok," I, 16.
[69] "Song of Myself," I, 91.
[70] *Ibid.*, p. 98.
[71] *Ibid.*, p. 103.
[72] "Full of Life Now," I, 162.
[73] "The Base of all Metaphysics," I, 147.
[74] "Trickle Drops," I, 151.
[75] "The Wound-Dresser," II, 75.
[76] "Salut au Monde!" I, 168.

young and strong in another country."[77] "My gait is no fault-finder's or rejecter's gait, . . ."[78] "Thither we also . . . As a father to his father going takes his children along with him."[79] "Who was not proud of his songs, but of the measureless ocean of love within him, and freely pour'd it forth."[80] But let us turn from isolated quotations for a moment, and look at the broader aspects suggested by them.

The religion of *Leaves of Grass* has at its center a single personality strikingly like the Christ of the Hebrew Bible. Edna D. Romig has analyzed this personality as it is expressed in an egotism of three kinds: first, there is the autobiographical *I*; second, there is the ego which recognizes itself as a part of God, the transcendental ego; and third, there is the ego that is keenly aware of innumerable equal identities, the social ego.[81] This is the personal trinity which justifies that "great pride of man in himself" of which Whitman remarks, "I think it not inconsistent with obedience, humility, deference, and self-questioning."[82] The analysis is clearly applicable to the presentation of Christ in the New Testament. In this study we are interested in the transcendental and the social egos only. Whitman himself recognized these two elements in his poetry and his comment on them suggests Christ's statement of the great commandment and the "second like unto it": "One main contrast of the ideas behind every page of my verses, compared with establish'd poems, is their different relative attitude towards God, towards the objective universe, and still more . . . the quite changed attitude of the ego, the one chanting or talking, towards himself and towards his fellow-humanity."[83]

First, the transcendental or spiritual ego of *Leaves of Grass* shares with Jesus that mysticism of awakening to a feeling of

[77] "Old Ireland," II, 138.
[78] "Song of Myself," I, 60.
[79] "Savantism," I, 13.
[80] "Recorders Ages Hence," II, 147.
[81] Edna D. Romig, "The Paradox of Walt Whitman," *University of Colorado Studies* 15 (1926), 112.
[82] "A Backward Glance O'er Travel'd Roads," III, 60.
[83] *Ibid.*, pp. 45–46.

oneness with the universe and its God. Following the initial mystical experience in "Song of Myself," the poet rejoices in his soul's ability to transcend time and space: "I pass death with the dying and birth with the new-washed babe, and am not contain'd between my hat and boots . . ."[84] Later in the same poem, struggling to express his mystical consciousness, he says:

There is that in me—I do not know what it is—
but I know it is in me.

.   .   .   .

Do you see O my brothers and sisters?
It is not chaos or death—it is form, union, plan—
it is eternal life—it is Happiness.[85]

It was this same sense of oneness with the universe and God that enabled the transcendental ego to see eternal lessons in even the simplest objects. As Christ considered the lilies of the field, so Whitman observed the more democratic spear of grass and saw it as "the scented gift and remembrancer" of the Lord "designedly dropt."[86]

Second, the parallels between Christ and the hero of *Leaves of Grass* as social beings are detailed. Whitman says, "This is what you shall do: Love the earth and sun and the animals, despise riches, give alms to every one that asks, stand up for the stupid and crazy, devote your income and labor to others, hate tyrants, argue not concerning God, have patience and indulgence toward the people, take off your hat to nothing known or unknown or to any man or number of men—go freely with powerful uneducated persons . . . re-examine all you have been told at school or church or in any book, and dismiss whatever insults your own soul; and your very flesh shall be a great poem and have the richest fluency. . . ."[87] The messages of great poets to each man and woman are, Come to us on equal terms, only

---

[84] See the fourth passage quoted on page 65 of this study, the essence of the mystic experience ("Song of Myself," I, 41).

[85] "Song of Myself," p. 107.

[86] *Ibid.*, p. 39.

[87] "Preface, 1855," V, 166–167.

then can you understand us, We are no better than you, What we enclose you enclose, What we enjoy you may enjoy."[88] "Literature is big only in one way—when used as an aid in the growth of the humanities—a furthering of the cause of the masses—a means whereby men may be revealed to each other as brothers."[89] "I do not seek those that love me; I would rather seek after some that hate me."[90] "I am the man, I suffer'd, I was there."[91] The social ego of *Leaves of Grass*, then, shares Christ's simplicity, his sense of brotherhood with all men, his capacity for forgiveness, and his compassion for human suffering. In one of Traubel's conversations with Whitman they discussed the critics' charges of an absence of a sense of humor in both Christ and Whitman.[92] If there is a similar absence of humor in the two heroes, there is a compensating optimism, even in the face of evil. They both accept the fact of evil and hope to cope with it as an inevitable part of life. "I walk with delinquents with passionate love, . . . I belong to those convicts and prostitutes myself, and henceforth I will not deny them."[93] "I have no mockings or arguments, I witness and wait."[94] There is no desire to attack, but rather the gentle desire to remold. And this is to be accomplished by example. The great prophet "proves himself by every step he takes." It is his presence that conquers—"not parleying, or struggling, or any prepared attempts. . . . Now he has passed that way, see after him."[95] It is in the desire to compel by example, to present for mankind the heroic life that knows no pettiness or triviality, that the central figures of the New Testament and *Leaves of Grass* seem most strikingly alike. Parallels in the accounts of their development will be indicated later when we turn to an analysis of *Leaves of Grass* itself.

[88] *Ibid.*, p. 171.
[89] Traubel, *With Walt Whitman in Camden*, I, 283.
[90] Furness, *Walt Whitman's Workshop*, p. 49.
[91] "Song of Myself," I, 80.
[92] Traubel, *With Walt Whitman in Camden*, IV, 8–9.
[93] "You Felons on Trial in Courts," II, 160.
[94] "Song of Myself," I, 37.
[95] "Preface, 1855," V, 164.

Third, the central personality of *Leaves of Grass* finds justification in his message—a message strikingly Christ-like in its
presentation and purport. In a note anticipating his poems
Whitman writes, "Ego-style, First person style . . . animated
. . . something involving self-esteem, decision, authority—as
opposed to the current *third person style*, essayism, didactic
. . . stating general truths in a didactic, well-smooth'd."[96] This
style is used to enhance the personal appeal. "Without effort,
and without exposing . . . how it is done, the greatest poet
brings the spirit of any or all events and passions and scenes
and persons . . . to bear on your individual character as you
hear or read. To do this well is to compete with the laws that
pursue and follow Time."[97] In *Leaves of Grass* the message is
addressed to the individual reader in such direct, forceful terms
that he is forced to accept or reject, is unable to remain indifferent or apart—a unique experience strangely similar to
that felt upon encountering the message of Christ. "For from
this book Yourself, before unknown, shall now rise up and be
revealed."[98] This effect is due in part to the positive quality of
the two gospels; they both seek to bring about change, not by
condemnation or argument, but by projected sympathy and
understanding.

> I give nothing as duties,
> What others give as duties I give as living impulses,
> (Shall I give the heart's action as a duty?)[99]

"You cannot define too clearly what it is you love in a poem
or in a man or woman. A great work of a great poet is not
remembered for its parts—but remembered as you remember
the complete person and spirit of him or her you love."[100] This
statement suggests the kind of reaction Whitman hoped to
evoke in his reader. In it are brought together the two major

---

[96] "Notes and Fragments," X, 34–35.
[97] "Preface, 1855," V, 169.
[98] Furness, *Walt Whitman's Workshop*, p. 132.
[99] "Myself and Mine," I, 290.
[100] "Notes and Fragments," IX, 158.

elements in *Leaves of Grass*: personal force, the essence of its
style or manner, and charity, the essence of its message. In
"Song of Prudence" Whitman speaks of these as "the only in-
vestments worth any thing."[101] Christ and poet-prophet, then,
are alike not only in their direct appeal to their brothers but in
their doctrine of love, finding its most appealing expression in
parables and its most disarming affirmation in undisturbed
paradoxes.

> I will write the evangel-poem of comrades and of love,
> For who but I should understand love with all its
>   sorrow and joy?
> And who but I should be the poet of comrades?[102]

Here are messages for the future. The prophet's message is
projected centuries ahead and must stand after the change of
time. Whitman asks these questions: "Have the marches of
tens and hundreds and thousands of years made willing detours
to the right hand and the left hand for his sake? Is he beloved
long and long after he is buried? . . . A great poem is for ages
and ages in common, and for all degrees and complexions. . . .
A great poem is no finish to a man or woman, but rather a beginning. . . . Whom he [the poet] takes with a firm grasp into
live regions previously unattained. . . . the elder encourages the
younger and shows him how."[103] Whitman's poem is obviously
more than a poem in the usual sense—like Christ's poem, it can
be called a gospel.

In just what way, then, does Whitman's new religion differ
from the old upon which it is based? The difference is primarily
one of degree, yet great enough to smack of heresy. Whitman
completely embraces the humanism of Christianity, and it is
in this sense that we define the religious spirit of his work as
Christ-like. His own statement of the matter was "Human-
istically speaking the Bible and *Leaves of Grass* are in every

---

[101] "Song of Prudence," II, 147.
[102] "Starting from Paumanok," I, 21.
[103] "Preface, 1855," V, 181–182.

way compatible."[104] In commenting on a pamphlet intended to prove the religion of Christ superior to his own, Whitman said, "I always thought that they came to about the same thing, but this woman evidently thinks they do not."[105] The nature of the poet's heresy is indicated in his asking just how Christian Jesus was, "if Christian at all?"[106] Whitman could not accept the supernatural elements in the dogma of the church and evidently felt that the real significance of the New Testament was obscured by them. "I have always looked about to discover a word to describe the situation: how Jesus and the churches have got divorced; how the institution has destroyed the spirit."[107]

> Silent and amazed even when a little boy,
> I remember I heard the preacher every Sunday put
>   God in his statements,
> As contending against some being or influence.[108]

To Whitman the orthodoxy of his time seemed small and piqued. "After you have got rid of all your dogmas then you can read the Bible—realize its immensity—not till then."[109] Whitman attacked the churches because he felt that they were clinging to old "fables, crudities, and superstitions" which denied the fundamental dignity and divinity of each human soul. "For all religions, divine, are but temporary journeys— subordinate to the eternal soul of the woman, the man supreme, the decider of all."[110] In *Democratic Vistas* Whitman says: "The ripeness of religion is doubtless to be looked for in the field of individuality and is a result that no organization or church can ever achieve. . . . Religion, although casually arrested, and after a fashion preserved in the churches and creeds,

---

[104] Traubel, *With Walt Whitman in Camden*, III, 470.
[105] *Ibid.*, I, 121.
[106] *Ibid.*, IV, 363.
[107] *Ibid.*, I, 98.
[108] "A Child's Amaze," II, 36.
[109] Traubel, *With Walt Whitman in Camden*, I, 454.
[110] Frey, *Catalogue of the Walt Whitman Collection*, Entry No. 22, p. 23.

does not depend upon them, but is a part of the identified soul, which when greatest, knows not bibles in old ways but in new ways."[111]

He asserts over and over again that God must be a present reality as well as a past and future one. He felt that Christian orthodoxy had bound religion to the past by its treatment of the Bible as primarily historical, to the point that it was alarmingly static and remote, that at best such a religion must entail elaborate supernatural concepts if it were to be in any way alive and vital for the present. It was this separation of the essence of religion from present reality and from its real abode, the vibrant human heart, that prompted the new religion. He praises Elias Hicks:

> Always Elias Hicks gives the service of pointing to the fountain of all naked theology, all religion, all worship, all truth to which you are possibly eligible—namely in *yourself* and your inherent relations. Others talk of bibles, saints, churches, exhortations, vicarious atonements—the canons outside of yourself and apart from man—Elias Hicks to the religion inside of man's very own nature. This he incessantly labors to kindle, nourish, educate, bring forward and strengthen. He is the most *democratic* of the religionists—the prophets.[112]

"The time has certainly come to begin to discharge the idea of religion, in the United States, from mere ecclesiasticism . . . and assign it to that general position, chiefest, most indispensable . . . inside of all human character, and education, and affairs."[113] *Leaves of Grass* is Whitman's attempt to express the Christ-idea once and for all in the form of a myth or symbol which overcomes the historical aspect and his serious objections to it. He accomplishes this by first identifying Walt Whitman, nineteenth-century American, with Everyman, and then relating his development in such a way as to identify him with

[111] *Democratic Vistas, Collect,* V, 104.

[112] "Notes (such as they are) Founded on E. H.," *November Boughs,* VI, 242.

[113] "Preface, 1872," V, 190–191.

Christ. Matthiessen declares, "This religious assurance, un-leashed from all control of dogma or creed, must be called no less than terrifying in the length to which it was to go in pro-claiming the individual as his own Messiah."[114] By so doing, Whitman feels that he has modernized and revitalized the true significance of the Christ-symbol. "In the domain of literature loftily consider'd . . . 'the kingdom of the Father has pass'd; the kingdom of the Son is passing; the kingdom of the Spirit begins.' "[115]

But Whitman's desire to free the Christ-concept from its historical orientation involves considerations more profound than that of making an immediate application of it to himself or his contemporaries. It relates in a real way to his poet-prophet's cosmic concern and his delight in *cosmic* or *mythical time*, the truly *sacred time*, indefinitely recoverable and repeat-able, as opposed to *historical time*, the only time which non-religious man can know, noncyclic and irreversible. Eliade points out the way in which Christianity in affirming the his-toricity of the person of Christ radically changes the whole experience and concept of liturgical time by divorcing it from the ancient concept of the cosmic and mythical.[116] It is the fact that such a historical orientation of the Christ-figure does vio-lence to the ancient, cosmic elements in *Leaves of Grass* that further encouraged Whitman in his desire to break with it.

Whitman follows the biblical tradition in many ways. He re-tains the idea that God, in order to reveal himself, must become man, that such a revelation requires a time and a place and a people, that it is in the light of this fact that the entire history of the Hebrew people exists—in order to accommodate the ap-pearance of the personality of Christ. While he recognizes the function of the Old Testament, it is too much history, and Christ, too much the historical figure. He overcomes this by a

[114] F. O. Matthiessen, *American Renaissance*, p. 546.
[115] "An Old Man's Rejoinder," VI, 283 (quoted from John Addington Sy-monds).
[116] Mircea Eliade, *The Sacred and the Profane*, pp. 72–78, 110–111.

simple, but ingenious, reorganization; he takes himself as the poet-prophet Christ, and America as his country. He develops the two simultaneously in *Leaves of Grass*. Not only is this two-fold development simultaneous, it is harmonious. The results are amazing. He saves both the nation and the poet-prophet of *Leaves* from the historical sense—makes them symbolical and mythical. The implications are limitless and account for the complexity and the thematic elements which give *Leaves of Grass* a sense of magnitude and sweeping thought that still re-mains primarily poetic and spiritual. Whitman does not neglect the sense of history, as too many critics have implied; rather, he transcends it. The poet-prophet must have a community in order to make his autobiography a real center of a religion. It is through an analysis of Whitman's skillful handling of the simultaneous development of this national element and the per-sonal element, made logical and possible through his use of the Christ-like poet-prophet, that we begin to arrive at an under-standing of the structural pattern of *Leaves of Grass*. This basic pattern is sustained throughout by an intricate system of "poem clusters" in which the personal and the national themes are intermingled in such a way that neither can be lost sight of for long. To become involved with one of these themes at the expense of the other, to fail to see them advance together, is to destroy a balance and to miss a concept of structure, leav-ing much in *Leaves* rather disjointed and seemingly chaotic. It is through the careful development of the poet-prophet con-cept and its persistent use throughout *Leaves of Grass* that the national element is held in meaningful focus.

There has been a tendency, during the last few decades in particular, to shy away from any serious consideration of Whit-man's intense national feeling. Referring to this aspect of Whit-man's poetry, Milton Hindus says, "The very qualities of Whitman which once made me suspicious of his motivations in the days when Hitler and Mussolini gave a bad name to every legitimate national aspiration have become increasingly

the most important in my mind."[117] There is no question but
that a cynical generation has distrusted Whitman's nationalism,
not understanding that it is primarily an outgrowth of his
whole concept of art—a fact Hindus makes quite clear, placing
Whitman in the company of Wagner and Dostoevski in this
respect.[118] This vague distrust has lingered and may explain
why extended studies of Whitman have not effectively sustained the national element and made it integral to all *Leaves
of Grass* as the poet himself has done. This is the case in the
work of both Miller and Asselineau, granting, of course, that
it is dealt with in scattered passages by each and is given considerable emphasis in Miller's concluding chapter.[119] It is also
present by implication in Miller's section entitled "Mystic
Evolution: The Self and History."[120] The shying away from
this aspect of Whitman's poetry in the past is understandable
in the light of Hindus's statement; however, it is time for some-
one to say "let us stand up." That has been done and needs
only to be heeded. There are a number of recent articles which
should give a liberating perspective to this whole matter. Probably the most forceful of these is J. Middleton Murry's "Walt
Whitman: The Prophet of Democracy." Murry says that it is in
this role that Whitman can best be comprehended. He gets to
the core of Whitman's involvement: "Democracy can be justified and believed in only on the basis of a prior conviction of
the infinite worth of the individual. . . . He [Whitman] vitally
renewed the religious revelation on which the justification and
continued existence of Democracy depends." And later Murry
concludes that it is through this unique aspect of his poetry
that Whitman earns our deepest homage.[121] Similar themes are

---

[117] Hindus, ed., *Leaves of Grass One Hundred Years After*, pp. 16–17.
[118] *Ibid.*, p. 19.
[119] Roger Asselineau, *The Evolution of Walt Whitman: The Creation of a Book*.
[120] James E. Miller, Jr., *A Critical Guide to Leaves of Grass*, pp. 209–218.
[121] J. Middleton Murry, "Walt Whitman: The Prophet of Democracy," in *Leaves of Grass One Hundred Years After*, Hindus, ed., pp. 127, 144.

sounded in essays by Daiches, Lovell, Randel, and Stovall.[122] Without stressing the concept of prophet, two recent essayists, Brown and Shapiro, have championed Whitman's involvement of himself and his poetry in an attempt to "adumbrate the meaning of America." Shapiro laments: "The twentieth century poet avoids this commitment."[123]

Whitman saw the humanism inherent in the Christian tradition as the chief inspiration and source of our democratic ideals. In making the Christ-like poet-prophet the central figure in *Leaves of Grass* he was attempting to revitalize and render immediate that ancient humanism, free of any subsequent dogmatizing or theologizing as he saw it. In his attempt at the expression of a new and fresh religion he sought to give to old forms new meanings appropriate to a democratized society. He reaches back into the past for nourishment appropriate to our national aspirations as he saw them. Through the Christ-like poet-prophet, religion and national aspiration meet.

We have seen that out of Whitman's organic theory of art grew naturally his concept of the poet-prophet; in much the same way his development of the Christ-like prophet as the central figure in *Leaves of Grass* led to his involvement with the great national themes. The Christ-symbol, then, has a unifying effect reaching far beyond the fact that it is the most fully developed and frequently recurring symbol in *Leaves of Grass*. It is a unifying element in that it is the source of the unique spirit permeating Whitman's poetry, manifest strikingly in terms of the poet-reader relationship, Rountree's

[122] David Daiches, "The Philosopher," in *Walt Whitman: Man, Poet, Philosopher. Three Lectures*, L. Quincy Mumford, ed., pp. 35–53; John Lovell, Jr., "Appreciating Whitman: 'Passage to India,'" *MLQ* 21 (June 1960), 131–141; William Randel, "Walt Whitman and American Myths," *South Atlantic Quarterly* 59 (Winter 1960), 103–113; Floyd Stovall, "Walt Whitman and the American Tradition," *Virginia Quarterly Review* 31 (1955), 540–557.

[123] Clarence A. Brown, "Walt Whitman and 'The New Poetry,'" *AL* 33 (March 1961), 33–45; Karl Shapiro, "The First White Aboriginal," *Walt Whitman Review* 5 (September 1959), 43–52 (later included in *Start with the Sun*).

"unity of reciprocity," and the means whereby the personal and religious and national themes are fused into a whole exceeding the sum of its parts. Just how this is accomplished is the concern of Chapter IV, "A Structural Analysis of *Leaves of Grass.*"

A Structural Analysis

of *Leaves of Grass*

In any study of the structure of *Leaves of Grass* the seventh edition, published in 1881, is the key volume. In a letter to John Burroughs anticipating the publication of that edition, Whitman writes, "The bulk of the pieces will be the same as hitherto —only I shall secure now the consecutiveness and *ensemble* I am always thinking of."[1] As we shall see later, most of his efforts between 1876 and 1881 were given to the rearrangement of his poems. The analysis to follow is based upon the grouping established in the 1881 edition, which he recognized as the fulfillment of his poetic purpose. In it, for the first time, Whit-

[1]Clara Barrus, *Whitman and Burroughs: Comrades*, p. 205.

man succeeded in arranging his poems as he desired them. He never changed that arrangement and he left instructions that any poems added be placed in annexes.[2] He initiated these annexes himself in the 1892 edition. They are of little concern to us here in view of the fact that they supplement rather than form an integral part of the *Leaves* as an organic whole. Whitman's request that any additions be placed in annexes, whereby he sought to preserve the structure of the 1881 edition, has been respected. The irony of the situation is that in all his care Whitman did not foresee the reprinting of the earlier editions, a recent trend; the manner in which this is sometimes done in a sense thwarts the old poet's wish to have each individual reader, each dear to him in a very special way, confronted with the book as he would have it.

This reprinting of earlier editions has, for the most part, accompanied the contemporary trend toward a fuller appreciation of the early poems at the expense of the later ones, an interesting reversal of the tendency of most scholars and critics of the past, who have wished to justify the materialism and excesses of the former by emphasizing the progression toward spirituality and moderation of the latter. Asselineau, for example, shows an enthusiasm for the early Whitman which is noticeably absent when he turns his attention to the post–"Drum-Taps" poet. More than once he speaks of Whitman's increasing concern with social and national themes, his decline in poetic inspiration and power, and his readiness to intellectualize and philosophize.[3] The most positive and effective statement of this new enthusiasm for the early poetry is Pearce's introduction to *Leaves of Grass: Facsimile of the 1860 Text*. In a lucid expression of his preference for the humane Whitman, as opposed to the prophetic Whitman who hopes "to look beyond the end of the journey," Pearce declares not only the poetry but also the arrangement of 1860 superior to that of

---

[2] "An Executor's Diary Note, 1891," III, 30.

[3] Roger Asselineau, *The Evolution of Walt Whitman: The Creation of a Personality*, pp. 204, 222–223.

later editions, which he says are dominated by Whitman's increasing tendency to mentalize and prophesy.[4] This straightforward, bold evaluation of the achievements of 1860 is timely; however, in the light of Whitman's claims one might wish that somehow the pitting of that edition against later ones had been avoided. Stovall issues a warning pertinent here, "The Bohemianism of *Leaves of Grass* in the editions of 1855, 1856, and 1860 is sometimes thought to be a truer expression of Whitman's real personality than the spiritual power of later years. This is certainly not the case; it is but one of many phases of the character of Whitman's hero."[5] Certainly a valid objection can be raised to the assumption that the progression toward intellectualization, spiritualization, or emphasis upon social and national themes is the result of a change, whether for better or for worse, in Whitman the man. Such an approach neglects any consideration of the sweep, the main drifts, of *Leaves* itself. In particular it neglects Whitman's concept of the poet-prophet and his mission, thus violating basic relationships characteristic of Whitman's theory of poetry, of his thoughts on the role of the poet, and of their realization in *Leaves*. The result is a distortion of *Leaves of Grass* as Whitman intended it. One of the merits of Miller's *Critical Guide* is his recognition of quality throughout Whitman's poetry. The youthful exuberance inherent in "Song of Myself" has great charm, but had it persisted in "Passage to India" it would have constituted an artistic flaw of monstrous proportions. This is not to be lamented; in the latter there is "abundant recompense."

Calling attention to this irony is not to question the value of such reprints and the attendant scholarship. But the irony is there, and it justifies an objection to the practice of setting the

---

[4] Roy Harvey Pearce, *Leaves of Grass: Facsimile of the 1860 Text*, pp. xiii–xiv, xvi–xviii, xxv, xlvii, l–li.

[5] Floyd Stovall, "Walt Whitman and the American Tradition," *Virginia Quarterly Review* 31 (1955), 555; S. K. Coffman, Jr., "Form and Meaning in Whitman's 'Passage to India,'" *PMLA* 70 (June 1955), 337–349; John Lovell, Jr., "Appreciating Whitman: 'Passage to India,'" *MLQ* 21 (June 1960), pp. 131–141.

early against the late. There is at least a possibility that any preference for an early edition—a preference Whitman did not share—might be the result of a failure to see fully the true nature and implication of the 1881 structure, which claimed his allegiance. We have noted Pearce's preference for the 1860 text, expressed in his introduction to the facsimile edition. In *The Continuity of American Poetry*, published in the same year, he writes, "He may have in the end wanted *Leaves of Grass* to be a 'cathedral.' But he could make it into nothing other than a series of private antinomian chapels, each reflecting a momentary impulse toward structure, each a success in so far as the impulse was carried through." And then Pearce, rather unexpectedly, redeems himself when he adds, "The impulse was that of the self fully engaged in the act of creating a structure which would make for the possibility of further creation: an infinite series of those chapels, as it were—each to be the locale, the occasion, and the means to the creative, self-assertive, self-discovering act of that infinite number of Americans who would be drawn into them."[6] This is superb as far as it goes. But Whitman summoned himself to the task of suggesting a whole exceeding the individual parts, and in doing so he places before the imaginative reader the final and most important challenge of all. It is obvious that the task was strenuous for the poet, and the response of the reader needs be correspondingly so. This is the kind of strenuous excitement peculiar to the reading of *Leaves of Grass*. Too often the difficulty of the challenge encourages the questioning of the challenger.

No dainty dolce affettuoso I,
Bearded, sun-burnt, gray-neck'd, forbidding, I
   have arrived,
To be wrestled with as I pass for the solid prizes
   of the universe,
For such I afford whoever can persevere to win them.[7]

[6] Roy Harvey Pearce, *The Continuity of American Poetry*, p. 165.
[7] "Starting from Paumanok," I, 29.

Whitman's preference for the 1881 edition, then, was based upon its structure. As has been suggested, in this edition he achieved the arrangement, the precise balance of directness and suggestiveness, and the degree of unity which he desired. His doctrine of indirection and the creative participation of the reader, his delight in the 1881 edition and his statement that regardless of what the world might do with his book this is what he would have it be, suggest that the necessary clews and indirections are here, just as surely as they are "under [our] boot-soles."

The pattern established in 1881 is made obvious and enforced by numerous allusions, transitional poems, contrasting poetic styles and moods, and, most important of all, by a careful handling of imagery. In this discussion of these devices and of the poem clusters, everything has been subordinated to a consideration of the organization of each group of poems and of its relationship to *Leaves* as a whole. Such an approach has been prompted by the conviction that *Leaves of Grass* is a great work of art, the component parts of which can be accounted for by their relation to the whole, independent of any particular biographical or psychological circumstances.

INSCRIPTIONS (24 POEMS)

"Inscriptions" is a group of twenty-four prefatory poems. The first twenty-one anticipate the principal themes and symbols that run throughout *Leaves of Grass*; the final three are dedications, of which the first is to poets to come and the others are to the reader. "One's-Self I Sing," the first poem of the group, announces the main themes of the entire volume as it sets forth apparent paradoxes which lie at the heart of the songs to follow, that of the simple separate person and the democratic word "En-Masse," and that of powerful freedom under divine law. The great individual is identified only to recognize himself as one with those around him in a brotherhood of love and equality—the recognition which distinguishes

the "Modern Man."[8] "He that findeth his life shall lose it, and
he that loseth his life for my sake shall find it." The lyrics which
follow introduce more specific themes. In "As I Ponder'd in
Silence" Whitman professes a reverence for the old epic themes
of war, waged for life and death, body and soul, above all pro-
moting brave soldiers.[9] The poem introduces the war symbol
and the epic quality to run throughout the volume. "In Cabin'd
Ships at Sea" anticipates two major symbols which are to act
as structural devices in unifying *Leaves of Grass*, the journey-
voyage-symbol and the land-sea-symbol. The poem itself, coming early in the volume, cannot be fully appreciated until one
is acquainted with the extended use of these two symbols by
Whitman: the land represents the material world and mortality,
and the journey, man's mundane experience; the sea represents the spiritual world and immortality, and the voyage, man's
venture into that mystic realm. It is only after we have become aware of Whitman's consistent use of these contrasting
symbols in *Leaves of Grass* as a unity, that we grasp the full
purport and beauty of his thought "By sailors young and old
haply will I, a reminiscence of the land, be read, In full rapport
at last." It is important that we be told at the start that this is
more than a reminiscence of the land, that these are voyagers'
thoughts—*"this is ocean's poem."*[10] It is the true artist who
recognizes the desirability of couching this anticipatory evaluation of his work in a symbolism which the reader is to comprehend fully only in retrospect, as he discovers the concluding
poems of *Leaves of Grass*. Following these three major poems
are two minor ones: the first proclaiming America's democracy
for all lands and the second proclaiming Whitman as the chanter of personality, projecting the history of the future.[11] The
sixth poem sets forth the cause to which the book is dedicated,

8 "One's-Self I Sing," I, 1.
9 "As I Ponder'd in Silence," I, 2.
10 "In Cabin'd Ships at Sea," I, 3.
11 "To Foreign Lands," "To a Historian," I, 4.

Freedom. The war symbol is used and "Drum-Taps" is foreshadowed when he says "my book and the war are one" revolving "Around the idea of thee," old cause.[12] "Eidólons" is a key poem of the "Inscriptions." In stating Whitman's concept of the relationship of the material and the spiritual, it is an initial justification of the dominant materialism of the poems preceding "Sea-Drift."[13] "Every material object . . . has spiritual effluxes which remain changeless and eternal after the dissolution of the object itself. . . . These effluxes unite to produce an eidolon of that form," which is its eternal soul.[14] The material is the source of the true reality, the eidolon. The remainder of the poems of the group are brief foreshadowings of themes of individuality, materialism, creativity, nationality, equality, natural placidity, science, singing America, suffering America, insurrection, and reconciliation—themes for "untold latencies" who will thrill to every page.[15] The three final poems draw the reader into an intimate relationship with the poet—a relationship to be cherished throughout *Leaves of Grass.*[16]

INTRODUCTIONS (2 POEMS)

Following "Inscriptions" are two major poems which, although left outside any given group by Whitman, might well be grouped together as introductory. They are the basic poems of the entire volume and, as might be expected, are dominated by the Christ-symbol. In them Whitman gives this unifying figure its fullest development, establishing the desired poet-reader relationship and defining the nature and mission of the poet-prophet. The reader is vividly introduced to the Christ-like poet-

---

[12] "To Thee Old Cause," I, 5.
[13] "Eidólons," I, 5–9.
[14] Floyd Stovall, ed. *Walt Whitman*, p. 467.
[15] "For Him I Sing," "When I Read the Book," I, 9; "Beginning My Studies," "Beginners," "To the States," I, 10; "On Journeys through the States," I, 11; "To a Certain Cantatrice," "Me Imperturbe," "Savantism," I, 12; "The Ship Starting," I, 13; "I Hear America Singing," I, 13–14; "What Place Is Besieged?" "Still Though the One I Sing," "Shut Not Your Doors," I, 14.
[16] "Poets to Come," "To You," "Thou Reader," I, 15.

prophet who is the *I* of the entire volume, whether engaged in introspective soliloquies, intimate confidences, grand and mystical visions, or rhapsodic prophecy. A sustained awareness of this *I* is essential in getting at the intricate implications and relationships of the varied themes and moods contained in the poetry he pours forth. Whitman assists us in this by recurring to the Christ-symbol at strategic points throughout *Leaves of Grass.*

The first of the two poems "Starting from Paumanok" gives background about the poet and in that sense prepares the way for "Song of Myself." It functions primarily, however, as an introduction to the book as a whole. In view of the fact that *Leaves of Grass* is more than poetry in the usual sense, that it is a gospel as well, an introduction is necessary. The poet is hailed as a prophet of a new religion, a religion for Democratic America, a new land, Eden-like, yet taking to herself all the heritage of the past, promising even greater things for the future. This rich, abundant nation, the culmination of all that has gone before, the great hope of all humanity, is the inspiration of the new poet of love, democracy, and religion.[17] That poet cries out for comrades, for kindred spirits to haste on with him, hand in hand, into the twilight of morning. He would address each comrade individually, as an equal, and draw him close to himself.[18] The appeal of "Starting from Paumanok" recalls one of Whitman's observations about Elias Hicks. "They [old persons] think Elias Hicks had a large element of personal ambition, the pride of leadership, of establishing perhaps a sect that should reflect his own name, and to which he should give special form and character. Very likely. Such indeed seems the means, all through progress and civilization, by which strong men and strong convictions achieve anything definite. But the basic foundation of Elias was undoubtedly genuine religious fervor. He was like [a]Hebrew prophet."[19]

[17] "Starting from Paumanok," I, 21–23.
[18] *Ibid.*, p. 32.
[19] "Notes (such as they are) founded on E. H.," *November Boughs*, VI, 268.

"Starting from Paumanok" is a poem of major importance in considering the over-all structure of *Leaves*. In it are initiated, as a preparation for what is to follow, a large number of the major themes and symbols of the entire volume. An early awareness of the recurring presence of these themes and symbols is essential to an intelligent reading of *Leaves of Grass*. Whitman believed that the profoundest realities lie beyond mere human understanding and become vital in the life of man only when dimly perceived through intuition or through the sensitive interplay of all of man's faculties. Hence his emphasis upon "faint clews and indirections," or suggestiveness, in poetic communication. The greatest truths can be expressed only indirectly by symbols or themes. These are clarified by constant restatement and reorchestration until they convey that positive vitality and opulence which Whitman perceived and loved as characteristic of all realities both material and spiritual. Whitman's symbols and themes are dynamic; no small part of their peculiar forcefulness is achieved by their continual growth and expansion. This can be seen to a limited degree in the Christ-symbol in "Starting from Paumanok." It is suggested in the second line of the poem: "Well-begotten and raised by a perfect mother."[20] It recurs throughout the poem in these passages: "I sat studying at the feet of the great masters, . . . O that the great masters might return and study me. . . . I will write the evangel-poem of comrades and of love. . . . I, too, . . . inaugurate a religion, I descend into the arena . . . I will show that whatever happens to anybody . . . may be turned to beautiful results . . . that nothing can happen to anybody more beautiful than death . . . that all the things of the universe are perfect miracles. . . . I will not sing with reference to a day, but with reference to all days. . . . Did you wait for one with a flowing mouth and indicative hand? . . . [I come] personally to you . . . enjoining you to acts, characters, spectacles, with me. . . . For your life adhere to me. . . . I have arranged to be wrestled with as I pass for the solid prizes of the universe . . . such I afford whoever

[20] "Starting from Paumanok," I, 16.

can persevere to win them. . . . Now I triumph—and you shall also."[21] These passages, somewhat insignificant if taken singly, combine to produce a cumulative effect which renders the Christ-symbol the dominant element in the poem. Other symbols introduced here and destined to play a significant part in later poems are the grass-symbol inherent in the line "take my leaves America"; the bird-poet-symbol in "Democracy! near at hand to you a throat inflating itself and joyfully singing . . . for the brood beyond us and of us"; the journey-symbol in "With me with firm holding, yet haste, haste on"; and the Eden-symbol in "a world primal again."[22] Akin to these symbols is a second device destined to play an important part in the unification of *Leaves of Grass* as a whole, the catalogue; as we shall see later this device is utilized in connection with the journey-symbol.[23]

Finally, in "Starting from Paumanok" many of the major themes of the volume are swiftly introduced: the attachment of the poet to his nation in "Solitary, singing in the West, I strike up for a New World. . . . Americanos . . . for you a programme of chants"; the cosmic nature of America's rich materiality and potential spirituality in "Here the heir-ship and heiress-ship of the world, here the flame of materials,/ Here spirituality the translatress"; companionship and manly love, the only basis for a united nation, in "these are to found their own ideal of manly love"; the necessary acceptance of all things, evil included, in "I make the poem of evil also, I commemorate that part also"; the three major themes of *Leaves* as a whole, love, democracy, and most important of all, religion in "the greatness of Love and Democracy, and the greatness of Religion"; the spiritual foundation of the principle of equality in "O such themes—equalities! O divine average"; these songs ever for the present and the future in "For those who belong here and those to come"; the true significance of sex in "And sexual organs and acts! do you concentrate in me, for I am

[21] *Ibid.*, pp. 18, 21, 25, 26, 27, 29, 32.
[22] *Ibid.*, pp. 18, 24, 29, 30.
[23] *Ibid.*, pp. 27–28, 31.

determin'd to tell you with courageous clear voice to prove you illustrious"; and the praise of the body in "Behold, the body includes and is the meaning, the main concern and includes and is the soul."[24] To one acquainted with *Leaves of Grass* generally, this review of the symbols and themes introduced in "Starting from Paumanok," symbols and themes which are either of major importance or else controversial and misleading unless seen in relation to the whole, substantiates the declaration:

> I will not make poems with reference to parts,
> But I will make poems, songs, thoughts, with
>   reference to ensemble . . .[25]

"Song of Myself" is the nuclear poem of the book. In "A Backward Glance O'er Travel'd Roads" Whitman offers the following explanation: "I saw, from the time my enterprise and questionings positively shaped themselves (how best can I express my own distinctive era and surroundings, America, democracy) that the trunk and center whence the answer was to radiate . . . must be an identical body and soul, a personality— which personality, after many . . . ponderings I deliberately settled should be myself—indeed could not be any other."[26] That Whitman's great song of the ego comes early in *Leaves of Grass* is a necessity. In the light of the observations preparatory to this analysis, further discussion of this fact would be superfluous. The great appeal of Elias Hicks to Whitman grew out of his doctrine that "the fountain of all naked theology, all religion, all worship," is in the individual himself.[27] Whitman's seemingly crass egotism is tempered when we are aware of its true function. It possesses pride; but it also possesses great sympathy. His compassion and his uninhibited exaltation of selfhood alike sprang from his belief in the potential greatness

[24] *Ibid.*, pp. 17, 18, 19, 20, 23, 24, 25, 27.
[25] *Ibid.*, p. 25.
[26] "A Backward Glance O'er Travel'd Roads," III, 56–57.
[27] "Notes (such as they are) founded on E. H.," *November Boughs*, VI, 242.

in man, a greatness to be divined where it was not yet made
flesh. Here in "Song of Myself" is the great composite democratic individual, the great example. True, it is Walt Whitman
—God made flesh. But he proclaims all men equal to himself.
"I show that size is only development./ . . . I know perfectly
well my egotism . . . and would fetch you, whoever you are,
flush with myself."[28] Even more, Whitman (and in this respect
he goes beyond the Christ-concept) wanted *Leaves of Grass*
to compel every reader to transpose himself into the central
position and become the living fountain. Selincourt, it seems
to me, sees "Song of Myself" clearly in relation to the whole.
"The general purpose of his book, of course, is that it shall be
the deliberate and progressive unfolding of the conscious life
of a man who is at once individual and typical; and it is so arranged as to present first the foundation and implication of
such a life and to fill in afterwards the various stages of experience and reflection."[29] Knowledge of the prophet himself
is prerequisite to the comprehension and acceptance of any
prophecy. Self-revelation, then, as anticipated in "Starting from
Paumanok" and fully recorded in "Song of Myself," is the first
phase of *Leaves of Grass.*

It is significant that the foundation poem of *Leaves of Grass,*
the germ from which it springs, is given primarily to the establishment of the Christ-symbol. Having qualified the central
personality of *Leaves* by such a device in "Song of Myself,"
Whitman shifts emphasis somewhat and proceeds to reveal
him in relation to a time and a place and a society, his development paralleling that of his nation. In other words, "Song of
Myself" is preparatory to the gospel of *Leaves of Grass* in much
the same way that the prophecies of the Old Testament are
preparatory and essential to our full understanding of the Christ
who actually lives and proves himself among the peoples and
events of his age.

Let us look for a moment at the prophetic picture, the Christ-

[28] "Song of Myself," I, 58, 94.
[29] Basil de Selincourt, *Walt Whitman: A Critical Study,* p. 165.

symbol, in "Song of Myself." A series of partial quotations running throughout the poem will indicate its significance. Following the first climactic passage of the poem, the budding prophet's mystical awakening, he exclaims, "Swiftly arose and spread
around me the peace and knowledge that pass all the argument
of the earth, . . . I know that the hand of God is the promise of
my own, . . . that all men . . . are also my brothers. . . . that a Kelson of the creation is love."[30] He testifies further as the poem
progresses: "I pass death with the dying and birth with the
new-wash'd babe. . . . I am the . . . companion of the people . . .
immortal . . . (They do not know how immortal, but I know.)"
The last supper is suggested in the lines "[I] brought water
and fill'd a tub for his sweated body and bruis'd feet. . . . This
is the meal equally set, . . . I will not have a single person slighted
or left away." Allusions to the resurrection, second coming, de-
scent into hell follow: "I know I am deathless. . . . I come to
my own to-day or in ten thousand or ten million years, . . .
take it now, or with equal cheerfulness . . . wait. . . . The pleas-
ures of heaven are with me and the pains of hell, . . . the first I
grasp and increase upon myself, the latter I translate into a new
tongue."

Attitudes and relationships are described in terms reminiscent of New Testament revelation: "My gait is no fault-finder's
or rejecter's gait. . . . I find . . . soft doctrine as steady help
as stable doctrine. . . . Whoever degrades another degrades
me. . . . Divine am I inside and out, and I make holy whatever
I touch or am touch'd from. . . . Writing and talk do not prove
me. . . . I wholly confound the skeptic. . . . Logic and sermons
never convince."

Scenes and experiences from the life of Christ are echoed.
"[I walk] the hills of Judea with the beautiful gentle God by
my side. . . . I am the man, I suffer'd, I was there. . . . That I
could look with a separate look on my own crucifixion and
bloody crowning. . . . Corpses rise, gashes heal, fastenings roll
from me. . . . Eleves, I salute you! come forward! . . . Wherever

[30] "Song of Myself," I, 38.

he goes men and women . . . desire he should like them, touch
them, speak to them, stay with them. . . . When I give I give
myself. . . . Let the physician and the priest go. . . . I seize the
descending man and raise him with resistless will. . . . hang
your whole weight upon me. . . . I am he bringing help for the
sick . . . and for the strong upright men . . . yet more needed
help."

Similarly, there are echoes in passages suggesting the inclusive nature of his experience and sympathy: "A call in the
midst of the crowd, . . . orotund sweeping and final, . . . Come
my children. . . . Ever that thorn'd thumb . . . ever the vexer's
hoot! . . . ever love . . . ever the trestles of death. . . . The weak-
est and shallowest is deathless with me. . . . I do not despise
you priests. . . . my faith is the greatest of faiths and the least
of faiths, . . . I shall come again upon the earth after five thousand years. . . . [I accept] the Gospels, accepting him that was
crucified, knowing assuredly that he is divine. . . . I know the
sea of torment, doubt, despair and unbelief. . . . I launch all
men and women forward with me into the Unknown. . . . Other
births will bring us richness and variety. . . . I am the acme of
things accomplished, and I am encloser of things to be."

There are even suggestions of the Word which was in the
beginning and is now at the right hand of God: "Afar down I
see the huge first Nothing, I know I was even there. . . . Long
I was hugg'd close. . . . My rendezvous is appointed . . . the
Lord will be there and wait till I come . . . the great Camerado,
the lover true for whom I pine will be there."

Finally, there is the Christ-like offer of comfort and aid and
challenge and the Christ-like mysticism. "If you tire, give me
both burdens. . . . Here are biscuits to eat and here is milk
to drink . . . as soon as you sleep and renew yourself . . . I . . .
open the gate for your egress hence. . . . Now I will you to be
a bold swimmer. . . . Who can stray from me? . . . My words
itch at your ears till you understand them. . . . But roughs and
little children better than they. . . . I go forth with fishermen
and seamen and love them. . . . On that solemn night (it may be

their last) those that know me seek me. . . . I am at peace about
God and about death. . . . I see something of God each hour of
the twenty-four, and each moment then. . . . I plead for my
brothers and sisters. . . . It is not chaos or death—it is form,
union, plan—it is eternal life—it is Happiness. . . . Listener up
there! . . . (Talk honestly, no one else hears you, and I stay
only a minute longer.)"[31] The concluding stanzas are:

> You will hardly know who I am or what I mean,
> But I shall be good health to you nevertheless,
> And filter and fibre your blood.

> Failing to fetch me at first keep encouraged,
> Missing me one place search another,
> I stop somewhere waiting for you.[32]

We need not agree on all these echoes or allusions (given
here in the order in which they occur in "Song of Myself") in
order to see how thoroughly the Christ-image permeates this
key poem. Suffice it to say that among these passages the crucifixion allusion is the most significant. It is the climax of the
entire poem toward which all of the prophet's sympathetic iden-
tifications of himself with the experience and suffering of all
men carefully progress—the progression whereby crucifixion
and resurrection are his own and whereby he is qualified for
the exalted role he is to play.

The grass-symbol is the second important symbol in "Song
of Myself" which is to recur throughout the volume, gradually
revealing the full significance of the title. The grass is fittingly
symbolic of Whitman's poems because it grows, contains hints
of the mystery of life, is of "hopeful green," is of God, is a
"uniform hieroglyphic," springs mysteriously out of the dead,
is common and democratic ("growing wherever the land is and
the water is"), and yet is "no less than the journey-work of the

[31] *Ibid.*, pp. 41, 44, 55, 57, 58, 60, 62, 63, 66, 70, 78, 80, 88, 89, 90, 92, 93, 94,
95, 96, 97, 98, 100, 101, 102, 103, 104, 105, 106, 107, 108.
[32] *Ibid.*, p. 109.

stars."[33] A third symbol of structural significance, that of the
journey ("I tramp a perpetual journey"), and the repeated
use of the catalogue contribute to the expansive spirit of the
poem, and as we shall see, relate it in this respect to most of the
other pre–"Sea-Drift" poems.[34] Finally, for a review of the
themes developed in "Song of Myself" we need only turn back
to Chapter III and its discussion of the Christ-symbol; there
the main themes have already been suggested in the passages
on the likeness of the hero of *Leaves* to Christ as a mystic, social
being, and gospel bearer. This fact, it seems to me, is ample justification for the emphasis we have placed upon that particular
symbol.

CHILDREN OF ADAM (16 POEMS)

Following, and closely associated with these two songs, are
"Children of Adam" and "Calamus." The "Children of Adam"
poems are poems of the natural man and sex. In attempting to
understand these lyrics and justify their position in *Leaves of
Grass*, there are two important features of the group to keep
in mind: (1) the identification of the self with Adam in his
state of innocence, and (2) the clearly related experiences of
procreation and love. In the light of the biblical backgrounds
that we have suggested, Whitman's identification of himself
with Adam in Eden is interesting. R. W. B. Lewis provides helpful hints regarding this subject:

> From about 1820 onward, editorials, orations, stories, and poems
> spread the good news that since the American, inhabitant of a
> virgin continent, was born into the world free of inherited fault,
> his moral course must be one of self-development, the expansion
> of natural faculties, rather than one of redemption. . . . The
> symbol collecting and unifying these concepts was found at last
> in the figure of Adam before the fall: prototype of the American,

---

[33] *Ibid.*, pp. 39–40, 54, 70.
[34] *Ibid.*, pp. 101, 48–52, 73–78.

miraculously free of family and race, emancipated from history and born, as it were, at the second dawn of time. Humanity in the new world was to be given a second chance.[35]

The American in *Leaves of Grass* is the new unfallen Adam in the western garden. That this idea is inherent in most of Whitman's poetry is undeniable. In view of the fact that the Eden-symbol is used in the first and last poems of "Children of Adam," it would seem that the idea is attached to this section in particular. Miller develops this Eden theme into something more than a point of reference or frame, seeing in Whitman's unique use of it the reversal of the myth and the concept of rebirth. In addition he sees a spirituality in the poems, implicit in Whitman's use of "electric," which escapes me.[36] In both *Start with the Sun* and *Walt Whitman* Miller identifies Whitman's concept of sexual force with "the neglected historical force" and the life force of cosmic dimensions.[37]

Throughout "Children of Adam" the Eden-symbol is reinforced by Whitman's elaborate use of Eden-like scenery and his subtle intermingling of the sensuality of man and the lusciousness of nature. "From Pent-up Aching Rivers" and "Spontaneous Me" demonstrate the effectiveness of these techniques. There are a number of prose passages that may prove helpful here. After quoting Marcus Aurelius' concept that virtue is "only a living and enthusiastic sympathy with nature," Whitman adds, "Perhaps indeed, the efforts of the true poets . . . have been, and ever will be, . . . to bring people back from their persistent strayings and sickly abstractions to the costless average, divine, original concrete."[38] And at the other places he states:

[35] R. W. B. Lewis, "The Danger of Innocence: Adam as Hero in American Literature," *Yale Review* 39 (1950), 473.

[36] James E. Miller, Jr., *A Critical Guide to Leaves of Grass*, pp. 36–51.

[37] James E. Miller, Jr., Karl Shapiro, and Bernice Slote, *Start with the Sun*, pp. 24–26; James E. Miller, Jr., *Walt Whitman*, pp. 145–150. An interesting contrast can be seen in Asselineau's treatment of the section as little more than an afterthought (Roger Asselineau, *The Evolution of Walt Whitman: The Creation of a Book*, p. 114).

[38] *Specimen Days*, V, 44.

A strong-fiber'd joyousness and faith, and the sense of health *al fresco*, may well enter into the preparation of future noble American authorship. Part of the test of a great literatus shall be the absence in him of the idea of the covert, the lurid, the maleficent, the devil, the grim estimates inherited from the Puritans, hell, natural depravity, and the like. . . . Man has long enough realized how bad he is. I would not so much disturb or demolish that conviction, only to resume and keep unerringly with it the spinal meaning of the Scriptural text, "God overlook'd all that he made, '(including the apex of the whole—humanity—with its elements, passions, appetites)' and behold, it was very good.[39]

"Puritanism and what radiates from it must always be mention'd by me with respect; then I should say, for this vast and varied Commonwealth, geographically and artistically, the Puritanical standards are constipated, narrow, and non-philosophic."[40] Certainly there is no place in Whitman's new religion for the idea of original sin. This is one of his sharp departures from the Christian doctrine, and he wanted it to be made clear in *Leaves of Grass* as swiftly and deftly as possible. What more prompt, positive, poetic (nonargumentative) device could be found than that of identifying his hero, at the start, with Adam in Eden. The implications of the allusion are unmistakable, its connotative values rich and disarmingly beautiful. All that the poet needs to do in order to accomplish subtly his purpose is to sing in all his uninhibited innocence exuberant songs of sex.

To the garden the world anew ascending,

.   .   .   .

The revolving cycles in their wide sweep having
     brought me again,
Amorous, mature, all beautiful to me, all wondrous,
My limbs and the quivering fire that ever plays

[39] "Democratic Vistas," "A Memorandum at a Venture," *Collect*, V, 132, 238.
[40] "American National Literature," *Good-Bye My Fancy*, VII, 9.

through them, for reasons, most wondrous,
Existing I peer and penetrate still,
Content with the present, content with the past,
By my side or back of me Eve following,
Or in front, and I following her just the same.[41]

As Adam early in the morning,
Walking forth from the bower refresh'd with sleep,
Behold me where I pass, hear my voice, approach,
Touch me, touch the palm of your hand to my body
    as I pass,
Be not afraid of my body.[42]

O to speed where there is space enough and air
    enough at last!
To be absolv'd from previous ties and conventions,
    I from mine and you from yours!
To find a new unthought-of nonchalance with the
    best of Nature!
To have the gag remov'd from one's mouth!
To have the feeling today or any day I am sufficient
    as I am.[43]

Whitman was able to slough off those inhibitions foreign to
the natural man and to celebrate sex in a way that Milton wished
but was unable to celebrate it in *Paradise Lost*. The tragedy of
"Children of Adam" as a part of *Leaves of Grass* is not so much
that it is a failure itself, but rather that the reader fails to meet
its challenge. Most critics have treated Whitman's expression
of the sex theme in these poems as superficial and nonpoetic,
while accepting his use of the sex symbol elsewhere in *Leaves
of Grass* where it is equally natural and free in expression, but
enhanced by spiritual significance. This fact suggests to me that
there has been a general failure to appreciate Whitman's peculiar problem. His *primary* purpose in this group of poems is to

[41] "To the Garden the World," I, 110.
[42] "As Adam Early in the Morning," I, 136.
[43] "One Hour to Madness and Joy," I, 130.

praise the physical act itself, preparatory to his enrichment of it by pointing out its emotional and spiritual values—its ultimate significance. Whitman's treatment of sex in these early poems seems limited only if we refuse to see it in relation to the developments that follow. In such a case, the mistake is the same as that which has led to a condemnation of his early materialism—a condemnation indicative of a failure to grasp the real significance of his message and purport in *Leaves* as a whole. "The Highest said: Don't let us begin so low—isn't our range too coarse—too gross? . . . The Soul answer'd: No. Not when we consider what it is all for—the end involved in Time and Space."[44] Whitman was a true poet in that he could not love things spiritual and despise the physical sources of their revelation and expression. "Children of Adam" is another effort on his part, unconscious perhaps, to make the reader himself a poet. More than any other poet, it seems to me, Whitman shares with his reader the actual materials and attitudes of poem making. In "Children of Adam," as he later proves to most critics' satisfaction, is at least the stuff of which poetry is made.

There is evidence that Whitman visualized the "Children of Adam" poems as trailblazers in the sense of clearing away unreal prejudices and obstacles to reality, and also as the vital poetic play establishing contact—an uninhibited, intimate, real contact—with his readers. Historically, at any rate, this function was not fully realized. Finally, "Children of Adam" should come first, according to simple chronology and logic, for it is concerned with beginnings, foundations. Whitman says:

> with reference to the whole construction, organism, and intentions of *Leaves of Grass,* anything short of confronting that theme [sex], and making myself clear upon it, as the enclosing basis of everything (as the sanity of everything was to be the atmosphere of the poems), I should beg the question in its most momentous aspect, and the superstructure that followed, pretensive as it might assume to be, would all rest on a poor foundation, or no

[44] "Memoranda," *Good-Bye My Fancy,* VII, 20.

foundation at all. In short, as the assumption of the sanity of birth, nature and humanity, is the key to any true theory of life and the universe—at any rate, the only theory out of which I wrote—it is, and must inevitably be, the only key to *Leaves of Grass,* and every part of it.[45]

But to see "Children of Adam" in relation to *Leaves* as a whole is to realize that here Whitman celebrates the physical act of procreation as something more than the origin of new life. Drawing heavily upon the Adam tradition, he shows how this significant, God-like, creative act, which is fundamentally physical, inevitably leads man into his most basic and natural spiritual experience—the spiritual experience at the heart of *Leaves of Grass*—the union of individual spirits in the act of love. This is the beginning of Adam's spiritual training in *Paradise Lost,* and the angel points it out before he turns scarlet. Stovall says of Whitman, "If he tried to lift sex out of its degradation and liberate it from taboos, it was because he believed it to be the most spiritual part of man's nature, the physical counterpart of the divine creative mind, and an integral part of the soul."[46] There are three significant elements here, related to the structural pattern of *Leaves*. There is the establishment of the characteristic Whitmanian progression from body to spirit, from material to spiritual. There is the implication that as basic as procreation in the physical world is love in the spiritual world. There is the foundation for the vivid sexual symbolism which is to persist throughout his work —a symbolism which represents to him, through the ecstasy of the basically physical sex experience, a transcending of all fixed forms in our most natural, exalted act of pure reality. Later Whitman is to point to love and death as the transcending of fixed form and to the resultant experience of reality. These approaches to the "Children of Adam" poems make them fundamental—a natural starting point for all of *Leaves of Grass*.

[45] "A Memorandum at a Venture," *Collect*, V, 233–234.
[46] Floyd Stovall, *American Idealism*, p. 93.

Whitman's refusal to discard or to modify them materially seems to indicate that he considered them as such. In "A Backward Glance O'er Travel'd Roads" Whitman says, "the spirit in which they are spoken, permeates all of *Leaves of Grass*, and the work must stand or fall with them, as the human body and soul must remain as an entirety."[47]

One final observation, "Children of Adam" is the one grouping of poems free of any suggestion of the Christ-symbol. Here, for special reasons, the identification is with the first Adam, rather than the second. The exclusion of the symbol is altogether appropriate. Milton's Satan knew better than to tempt Christ with woman.

CALAMUS (39 POEMS)

Viewed in the above light, "Children of Adam" leads naturally into the "Calamus" poems. Man first learns the spiritual act of love as Adam did (by slowly appreciating the significance of sexual attraction)—now the spiritual aspect expands and grows. Throughout the "Calamus" poems a keen awareness of the physical self exists; however, the physical obviously becomes more and more symbolic in function and less and less the literal instrument of self-realization that it is in "Children of Adam." Binns speaks of this progression in these terms, "The gospel of self-realization thus becomes a social gospel, and the thought gives a political significance to these, the most esoteric of all Whitman's poems."[48] A footnote in *Democratic Vistas*, stating Whitman's awareness of the novelty of his "adhesiveness" as a poetic theme, may throw some light on the "esoteric" quality that Binns mentions:

> It is to the development, identification, and general prevalence of that fervid comradeship (the adhesive love, at least rivaling the amative love hitherto possessing imaginative literature, if not going beyond it) that I look for the counterbalance and offset

[47] "A Backward Glance O'er Travel'd Roads," III, 62.
[48] Henry Bryan Binns, *A Life of Walt Whitman*, p. 162.

of our materialistic and vulgar American democracy, and for the spiritualization thereof. . . . I say democracy infers such loving comradeship, as its most inevitable twin and counterpart, without which it will be incomplete, in vain, and incapable of perpetuating itself.[49]

At any rate, it is this section of *Leaves of Grass* that contains the firm foundations of Whitman's concept of a vital, real, spiritual democracy. The essence of this democracy is the expression of friendship and brotherhood springing directly from the human heart. "Adhesiveness or love . . . fuses, ties and aggregates, making the races comrades and fraternizing all."[50] "Let diplomats, as ever, still deeply plan, seeking advantages, proposing treaties between governments, and to bind them, on paper: what I seek is different, simpler. I would inaugurate from America, for this purpose, new formulas—international poems. I have thought that the invisible root out of which the poetry deepest in, and dearest to, humanity grows, is friendship."[51] It is to this vibrant, sincere love of man for man as the true spirit of democracy that the "Calamus" poems are dedicated. Just as the crisp springs of religion are to be found in each individual heart rather than in creeds or codes, so it is with true brotherhood. Even that love which we project generally to all mankind must spring from the heart; it must bear its warmth and its sincerity; in fancying that it can be cool and calculated, we deceive ourselves.

> To hold men together by paper and seal or by compulsion
>   is no account,
> That only holds men together which aggregates all in a
>   living principle, as the hold of the limbs of the
>   body or the fibres of plants.[52]

49 *Democratic Vistas, Collect,* V, 131 (footnote).
50 *Ibid.,* p. 80.
51 "Poetry To-Day in America," *Collect,* V, 221.
52 "By Blue Ontario's Shore," II, 114.

This, it seems to me, is the long view that must be kept in mind in approaching the "Calamus" poems. If they are to form a genuine transition from "Children of Adam" to the democratic songs which immediately follow them, they must be characterized by the blending of concepts of intimate physical love and of general love of man for mankind. The purpose of this blending is to establish the naturalness of "adhesiveness." James Thomson is appreciative of Whitman's contribution: "He sings in the great section termed 'Calamus,' as it has scarcely been sung before, the perfect love of comrades, the superb friendship of man and man, as deep as life, stronger than death."[53]

One cannot deny that there are some vividly sensual passages in the "Calamus" poems which give grounds for charges of homosexuality. Some critics have magnified these out of all proportion. Malcolm Cowley seizes upon the symbol of the calamus plant and declares, "The sweet-flag or calamus root, the 'growth by the margin of pond-waters,' was simply Whitman's token of the male sexual organ. . . . The poems under this general title were poems of homosexual love, in its physical aspects and with its metaphysical lessons."[54] But Cowley does not rely upon the poems themselves in substantiating his charges; he embroiders on biography: "Feverish and disproportionate, it [Whitman's homosexuality] set him roving through the streets in search of young men, preferably rough and bearded, who might be interested in his type of affection." Asselineau's unhappy chapter happily entitled "Sex Life" pursues a similar theme.[55] In his lengthy treatment of the "Calamus" problem he accepts the charge of homosexuality and emphasizes a literal interpretation of symbolism and meaning characteristic of the Cowley position.[56] The extreme expression

[53] James Thomson, *Walt Whitman: The Man and the Poet*, p. 31.

[54] Malcolm Cowley, "Introduction," *The Complete Poetry and Prose of Walt Whitman*, I, 14.

[55] Asselineau, *The Evolution of Walt Whitman: The Creation of a Book*, pp. 107–128.

[56] Asselineau, *The Evolution of Walt Whitman: The Creation of a Personality*, pp. 107–114; 121–122.

of this point of view comes from Griffith, who says that Whitman viewed his calamus love as destructive and that this developed in him a deep sense of guilt, leading ultimately to the death wish. In this way Griffith accounts for the plaintive elements in "Calamus" and relates the group to the "death poems" of the 1860 edition.[57] Returning to Cowley, we find that he goes on to suggest that one group of Whitman's associates at Pfaff's was homosexual and concludes, "At this point we begin to see that Whitman is trying to identify, or at least confuse, homosexuality with Americanism."[58] A similar judgment by Van Doren, also based primarily on a subjective interpretation of biographical materials, is challenged by Fausset. He says, "This is an extreme judgement [that Whitman's poems of "adhesiveness" are invalidated by sexual abnormality], although it contains an element of truth. It would only be acceptable if homosexual love had been in fact the main spring of Whitman's gospel of democratic comradeship. . . . And there is no evidence that it was."[59] Blodgett summarizes Havelock Ellis's study in these words, "Ellis delivers the opinion that Whitman, who lacked the analytical power to comprehend his own nature, possessed unconsciously a tendency toward homosexuality."[60] It is difficult to preach a gospel of which one is unaware. Whether or not Whitman the man was homosexual is of no concern in this study; whether or not homosexuality is the major theme of "Calamus" is of considerable importance. I would like to advance the opinion that it definitely is not; that the sensual imagery in the poems does not necessitate such an interpretation; that it is precisely the spiritual quality of the love of man for man that causes Whitman to exalt it; that it is this particular quality upon which he clearly focuses attention;

[57] C. Griffith, "Sex and Death: The Significance of Whitman's Calamus Themes," *PQ* 39 (January 1960), 18–38.

[58] Cowley, "Introduction," *The Complete Poetry and Prose of Walt Whitman*, I, 16, 17, 27.

[59] Hugh l'Anson Fausset, *Walt Whitman: Poet of Democracy*, p. 151.

[60] Harold Blodgett, *Walt Whitman in England*, p. 208.

and that the ultimate purpose of the section is to proclaim the
doctrine of brotherhood based on the projected love of the
human heart. It is out of the experience of the love of the individual for the individual that man learns the real human relationship essential to spiritual democracy. In Whitman's own
words, what he hopes to accomplish can be realized only "by a
sublime and serious Religious Democracy sternly taking command, dissolving the old, sloughing off surfaces, and from its
own interior and vital principles, reconstructing, democratizing
society."[61] In the "Calamus" poems Whitman is continuing
his bold, frank attempt begun in "Children of Adam" to clear
the mind in preparation for the complete intellectual, spiritual,
and emotional emancipation essential to the realization of his
spiritual democracy.

Selincourt distinguishes between "Children of Adam" and
"Calamus" in this manner: "It [the former] is the praise of
sex as distinguished from the praise of love, while Calamus is
the praise of love as distinguished from the praise of sex."[62]
Whenever poets have dealt vividly with the theme of love, no
matter how spiritual, they have inevitably resorted to sensual,
sexual imagery. We need go no further than the so-called
"metaphysical poetry" of the seventeenth century or the Bible
to see that such a practice is traditional. The presence of such
imagery does not lead one to suppose that either sensuality or
sex is the theme of Donne's *Holy Sonnets*, for instance. Rather,
it is viewed as his unique manner of speaking, of giving new
vitality to the concept of Christian love. "Calamus" can be, and
I believe should be, viewed in a similar light. G. W. Mathews
says: "A very careful study of these poems leads me to the
theory that in them Whitman was seeking a basis for his great
conception of Democracy. . . . What then is the element in these
poems of Whitman's before which we recoil? It is due, I think,
to Whitman's intense vitality and to what to most people seems

[61] "Democratic Vistas," *Collect*, V, 125.
[62] Selincourt, *Walt Whitman*, p. 208.

the grossness of his symbolism. It is a question of method. He thought in pictures, not in ideas, and hence when he portrays affection it tends to run into terms of contact."[63]

Stovall makes a similar observation, "In him more than in others emotion was directly allied with sense perception; hence the extreme sensuousness of his nature was the source and final determinant of his songs of love."[64] Holloway goes a little deeper into the psychology of the matter when he states: "The artist is expected to pass in his imagination from the man's point of view to the woman's, and back again, at will; Whitman is almost solitary among major poets of the world—unless Shakespeare be an exception—in his tendency to do this with his heart. The peculiarity, he seems to have thought, was what made him akin to the great religious teachers of the past."[65]

Even if homosexuality alone can explain the source of the symbolism in "Calamus" (and such an assumption is obviously open to serious questioning), it does not necessarily follow that it is the theme or gospel expounded therein; rather these poems are a magnificent example of a sublimation whereby a great spiritual theme, the love of man for man, is given a new and vital expression. Few students of Whitman have questioned this fact. The "Calamus" poems, according to most critics, possess a unique sincerity, tenderness, and delicacy, a delicacy not unlike the aroma which Whitman himself associated with the calamus plant. This, I think, is significant in attempting to understand the title of the group. As demonstrated in "When Lilacs Last in the Dooryard Bloom'd" and other poems of the spirit, fragrance is used by Whitman as a symbol of spiritual love.[66] A second, and related, observation

[63] Godfrey W. Mathews, *Walt Whitman*, pp. 37–39.

[64] Stovall, ed., *Walt Whitman*, pp. xxx–xxxi.

[65] "Introduction," *Uncollected Poetry and Prose*, I, xlix.

[66] See Kenneth Burke, "Policy Made Personal," in *Leaves of Grass One Hundred Years After*, ed. Hindus, pp. 99–106; Miller, *A Critical Guide to Leaves of Grass*, pp. 52–79. Included in Miller's chapter are other interesting parallels to this treatment, though there is considerable difference in over-all purpose and point of view. Miller is concerned primarily with relationships within the group itself and becomes somewhat involved in biographical considerations.

is the fact that the poet must depart the shore and wade out into the water in order to possess the calamus plant. In *Leaves of Grass* this departure from the land is always the symbol of passage into the spiritual world. Such tender and subtle interpretations of the significance of Whitman's title are certainly more in keeping with the delicate and esoteric quality which is characteristic of these poems than is the gross interpretation suggested by Cowley, that the root is the symbol of the male sexual organ. I doubt that either Whitman's poetic imagination or his indirect, suggestive manner of poetic expression could tolerate a symbol so insensate and so foreign to the tone of these sensitive love poems. Whitman himself explained the connotative values of his title to Rossetti in the following terms: "Calamus is the very large and aromatic grass, or rush, growing about the water ponds in the valleys—spears about three feet high; often called Sweet Flag; grows all over the Northern and Middle States. The recherché or ethereal sense of the term, as used in my book, arises probably from the actual Calamus presenting the biggest and hardiest kind of spears of grass, and their fresh, aquatic, pungent *bouquet*."[67] Certainly this testimony overshadows the rather obscure line from "Song of Myself," written long before the "Calamus" poems had been conceived and in an utterly different mood and context, upon which Cowley attempts to base his interpretation:

> Root of wash'd sweet-flag! timorous pond-snipe! nest
> of guarded duplicate eggs! it shall be you![68]

Just as we observe the turning out and expansion of the "Children of Adam" concept of love in the "Calamus" poems, so we encounter in them the first long Whitmanian progression from the material to the spiritual. When seen in this manner it is not difficult to understand the zeal with which Whitman defended them as elemental in his creed. One cannot question the

---

[67] W. S. Kennedy, *The Fight of a Book for the World*, p. 177.
[68] "Song of Myself," I, 63.

sincerity of one of his most eloquent passages on the subject:

> While I am about it, I would make a full confession. I also sent
> out *Leaves of Grass* to arouse and set flowing in men's and
> women's hearts, young and old, endless streams of living pulsat-
> ing love and friendship, directly from them to myself, now and
> ever. To this terrible, inexpressible yearning, (surely more or less
> down underneath in most human souls)—this never-satisfied ap-
> petite for sympathy, and this boundless offering of sympathy—
> this universal democratic comradeship—this old, eternal, yet
> ever-new interchange of adhesiveness, so fitly emblematic of
> America—I have given in that book, undisguisedly, declaredly,
> the openest expression. Besides, important as they are in my pur-
> pose as emotional expressions for humanity, the special meaning
> of the "Calamus" cluster of *Leaves of Grass* . . . mainly resides
> in its political significance. In my opinion, it is by a fervent, ac-
> cepted development of comradeship . . . that the United States
> of the future . . . are to be most effectually welded together, in-
> tercalated, anneal'd into a living union. Then, for enclosing clew
> of all, it is imperatively and ever to be borne in mind that *Leaves
> of Grass* entire is not to be construed as an intellectual or scho-
> lastic effort or poem mainly, but more a radical utterance out
> of the Emotions and Physique—an utterance adjusted to, per-
> haps born of, Democracy and the Modern—in its very nature
> regardless of the old conventions, and, under the great laws, fol-
> lowing only its own impulses.[69]

Myers's statement, that for Whitman "the problem of reconciling the free citizen with the power of the state is solved when
the individual treats the state as a projection of one part of his
personality, that part which unites him with other individuals,"
suggests the particular significance of the "Calamus" contribution to *Leaves of Grass* as a whole.[70] It is unjust to consider the
group out of context.

The first five poems of "Calamus" seem to anticipate the

---

[69] "Preface, 1876," *Collect*, V, 199 (footnote).
[70] H. A. Myers, "Whitman's Consistency," *AL* 8 (November 1936), 256.

problem that arises when one loses sight of the group's particular function in the structure of the work as a whole, encouraged to do so by passages of frank sensuality. When we remember the opening poem of "Children of Adam" with its picture of Adam walking in the garden, Eve following—a picture again evoked in the concluding poem—it becomes obvious that the title of the first poem in the "Calamus" group, "In Paths Untrodden," is intended to denote a progression. Whitman's symbolism suggests that the progression is in the direction of a new spirituality. The paths hitherto untrodden lead to the margins of waters, where the poet hears the whispers of the "tongues aromatic" of the aquatic calamus plant. There is a striking similarity to the symbolism of "Out of the Cradle Endlessly Rocking," in which the child wanders alone to the shore and hears the whisper of the sea. This is significant for two reasons: first, it associates "Calamus" with the great poem which records Whitman's spiritual awakening; and second, it calls attention to the fact that these poems were written during the same short period of composition. The "paths untrodden" are an escape "from the life that exhibits itself" into a new spiritual awareness described in the lines:

> Clear to me now standards not yet publish'd, clear
>   to me that my soul,
> That the soul of the man I speak for rejoices in
>   comrades.[71]

Thus the central theme of "Calamus" is announced.

In the second poem of the group, "Scented Herbage of My Breast," Whitman continues to emphasize the spirituality of this new love. In the title itself we find the word *scented*, echoing the word *aromatic* and anticipating the lilac fragrance of the great Lincoln poem. The spirituality of this symbol is borne out by the epithets:

> Tomb-leaves, body-leaves growing up above me
>   above death,

[71] "In Paths Untrodden," I, 137.

Perennial roots, tall leaves, O the winter shall
   not freeze you delicate leaves.
Every year shall you bloom again . . . [72]

This is the first great "Calamus" poem in which we encounter
at the full Whitman's use of unique, vividly sensual symbolism
for expressing highly spiritualized concepts. The slender leaves,
the "blossoms of blood," leaves springing from the very heart
of him, are (like the "beautiful uncut hair of graves") expressions of that spiritualized love "folded inseparably" with
death, which will become the "real reality" and will "one day
perhaps take control of all" and "dissipate this entire show of
appearances."[73] Thus, in the second poem, probably the most
esoteric of the "Calamus" lyrics, the theme of the group is
identified with the earlier grass-symbol and with the love-death
theme which later becomes the spiritual climax of the entire
work.

   "Whoever You Are Holding Me Now in Hand" identifies the
"Calamus" theme with the Christ-like idea that faith and the
spirit of self-denial and surrender are necessary if one is to
"prove victorious" in laying hold of this new gospel of love.
This idea dominates the entire poem. The passage

Here to put your lips upon mine I permit you,
With the comrade's long-dwelling kiss or the new
   husband's kiss,
For I am the new husband and I am the comrade.[74]

weds highly sensual imagery and unmistakable allusion to the
Christ of the New Testament. It demonstrates the danger of
giving too literal an interpretation to such complex, sensual
passages, for here the symbolic expression is that of the relationship of the reader to the book.

   "For You O Democracy" is the dedicatory poem of the section; it is the poetic counterpart of Whitman's prose statement

[72] "Scented Herbage of My Breast," I, 138.
[73] *Ibid.*, p. 139.
[74] "Whoever You Are Holding Me Now in Hand," I, 140–141.

that the special meaning of the "Calamus" group "mainly re-
sides in its political significance."

> I will make the most splendid race the sun ever
> > shone upon,
> I will make divine magnetic lands,
> > With the love of comrades,
> > > With the life-long love of comrades.
>
> . . . .
>
> For you these from me, O Democracy, to serve you
> > ma femme!
> For you, for you I am trilling these songs.[75]

Parrington stresses this phase of "Calamus":

> But in Whitman all limitations and skepticisms were swept away
> by the feeling of comradeship. Flesh is kin to flesh, and out of
> the great reserves of life is born the average man "with his ex-
> cellent good manliness." Not in distinction but in oneness with
> the whole is found the good life, for in fellowship is love and in
> the whole is freedom: and love and freedom are the law and the
> prophets. The disintegrations of the earlier individualism must
> be succeeded by a new integration; fear and hate and jealousy
> and pride have held men apart hitherto, but love will draw them
> together. After all solidarity—the children of America merging
> in the fellowship, sympathetic, responsive, manlike yet divine, of
> which the poet should be the prophet and literature provide the
> sermons.[76]

"These I Singing in Spring" is probably intended to be the
key poem of the "Calamus" group. In it the calamus-symbol,
from which the section takes its name, is developed. Here Whitman emphasizes the significant fact (already discussed in this
study) that the poet must depart the shore, "fearing not the
wet," and wade out in order to obtain the calamus root. This

[75] "For You O Democracy," I, 142.
[76] Vernon Louis Parrington, *Main Currents in American Thought*, III,
76–77.

symbolism is reinforced by the line "Collecting I traverse the garden the world [the physical], but soon I pass the gates [into the spiritual]."[77] That all is spirit is clearly indicated in the lines which follow:

> Alone I had thought, yet soon a troop gathers around me,
> Some walk by my side and some behind, and some
>   embrace my arms or neck,
> They the spirits of dear friends dead or alive,
>   thicker they come, a great crowd, and I in
>   the middle.[78]

It is to these presences that the poet offers his *fragrant* tokens of lilac, pine, pinks, sage, wild orange, plum-blows, aromatic cedar, and ultimately, of calamus. The entire poem moves consciously in an atmosphere of fragrance. Finally, the line "These I compass'd around by a thick cloud of spirits" is an obvious biblical allusion preparing us for the concluding Christ-like idea that only those with receptive hearts, with the spirit of love within them, are prepared to receive the ultimate gift, the calamus root—the token of perfect, reconciling love.[79] The meeting of these three major symbols of the "Calamus" group (the land-water, the fragrance, and the Christ symbols) in this single lyric makes it appear to be the key poem of the section. To associate it with any crude, sensuous interpretation of the calamus-symbol is to miss the mystical beauty of one of the most poignant lyrics in *Leaves of Grass*.

The remainder of the "Calamus" poems serve as variations on the themes introduced in these first five. For our consideration here they can be conveniently gathered according to poetic techniques into three groups: philosophic poems, symbolic poems, and picture-poems. In *Leaves of Grass*, undoubtedly for the sake of variety, the three types are carefully intermingled so that only once do as many as three of one type fall

---

[77] "These I Singing in Spring," I, 142.
[78] *Ibid.*, p. 143.
[79] *Ibid.*, p. 144.

together. A few poems in each category deserve particular mention in this study.

Most significant of the philosophical poems are "Of the Terrible Doubt of Appearances," "The Base of All Metaphysics," "This Moment Yearning and Thoughtful," "Sometimes with One I Love," and "That Shadow My Likeness." The first and the last of these are closely related in theme. In "Of the Terrible Doubt of Appearances" it is the experience of love that gives the poet assurance of the rightness of things spiritual and physical, an intuitive assurance beyond reason and verbal expression. This poem is related to the picture poems in that the experience of love is represented by the image of two men side by side, holding hands. The triumph of spiritual love over all things is expressed in the concluding lines:

> I cannot answer the question of appearances or
>   that of identity beyond the grave,
> But I walk or sit indifferent, I am satisfied,
> He ahold of my hand has completely satisfied me.[80]

In "That Shadow My Likeness" love is presented as the "real reality," the only means of complete self-realization. In a similar mood "Sometimes with One I Love" depicts the frustrated, perturbed lover who in a brief moment of revelation rises above the immediate and realizes that love is its own reward. "But now I think there is no unreturn'd love, the pay is certain one way or another."[81] Certainly the significance of each of these three experiences is a spiritual significance. The lines

> (I loved a certain person ardently and my love
>   was not return'd,
> Yet out of that I have written these songs.)[82]

suggest a spiritual triumph not unlike that of a Christ "despised and rejected of men." The identification of the love celebrated

---

[80] "Of the Terrible Doubt of Appearances," I, 146.
[81] "Sometimes with One I Love," I, 160.
[82] *Ibid.*, p. 160.

in "Calamus" with Christ-like love is the climax of "The Base of All Metaphysics." It is significant that the metaphysics of Christ is pointed to as the greatest of all the optimistic philosophies which Whitman loved.

> . . . and underneath Christ the divine I see,
> The dear love of man for his comrade, the attraction
>   of friend to friend,
> Of the well-married husband and wife, of children
>   and parents,
> Of city for city and land for land.[83]

This list of relationships suggests the general nature of the love Whitman is celebrating. The final line relates the poem to "This Moment Yearning and Thoughtful" in which the friendship of man for man is expanded into the theme of international brotherhood.

The symbolic poems fall roughly into two groups: that group dominated by the fragrance-symbol and that dominated by the Christ-symbol. Three poems belong to the former. "Roots and Leaves Themselves Alone" begins

> Roots and leaves themselves alone are these,
> Scents brought to men and women from the wild
>   woods and pond-side . . .

and ends

> If you bring the warmth of the sun to them they
>   will open and bring form, color, perfume, to you,
> If you become the aliment and the wet they will
>   become flowers, fruits, tall branches and trees.[84]

"The Prairie-Grass Dividing" is quite specific in indicating the fragrance-spirit association in Whitman's mind:

> The prairie-grass dividing, its special odor breathing,
> I demand of it the spiritual corresponding, . . .[85]

---

[83] "The Base of All Metaphysics," I, 147.
[84] "Roots and Leaves Themselves Alone," I, 149–150.
[85] "The Prairie-Grass Dividing," I, 155.

In "Not Heat Flames Up and Consumes" Whitman stresses the
ethereal nature of the symbol and of the love:

> Not the air delicious and dry, the air of ripe
>   summer, bears lightly along white down-balls
>   of myriads of seeds,
>
> .   .   .   .
>
> O nor down-balls nor perfumes, nor the high
>   rain-emitting clouds, are borne through the open air,
> Any more than my soul is borne through the open air,
> Wafted in all directions O love, for friendship,
>   for you.[86]

The connotations of these lines bring to mind another important symbolic poem, "Fast-Anchor'd Eternal O Love!"
which, though it does not make specific use of the fragrance
symbol, does relate to it. As Symonds has pointed out, this
poem contrasts the love of man and woman and the love of
man and man, using the term "fast-anchor'd" for the former
and the terms "disembodied, ethereal" for the latter. The last
lines read:

> I ascend, I float in the regions of your love O man,
> O sharer of my roving life.[87]

The figure here of ascending recalls at once the similar figure
used in the highly mystical poem "The Sleepers." Symonds
explicates the lines as follows: "He [Whitman] hints that we
have left the realm of sex and sense and have ascended into a
different and rarer atmosphere, where passion, though it has
not lost its strength, is clarified."[88]

Only two of the "Calamus" poems introducing the Christ-
symbol need be mentioned here. In the first of these, "Trickle
Drops," Whitman identifies the love that brought forth the
"Calamus" poems with the love that brought forth the shed

[86] "Not Heat Flames Up and Consumes," I, 150.
[87] "Fast-Anchor'd Eternal O Love!" I, 160.
[88] John Addington Symonds, *Walt Whitman: A Study*, p. 86.

blood of Christ. The poem deserves to be quoted in its entirety.

> Trickle drops! my blue veins leaving!
> O drops of me! trickle, slow drops,
> Candid from me falling, drip, bleeding drops,
> From wounds made to free you whence you were prison'd,
> From my face, from my forehead and lips,
> From my breast, from within where I was conceal'd,
>   press forth red drops, confession drops,
> Stain every page, stain every song I sing, every
>   word I say, bloody drops,
> Let them know your scarlet heat, let them glisten,
> Saturate them with yourself all ashamed and wet,
> Glow upon all I have written or shall write,
>   bleeding drops,
> Let all be seen in your light, blushing drops.[89]

The final poem of the "Calamus" group, "Full of Life Now," is addressed to the distant future and carries with it something of the idea of a "second coming" when this revitalized gospel of love is realized.

> When you read these I that was visible am become
>   invisible,
> Now it is you, compact, visible, realizing my
>   poems, seeking me,
> Fancying how happy you were if I could be with
>   you and become your comrade;
> Be it as if I were with you. (Be not too certain
>   but I am now with you.)[90]

Only eight of the thirty-nine "Calamus" poems can be classified as picture-poems: "Recorders Ages Hence," "When I Heard at the Close of the Day," "Behold This Swarthy Face," "To a Stranger," "We Two Boys Together Clinging," "A Glimpse," "What Think You I Take My Pen in Hand?" and

---

[89] "Trickle Drops," I, 151.
[90] "Full of Life Now," I, 162.

"Among the Multitude." Only one of these, "When I Heard at the Close of the Day," has any great poetic merit. In spite of these facts, these are the poems that are invariably dwelt upon in discussions of the meaning and significance of the group as a whole. This misplaced emphasis is misleading. Anyone even casually acquainted with *Leaves of Grass* must be aware of Whitman's tendency as a poet to think in pictures. These poems are briefly sketched scenes symbolic of the love celebrated in "Calamus." To take them as literal expressions of that love, as such critics as Cowley have done, is to divorce them entirely from the atmosphere in which Whitman placed them, scattering them lightly among the thirty-one poems (most of which we have discussed) which are artistically superior and are obviously intended to set the dominant tone of the "Calamus" group. Whitman writes poetry like a musician: the picture-poems, the philosophic poems, and the symbolic poems are contrasting groups of instruments whereby he reorchestrates and produces variations until the potentialities of his theme are exhausted. The picture-poems are a comparatively small part of the whole; they are the least melodic passages in "Calamus" and lack artistic significance when detached from the soaring, eloquent qualities of passages like "These I Singing in Spring" or "Roots and Leaves Themselves Alone." While it may serve some biographical purpose to stress these poems and to drive home their psychological significance by bringing in consideration of similar poems which Whitman deleted from the group, such procedure, it seems to me, is invalid from the standpoint of literary criticism. The critic has no right to base a positive interpretation of a work of art upon poetic passages which the artist saw fit to remove from it. If Whitman carefully removed poems and passages which he came to feel revealed the erotic sources rather than the spiritual and social purpose of his work, that fact would strengthen the interpretation of "Calamus" given here, an interpretation which insists that *Leaves of Grass* be viewed as a work of art complete in itself as Whitman intended it, capable of being

understood and admired on its own terms.[91] "Here the Frailest
Leaves of Me" and "Earth, My Likeness" are frequently associated with the picture-poems and used as evidence in favor
of an erotic interpretation. While the literal mind can hardly
escape such an interpretation, the fact remains that when considered in context they can be easily taken as expressions of
an old, conventional theme of the lyrist—a lament over an in-
capacity to express fully all that is felt within. This idea is
unmistakable in "Earth, My Likeness." The suggestion that
neither the vegetation of the earth nor the poems adequately
express the tremendous forces within relates this lyric in a
very significant way to "Scented Herbage of My Breast." In fact
the title "Earth, My Likeness" remains rather empty until this
relationship is seen. The central idea of the poem, that love is
the force within "eligible to burst forth" in leaves or songs, is
a major theme of "Calamus" as a whole: it finds expression in
the final poem to be discussed, "I Saw in Louisiana a Live-
Oak Growing."

The significance of the botanical imagery characteristic of
the "Calamus" poems is revealed in the concluding lines of
"I Saw in Louisiana a Live-Oak Growing":

> For all that, and though the live-oak glistens there
>   in Louisiana solitary in a wide flat space,
> Uttering joyous leaves all its life without a
>   friend a lover near,
> I know very well I could not.[92]

At first Whitman intended to make this the title poem of his
songs of manly love and to call the group "Live-Oaks, with
Moss." His shift in titles to "Calamus-Leaves" and later to
"Calamus" was fortunate.[93] Though he never forsook the botanical imagery, he must have seen the obvious flaw in using

---

[91] Frederik Schyberg, *Walt Whitman*, pp. 159–165. Schyberg's treatment,
unavailable to me until after this chapter was written, is an interesting contrast in interpretation, based primarily on psychological considerations.

[92] "I Saw in Louisiana a Live-Oak Growing," I, 153.

[93] The first two titles never actually appeared in *Leaves of Grass*.

the live-oak as the central symbol. As treated in his poem, it
is a negation of his message in its ability to utter "joyous
leaves" though solitary. He finally struck upon the calamus
plant as more appropriate. We have already discussed its perfume, its hardihood, and its aquatic nature. It beds and therefore utters its leaves in close harmony with its fellow plants.
Finally, Whitman seized upon the idea of the sweet root of
the plant, the source of its spear-shaped leaves, as the symbol
of manly love, the source of his songs. This root-leaf relationship (along with the fact that in structure the calamus, with its
single root and spearlike leaf, is glorified grass) is the true
explanation of the calamus-symbol; evidence of this is the fact
that the relationship persists in the imagery of two key poems
of the group "Scented Herbage of My Breast" and "Roots and
Leaves Themselves Alone" in which the calamus plant plays
no part.

At the time of writing "Calamus," Whitman was vitally
concerned with the reconciliation of his paradoxical ideas of
the supreme importance of the individual and the supreme importance of modern man en masse. In other words, he sought
a natural transition from the self-centered elements of "Song of
Myself" to the great themes of American and international
unity and brotherhood which were to follow. "Children of
Adam," as has been pointed out, is the first phase of this
transition; "Calamus," the second. In the sense of comradeship and brotherhood developed in the "Calamus" group, man
is seen turning out from himself. The group does not propose
a social or political program within itself so much as it records
the gradual awakening or self-realization essential to the development of such a program if it is to partake of that naturalness and human warmth which alone can assure its survival.
The striking resurgence of the Christ-symbol within the group
is of major importance. "Calamus" records a soul-searching,
a Christ-like sojourn "in the wilderness," which brings a fuller
meaning to the life of the individual as he turns out from himself and is stirred by an uncertain yearning to participate in

the life of his fellows and ultimately in the destiny of all mankind. Such a period of preparation has its moments of frustration and pathos, its moments of new certitude and vision, both
of which are moments "yearning and thoughtful." That the
poet experiences this sense of preparing, of a Christ-like tarry-
ing on the threshold of a great mission, is indicated in "A
Promise to California."

> A promise to California,
> Or inland to the great pastoral Plains, and on to
>   Puget sound and Oregon;
> Sojourning east a while longer, soon I travel
>   toward you, to remain, to teach robust American
>   love,
> For I know very well that I and robust love belong
>   to you, inland, and along the Western sea;
> For these States tend inland and toward the Western
>   sea, and I will also.[94]

The "Calamus" poems, then, commemorate days "in the wilderness" from which emerges a new, strengthened visionary.[95]
Immediately, in the optimistic songs which follow, we see this
new poet, for the first time, taking the open road westward into
the realm of broad social consciousness. He strikes out with
exuberance, pride, and complete confidence. And though his
understanding of this new life is to deepen, though unforeseen
events are to bring moments of faltering and remorse, this
early optimism is never utterly lost.

Songs of Democracy (11 poems)

The next eleven poems constitute an unnamed group (beginning with "Salut au Monde!" and ending with "A Song of
the Rolling Earth"). For convenience they will be referred to
in this study as "Songs of Democracy." These are the songs for

[94] "A Promise to California," I, 156.
[95] Schyberg, *Walt Whitman*, p. 158. Whitman, in "Calamus," is described by
Schyberg as "shy, hesitant, and wistfully stammering."

which "Calamus" is the immediate preparation; the bonds of comradeship have been clarified and established; there is no shyness, no hesitation here; from the very start the westward trek is characterized by a joyous sociability. Actually, this group of poems forms the final phase of the transition we have been discussing, from "Song of Myself" to such paeans of American unity as "A Broadway Pageant." There is marked advance from the position of the "Calamus" poems; nevertheless, the focus is on the society of great individuals rather than on the national identity. As the poet is showing the first flush of maturity, the nation is just beginning to become aware of itself. The "Songs of Democracy" are shot through with an awareness of the greatness of American individuals, of American materials, and of American concepts of democracy, but not with an awareness of a great democracy already unified.

"Salut au Monde!" follows nicely the "Calamus" poems as it reaches out to all men, all lands, with friendship and love. The opening line alludes to the picture of the clasped hands, which is used seven times in "Calamus":

> O take my hand Walt Whitman!
>
> .   .   .   .
>
> Such join'd unended links, each hook'd to the next,
> Each answering all, each sharing the earth with all.
>
> .   .   .   .
>
> What widens within you Walt Whitman?
>
> .   .   .   .
>
> Within me latitude widens, longitude lengthens,
> Asia, Africa, Europe, are to the east—America is
>   provided for in the west. . . .[96]

The climax of this extended identification of the self with all things comes in the final stanza. It is the fulfillment of the yearning for "other men in other lands" expressed in "Calamus."

[96] "Salut au Monde!" I, 163.

> My spirit has pass'd in compassion and determination
>   around the whole earth,
> I have look'd for equals and lovers and found them
>   ready for me in all lands,
> I think some divine rapport has equalized me with
>   them.[97]

To love individuals truly (as was the case first with the female mate, then with those humans in personal contact) inculcates the spirit of love toward all peoples.

There are two further aspects of the poem that should be mentioned here. The first is a significant passage in which the poet identifies himself with Christ, thus continuing one of the major "Calamus" symbols:

> I see Christ eating the bread of the last supper
>   in the midst of youths and old persons,
> I see where the strong divine young man Hercules
>   toil'd faithfully and long and then died,
>
> .   .   .   .
>
> I see Hermes, unsuspected, dying, well-belov'd,
>   saying to the people Do not weep for me,
> This is not my true country, I have lived banish'd
>   from my true country, I now go back there,
> I return to the celestial sphere where every one
>   goes in his turn.[98]

The second is the use of the catalogue for the first time in *Leaves of Grass* as the basic poetic technique for an entire long poem. The result is a quality of exuberance and opulence in sharp contrast to the tenderness and, sometimes, pathos of "Calamus." The significance of this technique and its relationship to the journey motif, which is also initiated in this poem, will be discussed later in summarizing the observations regarding the "Songs of Democracy" as a whole.

The sense of "going-forth" together, which runs throughout

[97] *Ibid.*, p. 175.
[98] *Ibid.*, pp. 168–169.

these songs, receives its fullest expression in "Song of the Open Road." Having saluted all men, so to speak, in the first poem, Whitman moves on in this second one to call his disciples, those special men who have the faith to move forward boldly and to share his life of liberty and love. The incident is strikingly Christ-like. Just a few passages will demonstrate this:

I think I could stop here myself and do miracles,

. . . .

I will scatter myself among men and women as I go,
I will toss a new gladness and roughness among them,
Whoever denies me it shall not trouble me,
Whoever accepts me he or she shall be blessed and
    shall bless me.

. . . .

Here a great personal deed has room,
(Such a deed seizes upon the hearts of the whole
    race of men,
Its effusion of strength and will overwhelms law
    and mocks all authority and all argument against
    it.)

. . . .

What is it I interchange so suddenly with
    strangers? ...
What with some fisherman drawing his seine by the
    shore as I walk by and pause?
What gives me to be free to a woman's and man's
    good-will? what gives them to be free to mine?

. . . .

Allons! from all formules!
From your formules, O bat-eyed and materialistic
    priests.

. . . .

(I and mine do not convince by arguments, similes,
    rhymes,
We convince by our presence.)

. . . .

Listen! I will be honest with you,
I do not offer the old smooth prizes, but offer
    rough new prizes, . . .
You shall not heap up what is call'd riches,
You shall scatter with lavish hand all that you
    earn or achieve,
You but arrive at the city to which you were destin'd,
    you hardly settle yourself to satisfaction before
    you are call'd by an irresistible call to depart,
You shall be treated to the ironical smiles and
    mockings of those who remain behind you.

. . . .

Allons! after the great Companions, . . .
Enjoyers of calms of seas and storms of seas, . . .
Trusters of men and women, observers of cities,
    solitary toilers,
Pausers and contemplators of tufts, blossoms,
    shells of the shore,
Dancers at wedding dances, kissers of brides,
    tender helpers of children, bearers of children,
Soldiers of revolts, standers by gaping graves,
    lowerers-down of coffins,

. . . .

Forever alive, forever forward,
Stately, solemn, sad, . . .
Desperate, proud, fond, sick, accepted by men,
    rejected by men,

. . . .

He going with me goes often with spare diet, poverty,
    angry enemies, desertions.

. . . .

Camerado, I give you my hand!
I give you my love more precious than money,
I give you myself before preaching or law;

Will you give me your self? will you come travel
    with me?
Shall we stick by each other as long as we live?[99]

"Crossing Brooklyn Ferry," the third poem of "Songs of
Democracy," extends love not only to future generations of
men, but to the materials, the "dumb, beautiful ministers,"
whereby all men—past, present, and future—have become and
will become identified. Time and space avail not, so far as the
brotherhood and equality of all mankind is concerned. What
is said of one man can be said of all others:

I too had been struck from the float forever held
    in solution,
I too had receiv'd identity by my body,
That I was I knew was of my body, and what I
    should be I knew I should be of my body.[100]

The divinity of all is reaffirmed in the line:

Diverge, fine spokes of light, from the shape of
    my head, or any one's head, in the sunlit water![101]

The "Song of the Answerer" proclaims the true poet as
the person capable of giving expression to these concepts of
brotherhood and equality in terms translatable to all men:

He resolves all tongues into his own and bestows
    it upon men, . . .
One part does not counteract another part, he is
    the joiner, he sees how they join.

. . . .

The maker of poems settles justice, reality, immortality,
His insight and power encircle things and the human race,
He is the glory and extract thus far of things and of
    the human race.[102]

[99] "Song of the Open Road," I, 180, 181, 183, 184, 185, 186, 188, 189, 190.
[100] "Crossing Brooklyn Ferry," I, 195.
[101] *Ibid.*, p. 198.
[102] "Song of the Answerer," I, 202, 204.

Whitman appropriately resorts to the technique of the extended catalogue used in "Salut au Monde!" for the development of his first important poem of this section praising the materials of America, "Our Old Feuillage." Out of the diversity and richness of these materials are to be shaped greater individual souls and a greater national soul "ONE IDENTITY" than ever known before. His catalogue is concluded with the invitation,

> How can I but here chanting, invite you for yourselves
> to collect bouquets of the incomparable feuillage
> of these States?[103]

A similar theme is pursued in "A Song of Joys." As the poet advances westward, he sings the beauty and significance of things along the way. The "vast elemental sympathy" generated and emitted by the human soul is not independent of those material objects which give each soul its identity. Man's final joy is the joy of death; he dies, and the physical body, having given form and beauty to the spiritual body, returns to the "eternal uses of the earth," and the real body, the spiritual, departs for other spheres.[104]

The creative, nondestructive nature of the advance is treated in "Song of the Broad-Axe." The motto of this hymn in praise of activity and energy might well be the short line "Muscle and pluck forever!"[105] All is power and creativity. In the new world of the west the broad-axe is no longer the bloody implement of headsmen, rather it is the glittering, "blue-gray" implement of great builders.

> I see the headsman withdraw and become useless,
> I see the scaffold untrodden and mouldy, I see
> no longer the axe upon it.
> I see the mighty and friendly emblem of the power
> of my own race, the newest, largest race.

[103] "Our Old Feuillage," I, 212.
[104] "A Song of Joys," I, 221–222.
[105] "Song of the Broad-Axe," I, 228.

.   .   .   .

The axe leaps!

.   .   .   .

The shapes arise![106]

The opening lines of "Song of the Exposition" are obviously
transitional:

> (Ah little recks the laborer,
> How near his work is holding him to God,
> The loving Laborer through space and time.)

> After all not to create only, or found only,
> But to bring perhaps from afar what is already
>   founded,
> To give it our own identity, average, limitless, free,
> To fill the gross the torpid bulk with vital
>   religious fire,
> Not to repel or destroy so much as accept, fuse,
>   rehabilitate,[107]

Thus the poet begins to see in this New World, which gives such
new and beautiful meanings to the dark symbols of old world
feudalism, the result of a cosmic evolution. Young and growing
America is the child of Europe and Asia and their daily hope.
The concept around which this poem is built is forcefully expressed in a passage from the preface of 1872:

> To me, the United States are important because in this colossal
> drama they are unquestionably designated for the leading parts,
> for many a century to come. In them history and humanity seem
> to seek to culminate. Our broad areas are even now the busy
> theatre of plots, passions, interests, and suspended problems,
> compared to which the intrigues of the past of Europe, the wars
> of dynasties, the scope of kings and kingdoms, and even the de-
> velopment of peoples, as hitherto, exhibit scales of measurement

---

[106] *Ibid.*, pp. 233–237.
[107] "Song of the Exposition," I, 238.

comparatively narrow and trivial. And on these areas of ours, as on a stage, sooner or later, something like an *éclaircissement* of all the past civilization of Europe and Asia is probably to be evolved.[108]

"Song of the Redwood-Tree" celebrates the natural grandeur of the New World as essential to the future greatness of modern man. The redwood tree becomes the symbol of the material richness and majesty of a land long in preparation for a "superber race" destined to "tally" its proportions. As the title might suggest, this poem is closely related to "Song of the Broad-Axe." One of its key passages alludes to this fact:

> Not wan from Asia's fetiches,
> Nor red from Europe's old dynastic slaughter-house,
> (Area of murder-plots of thrones, with scent left
>   yet of wars and scaffolds everywhere,)
> But come from Nature's long and harmless throes,
>   peacefully builded thence,
> These virgin lands, lands of the Western shore,
> To the new culminating man, to you, the empire new,
> You promis'd long, we pledge, we dedicate.[109]

Whereas "Song of the Broad-Axe" centers its attention upon the man of the new world in all his energy and creativity, "Song of the Redwood-Tree" centers upon the vast materials prepared for him, with their "unseen moral essence," their capacity to shape man as well as to be shaped by him.

> For man of you, your characteristic race,
> Here may he hardy, sweet, gigantic grow, here
>   tower proportionate to Nature,
> Here climb the vast pure spaces unconfined, unchecked
>   by wall or roof, . . .
> Here heed himself, unfold himself, (not others'
>   formulas heed,) here fill his time, . . .[110]

[108] "Preface, 1872," V, 186–187.
[109] "Song of the Redwood-Tree," I, 253.
[110] *Ibid.*, p. 254.

Nor is the theme of the intervening "Song of the Exposition" forgotten; its recognition of the importance of the past is alluded to in the concluding passage:

> But more in you than these, lands of the Western shore,
>   (These but the means, the implements, the standing
>   ground,)
> I see in you, certain to come, the promise of thousands
>   of years, till now deferr'd,
> Promis'd to be fulfill'd, our common kind, the race.
>
> The new society at last, proportionate to Nature,
>
> .   .   .   .
>
> Fresh come, to a new world indeed, yet long prepared,
> I see the genius of the modern, child of the real and ideal,
> Clearing the ground for broad humanity, the true
>   America, heir of the past so grand,
> To build a grander future.[111]

In "Song of the Redwood-Tree" three major themes of "Songs of Democracy" meet: the potential greatness of the modern man, the greatness of the past out of which he has evolved, and the greatness of the new world prepared for him. Out of these springs hope for a "grander future." Thus the poem becomes something of a summary preparing for the final theme of the group.

This final theme, equality, first introduced in "Crossing Brooklyn Ferry," receives full statement in "A Song For Occupations." In it, the doctrine of equality, inherent in Whitman's gospel of brotherhood, finds one of its subtlest and most effective expressions. Myers points out that the poem "presents an antithesis between the surface classification of people . . . and people as equal, infinite personalities of the spiritual democracy. . . . In society obvious differences exist between the laborer and the president. . . . These, however, are the surface turmoils and coverings; underneath them lies the community of

[111] *Ibid.*, p. 256.

equal and infinite souls, equal and infinite in that each soul is
commensurate with the world. . . . 'You and your soul enclose
all things, regardless of estimation.' "[112] Thus the progression,
whereby the celebration of great American individuals is reconciled with that of America en masse (Myers's spiritual democracy), is brought to a fitting climax.

The need for a new, real, powerful medium of expression for
these New World themes is presented in the final poem "A Song
of the Rolling Earth." In "Preface, 1872" Whitman declares:

> Our America today I consider in many respects as but indeed a
> vast seething mass of materials, ampler, better (worse also) than
> previously known—eligible to be used to carry towards its crown-
> ing stage, and build for good, the great ideal Nationality of the
> future . . .—but so far, no social, literary, religious, or esthetic
> organizations, consistent with our politics, or becoming to us—
> which organizations can only come, in time, through great dem-
> ocratic ideas, religion . . . and through our own begotten poets
> and literatuses.[113]

These poets, who are to present "the unspoken meanings of the
earth," are prophesied in "A Song of the Rolling Earth" as
the great architects of the future.

> Say on, sayers! sing on, singers!
> Delve! mould! pile the words of the earth!
> Work on, age after age, nothing is to be lost,
> It may have to wait long, but it will certainly
>   come in use,
> When the materials are all prepared and ready, the
>   architects shall appear.
> I swear to you the architects shall appear without
>   fail, . . .
> You shall be fully glorified in them.[114]

---

[112] H. A. Myers, "Whitman's Conception of the Spiritual Democracy, 1855–
56," *AL* 6 (November 1934) 247.
[113] "Preface, 1872," V, 187–188.
[114] "A Song of the Rolling Earth," I, 274–275.

There are two important aspects of these eleven democratic songs that should receive special consideration, for they are important devices in the over-all pattern of *Leaves of Grass.* The first of these is suggested in the foregoing discussion in terms of "going-forth"; it is the "journey motif." The concept as an extended figure is introduced in "Song of the Open Road" and continues through "Birds of Passage," taking on the particular connotation of pioneering America. The figure persists until we reach "Sea-Drift." Here we encounter a turning point; the nation has reached the West Coast in its westward push; simultaneously, the poet-prophet comes to the shore and launches into the unknown in "Out of the Cradle Endlessly Rocking." After this the "journey motif" is lost in the new figure of the voyage. This interesting conversion is significant when we realize how consistently Whitman uses the land as a symbol of the physical or material realm and the sea as the symbol of the spiritual. In *Leaves of Grass* we journey across a vast and teeming land, finding our true selves through the panorama of material America; but the successful journey inevitably brings us to the shore, where we launch out on a more significant passage—a voyage on the expansive, uncluttered, spiritual sea. The point at which the journey motif changes to the voyage motif is the point at which the emphasis in *Leaves of Grass* is shifted from the material to the spiritual.

The second aspect of particular interest here is the extended use of the catalogue. The journey motif is a key to this unique stylistic device. By repeated use of it Whitman conveys the impression of travel across a fabulous land, of life in a sprawling, complex society. In "Walt Whitman as Innovator" David Daiches points out Whitman's use of the catalogue for more subtle purposes than the panoramic effect—notably for the purification and expansion of the poet's sensibility.[115] Whitman's endless enumerations of practically everything under the sun suggest the vastness of existence itself and always con-

[115] David Daiches, "Walt Whitman As Innovator," in *The Young Rebel in American Literature*, ed. Carl Bode, pp. 25–48.

vey a sense of exhilarating expansion. It is interesting that the catalogues disappear when we reach the "Sea-Drift" poems and do not reappear until the crisis is passed and they burst again upon the scene with a welcomed exuberance in "By Blue Ontario's Shore," the poem which marks the beginning of renewed national progress following the spiritual crises and awakenings of the momentous war years. The return to such a panoramic device stands in sharp and effective contrast to the restricted, tight, intense, isolated word-pictures dominating "Drum-Taps." The artistry of the catalogue as Whitman employs it becomes suddenly apparent. The journey-voyage motif and the catalogue are devices thoughtfully and skillfully utilized in pointing up the over-all structural pattern of *Leaves of Grass*.[116]

It is important to note here that the concept of the westward movement is twofold in its application. It applies to both the poet and the nation. The final line of the "Calamus" poem "A Promise to California" reads

For these States tend inland and toward the Western
    sea, and I will also.[117]

From "Songs of Democracy" on to the end of *Leaves of Grass*, the development of the poet and of the nation are simultaneous. Within each cluster, poems stressing first one and then the other are carefully interspersed. As Selincourt suggests, the body of *Leaves of Grass* is given to recording "the various stages of experience and reflection" through which the poet of "Song of Myself" passes as he becomes more and more mature.[118] But Selincourt fails to point out that the same thing is being accomplished for the nation. As we have already warned, failure to recognize this twofold development and its signifi-

---

[116] Gay Wilson Allen, "Walt Whitman's 'Long Journey' Motif," *JEGP* 38 (January 1939), 76–95; Mattie Swayne, "Whitman's Catalogue Rhetoric," *University of Texas Studies* no. 4126 (1941), 162–178; A. N. Wiley, "Reiterative Devices in *Leaves of Grass*," *AL* 1 (March 1929), 161–170.

[117] "A Promise to California," I, 156.

[118] Selincourt, *Walt Whitman*, p. 165.

cance results in a rather chaotic reading of *Leaves of Grass*, devoid of an awareness of the basic organization which gives unity to the work as a whole.

Falling between "Songs of Democracy" and "Birds of Passage" is a brief poem "Youth, Day, Old Age and Night." It is one of four minor poems that were undoubtedly inserted by Whitman as space fillers.[119] Each of these is in one way or another related in content and theme to its surrounding poems; however, the relationship could hardly be described as immediate or organic.

BIRDS OF PASSAGE (7 POEMS)

"Birds of Passage" continues to depict the western movement of American life begun in "Songs of Democracy." It is a collection of songs of physical progress. The dominant image is that of the pioneer, of receding western frontiers. In pointing toward a strong sense of national identity it represents an advance in preparation for "A Broadway Pageant," the first great poem of nationalism. This national identity is alluded to in "Song of the Universal," the opening poem.

And thou America,

. . . .

The measur'd faiths of other lands, the grandeurs
    of the past,
Are not for thee, but grandeurs of thine own,
Deific faiths and amplitudes, absorbing, comprehending
    all,
All eligible to all.[120]

"Pioneers! O Pioneers!" is the key poem of "Birds of Passage," its title naming the dominant image of the cluster. "All the pulses of the world,/ Falling in they beat for us, with the Western movement beat."[121]

[119] The other three are "Reversals," "Transpositions," and "A Paumanok Picture."
[120] "Song of the Universal," I, 278.
[121] "Pioneers! O Pioneers!" I, 282.

All the past we leave behind,
We debouch upon a newer mightier world, varied world,
Fresh and strong the world we seize, world of labor
    and the march,
            Pioneers! O Pioneers![122]

The equality of the dynamic individuals from which the national identity of America is to emerge is the major theme of "To You." Its imagery is reminiscent of the "fine centrifugal spokes of light" in "Crossing Brooklyn Ferry."

Painters have painted their swarming groups and
    the centre-figure of all,
From the head of the centre-figure spreading a
    nimbus of gold-color'd light,
But I paint myriads of heads, but paint no head
    without its nimbus of gold-color'd light,
From my hand from the brain of every man and woman
    it streams, effulgently flowing forever.[123]

"France" is a salute to a sister nation struggling bloodily for a new identity under the laws of liberty and equality. It foresees similar crises for America. "Here too the blaze, the grapeshot and the axe, in reserve, to fetch them out in case of need."[124] The remainder of the poems restate the theme of individuality on the one hand and the theme of national unity on the other. The two meet in important lines from "With Antecedents"—the final poem of the group.

You and me arrived—America arrived and making
    this year,
This year! sending itself ahead countless years
    to come.[125]

At this crucial point the poem bursts into a rhapsodic sum-

---

[122] *Ibid.*, p. 280.
[123] "To You," I, 285.
[124] "France," I, 288.
[125] "With Antecedents," I, 293.

mation of all that has gone before, as if the poet-prophet becomes suddenly aware of a fusion of his themes of individuality, comradeship, and nationality, and of their cosmic origins and involvements.

> O but it is not the years—it is I, it is You,
> We touch all laws and tally all antecedents,
> We are the skald, the oracle, the monk and the knight
>
> .   .   .   .
>
> We stand amid time beginningless and endless, we stand
>   amid evil and good,
> All swings around us,
>
> .   .   .   .
>
> As for me, (torn, stormy, amid these vehement days,)
> I have the idea of all, and am all and believe in all,
> I believe materialism is true and spiritualism is true,
>   I reject no part.
>
> .   .   .   .
>
> I know that the past was great and the future will be
>   great,
> And I know that both curiously conjoint in the present
>   time,
>
> .   .   .   .
>
> And that where I am or you are this present day, there
>   is the centre of all days, all races,
> And there is the meaning to us of all that has ever
>   come of races and days, or ever will come.[126]

Most striking here are the cosmic implications. At this great moment of revelation the poet and his nation stand at the sacred center of time and space, sharing in the consecration of the cosmos. From this powerful recognition scene the fully identified poet-prophet steps forth to deliver the first of three great prophetic addresses to his nation. It is frequently in transitional passages such as this that Whitman makes his best use

[126] *Ibid.*, pp. 293–294.

of the poet-prophet as a means of having the personal and national and cosmic meet. And the framework is always religious.

A BROADWAY PAGEANT

"A Broadway Pageant" is the first important poem in *Leaves of Grass* which is primarily a prophecy of national greatness, a greatness first described in terms fundamentally materialistic. Here is the immediate America toward which the pioneers of "Birds of Passage" are moving. A satisfactory justification of this exaltation of materialism is impossible unless the poem is seen as part of a prophecy continued in "By Blue Ontario's Shore" and "Thou Mother with Thy Equal Brood." It is significant that these three lyrics, all prophesying national greatness, stand outside any titled group of poems, are spaced equidistantly throughout the volume, and are marked by similitude of imagery and spirit. When we see "A Broadway Pageant" in this light, its rank materialism becomes a part of an optimistic picture of a "nationality not only the richest, most inventive, most productive and materialistic the world has yet known, but compacted indissolubly, and out of whose ample and solid bulk, and giving purpose and finish to it, conscience, morals, and all the spiritual attributes, shall surely rise, like spires above some group of edifices, firm-footed on the earth, yet scaling space and heaven."[127]

It will not be enough to say that no nation ever achieved materialistic, political, and money-making successes, with the general physical comfort, as fully as the United States of America are today achieving them. I know very well that those are the indispensable foundations—the *sine qua non* of moral and heroic (poetic) fruitions to come. For if these pre-successes were all—if they ended at that—if nothing more were yielded than so far appears—a gross materialistic prosperity only—America, tried

[127] "Poetry To-Day in America," *Collect*, V, 226 (footnote).

by the subtlest tests were a failure—has not advanced the standard of humanity a bit further than other nations.[128]

In "Democratic Vistas" Whitman sees the advance of American democracy, following its actual political inception, in two phases: a materialistic development and a spiritual development. A careful reading, however, reveals a twofold development in the second phase. First, there emerges what Whitman calls a "native expression-spirit." Original, native authors and spokesmen are evolved who awaken the nation to new life as they plumb the meanings of her past and present experiences and formulate the desires and hopes that are to give her character. Second, there is the ultimate national response to these men of vision, whereby dreams are realized and all men become one in a thoroughly spiritualized democracy. "A Broadway Pageant" with its exaltation of materialism, "By Blue Ontario's Shore" with its exaltation of native voices, and "Thou Mother with Thy Equal Brood" with its exaltation of unity and spirituality are Whitman's poetic statement of the threefold development outlined in "Democratic Vistas."[129] The three poems are carefully placed to mark the advance of the nation (and as we shall see, the parallel advance of the poet) toward that sublime fulfillment anticipated in "Passage to India." It is significant that the theme which sweeps to such a grand climax in that prophetic poem is rather subtly introduced in "A Broadway Pageant" and restated in "By Blue Ontario's Shore" and "Thou Mother with Thy Equal Brood." Its introductory statement, in Stanza 3 of the first poem, follows:

And you Libertad of the world!
You shall sit in the middle well-pois'd thousands
    and thousands of years,
As to-day from one side the nobles of Asia come to you,
As to-morrow from the other side the queen of

[128] "Memoranda," *Good-Bye My Fancy*, VII, 69.
[129] "Democratic Vistas," *Collect*, V, 123–125.

England sends her eldest son to you.

The sign is reversing, the orb is enclosed,
The ring is circled, the journey is done.[130]

One last word on Whitman's materialism: his praise of material things is not accompanied by greed or any selfish desire to possess or own. It is always related to the poet-prophet's cosmic, rather than his personal, concern. Material things are dear because they are the "stuff" of reality. When they are praised they are invariably presented as residing at the *center of the world*. Here the poet says, "You shall sit in the middle well-poised." In ancient religions this *centrality* is, as already noted, symbolic of consecration, of sharing in the sacredness of the cosmos. To be at the center of the world, its navel, is to share its divine origins, to experience *the real*, to occupy that point at which the material and the spiritual meet, to be where communication with the transcendental world is possible. The poet-prophet's praise of things material, whether of the perfection of his own body or of the abundance of his own land or of the plenitude of all Creation, is invariably given some such orientation and invariably sweeps toward some cosmic, mystical revelation. Beck states that it is Whitman's view that "every holding of private property [by individual or state] and every particular achievement must be paid for by the loss of infinite riches of reality."[131] Whitman never denies the positive worth of earthly things. Nevertheless, through his praise of the excellence of materials sounds the warning "for what shall it profit a man?" Whitman's materialism, in this important respect, is a Christ-like materialism.

SEA-DRIFT (11 POEMS)

When we face the "Sea-Drift" group, it is suddenly as if the pioneers have met the sea. Here, as has already been suggested, is an important national turning point in the sense that the ex-

---

[130] "A Broadway Pageant," II, 4–5.
[131] M. Beck, "Walt Whitman's Intuition of Reality," *Ethics* 53 (October 1942), 18.

pansion of the nation's physical boundaries ceases, and introspection, self-analysis, begins. It is a personal turning point in
that it marks a keener spiritual awakening of the representative man, Walt Whitman. From this point on, the pioneering
symbolism is absent from *Leaves of Grass*. The exhilarating,
sweeping movement of "Birds of Passage" loses momentum
and for the first time begins to surge backward and forward.
The waters become deep; the sea speaks to us, in our soul-
searching, on themes of love, comradeship, brotherhood,
merged with the theme of death and creating a new and richer
harmony than before. It is in this section that the poet himself
begins to see into the life of things. "The personality of mortal
life is most important with reference to the immortal, the unknown, the spiritual, the only permanently real, which as the
ocean waits for and receives the rivers, waits for us each and
all."[132] It is interesting that the new spiritual depths, symbolized
by the sea, form the perfect image for combining the various
themes—the national aspect of loss of frontier—the personal
aspect as the poet in "Out of the Cradle Endlessly Rocking"
goes beyond the materialism of the shore and experiences a
sort of baptism and spiritual birth as he wades out into the sea.

> Whereto answering, the sea,
> Delaying not, hurrying not,
> Whisper'd me through the night, and very plainly
>   before daybreak,
> Lisp'd to me the low and delicious word death,
> And again death, death, death, death,
> Hissing melodious, neither like the bird nor like
>   my arous'd child's heart,
> But edging near as privately for me rustling at my feet,
> Creeping thence steadily up to my ears and laving me
>   softly all over,
> Death, death, death, death, death.[133]

[132] *Democratic Vistas, Collect*, V, 113.
[133] "Out of the Cradle Endlessly Rocking," II, 13.

It is the sea, "the old crone rocking the cradle," the old mother, the loving giver of life, that whispers the "low and delicious word" *death*. Here is the perfect symbolism for that "vast similitude" which "interlocks all." The key to life is death. This group of poems, then, effects an important shift in emphasis—from exploration to introspection, from materialism to spiritualism, from individuality to all-inclusive spirituality. "Sea-Drift" is the great awakening in *Leaves of Grass*; it is symbolic of the spiritual preparation of the nation and the poet for the central experiences of the volume as presented in "Drum-Taps." The indistinct whispers of the grass in the earlier poems have been lost in the more significant noises of the sea.

The importance of "Out of the Cradle Endlessly Rocking," the key poem of "Sea-Drift," in the structural pattern of *Leaves of Grass* is made obvious by the manner in which it evolves out of the earlier poems and anticipates the central themes of the later ones. Out of the poignant transiency of the concord of the "two feather'd guests from Alabama," a *physical* concord not unlike that of "Children of Adam," emerge intimations of a more satisfying and universal *spiritual* concord. Stovall sees "Out of the Cradle Endlessly Rocking" as at once Whitman's most beautiful love-poem and his first poem

> that is tragic in tone and that is concerned seriously with death. . . . In the experience here related he first discovered the true nature and meaning of the songs he should sing. . . . Death is the consoler, the clue to man's destiny, because it is the divine complement of human imperfection, through which love is made complete and immortal. . . . Having perceived the inadequacy of love and the imperfection of life without the fulfillment of death, he began to feel as a reality what at first he had conceived only as a theory; namely, that he was to be the poet of death and the soul as well as of life and the body.[134]

[134] Floyd Stovall, "Main Drifts in Whitman's Poetry," *AL* 4 (March 1932), 9–11; see also A. H. Marks, "Whitman's Triadic Imagery," *AL* 23 (March 1951), 99–126.

For the first time the central themes of *Leaves of Grass* are voiced—themes which are to be restated with the confidence and fullness of the master in "When Lilacs Last in the Dooryard Bloom'd."

Having caught the symbolism of the land and the journey on the one hand and of the sea and the voyage on the other, one is prepared for the fascination with the shore line which dominates "As I Ebb'd with the Ocean of Life." It becomes the shifting, uncertain boundary between the physical and the spiritual, between the known and the unknown—the symbol of a mysterious synthesis apprehended by the youthful poet, but not yet comprehended. On the one hand are the shores that he knows, and to look upon them is to think the "old thought of Likenesses"; on the other hand are the shores he knows not. It is his contemplation of this second vast and mysterious realm of ocean that reduces him in his own imagination to "a little wash'd-up drift" and evokes in him a hitherto unknown humility.

> O baffled, balk'd, bent to the very earth,
> Oppress'd with myself that I have dared to open
>   my mouth,
> Aware now that amid all that blab whose echoes
>   recoil upon me I have not once had the least
>   idea who or what I am,
> But that before all my arrogant poems the real
>   Me stands yet untouch'd, untold, altogether
>   unreach'd,
>
> .   .   .   .
>
> I perceive I have not really understood any thing,
>   not a single object, and that no man ever can,
> Nature here in sight of the sea taking advantage
>   of me to dart upon me and sting me,
> Because I have dared to open my mouth to sing
>   at all.[135]

135 "As I Ebb'd with the Ocean of Life," II, 15.

But these are little more than the first "stirrings of inquietude." The "outsetting bard" is timorous of the new realm before him. He turns from the new unknown.

> You friable shore with trails of debris
> You fish-shaped island, I take what is underfoot,
> What is yours is mine my father.
>
> .   .   .   .
>
> I throw myself upon your breast my father,
> I cling to you so that you cannot unloose me,
> I hold you so firm till you answer me something.[136]

The full significance of these lines can hardly be realized until one beholds the serenity of the aged poet on another shore when again "balk'd, bent" he prays:

> The voyage balk'd, the course disputed, lost,
> I yield my ships to Thee.[137]

Or again, the frantic clinging to the shore stands in sharp contrast to the tranquility of an eloquent two-line poem from "Songs of Parting."

> The untold want by life and land ne'er granted,
> Now voyager sail thou forth to seek and find.[138]

That Whitman was aware of this contrast is suggested by the way in which the title "The Untold Want" echoes a phrase from "Out of the Cradle Endlessly Rocking."

> O you singer solitary, singing by yourself,
>   projecting me,
> O solitary me listening, never more shall I cease
>   perpetuating you,
>
> .   .   .   .
>
> Never again leave me to be the peaceful child I
>   was before what there in the night,

[136] *Ibid.*, pp. 15–16.
[137] "Prayer of Columbus," II, 200.
[138] "The Untold Want," II, 285.

By the sea under the yellow and sagging moon,
The messenger there arous'd, the fire, the sweet
　　hell within,
The unknown want, the destiny of me.[139]

"As I Ebb'd with the Ocean of Life" is an eloquent expression of the inevitable period of sober and troubled reflection following the sudden and rhapsodic awakening in "Out of the Cradle Endlessly Rocking." The uncertainty and the hesitation of the "baffled, balk'd" poet anticipates the frustration of his nation in "By the Roadside." The apprehensive poet is just taking the long road to the comprehension finally attained in such spiritual utterances as "Passage to India."

This mood of stormy uncertainty broods over the remainder of the "Sea-Drift" poems as the poet faces the unknown, but not without the relief of an occasional bright symbol, such as the triumphant man-of-war-bird, "the radiant sisters the Pleiades," the "pennant universal," or, most significant of all, the gleaming, gurgling wake of the "stately and rapid" sea-ship which is the subject of the final poem. Each of the short poems in its own way catches some aspect of the challenge of the unknown. The vista is seaward, but the orientation is still of the shore.

By the Roadside (29 poems)

In "By the Roadside" we leave the personal attitudes of the "Sea-Drift" poems and return to the subject of America at large—a frontierless America. Pioneer exuberance is gone from the poetic treatment—the expansive catalogues of the earlier poems completely disappear in favor of meager, cramped, sharply focused pictures of American life. We encounter no more catalogues until the crisis is passed. The reckless, exciting push forward has given way to a study of a suddenly sullen and intense national life. The eye has taken on a "sober coloring" and we encounter thoughts on ownership rather than ex-

---

[139] "Out of the Cradle Endlessly Rocking," II, 12.

ploration, obedience rather than liberty, justice rather than
mercy, equality rather than brotherhood.

> I sit and look out upon all the sorrows of the world,
>   and upon all oppression and shame. . . .
> All these—all the meanness and agony without end
>   I sitting look out upon,
> See, hear, and am silent.[140]

> Then I will sleep awhile yet, for I see that these
>   States sleep, for reasons;
> (With gathering murk, with muttering thunder and
>   lambent shoots we all duly awake,
> South, North, East, West, inland and seaboard, we
>   will surely awake.)[141]

In this section we get a definite impression of the passing of
a considerable period of time—a time of troubled silence for
a nation preparing for war, for a poet waiting for his aroused
mind and spirit to find full expression. This is the somber
section of *Leaves of Grass*. More than any other it stands as a
warning to those critics who attempt to present Whitman as a
blind, foolhardy optimist. Asselineau writes eloquently of the
anguish with which Whitman pondered evil and of his final
acceptance of it.[142] Any good to be found in "By the Roadside"
is expressed in terms of anticipation—in terms of what is remote in time and space and experience. Sick of the learn'd
astronomer, the poet wanders off by himself and looks up "in
perfect silence at the stars."[143] When the poet turns to things
close at hand, his treatments are fragmentary and abrupt, and
experience seems shattered and chaotic. It is significant that
"A Boston Ballad," the first poem in the group, is the only
purely satiric poem in *Leaves of Grass*.

---

[140] "I Sit and Look Out," II, 34.
[141] "To The States," II, 39.
[142] Asselineau, *The Evolution of Walt Whitman: The Creation of a Book*,
pp. 52–61.
[143] "When I Heard the Learn'd Astronomer," II, 32.

The progression from the inquietudes of "Sea-Drift" to the resolution of "When Lilacs Last in the Dooryard Bloom'd" is not an easy one. But those first inquietudes are indeed blessed, for they are the basis for the philosophical acceptance of the evils and uncertainties that plague the "Roadside" poems.

> Though little or nothing can be absolutely known, perceived, except from a point of view which is evanescent, yet we know at least one permanency, that Time and Space, in the will of God, furnish successive chains, completions of material births and beginnings, solve all discrepancies, fears and doubts, and eventually fulfill happiness—and that the prophecy of those births, namely spiritual results, throws the true arch over all teaching, all science. The local considerations of sin, disease, deformity, ignorance, death, etc., and measurement by the superficial mind, and ordinary legislation and theology, are to be met by science, boldly accepting, promulging this faith, and planting the seeds of superber laws—of the explication of the physical universe through the spiritual—and clearing the way for a religion, sweet and unimpugnable alike to little child or great savan.[144]

DRUM-TAPS (43 POEMS)

The break of the troubled silence by "Drum-Taps" is a grim relief. Here is Whitman's account of a nation and a man at war. In it are poems depicting the call of drum and bugle, a people's fevered response to that call, and battlefield scenes, and intimate personal poems of the wound-dresser's experience. Not nearly enough has been made of the great contrasts in poetic style and tone within *Leaves of Grass*. Contrast the bleakness of "Drum-Taps" with the full flush of the "Calamus" poems. Surely the wound-dresser could never touch our hearts with such floods of warmth and pathos had he not been preceded by the spirited, sensuous lover and comrade of "Children of Adam" and "Calamus." "Drum-Taps" has its own peculiar force, both humane and artistic, but that it draws heavily upon

[144] "Democratic Vistas," *Collect*, V, 136 (footnote).

the earlier poems is a circumstance which too many nineteenth-century critics wished to deny.

Miller gives us an excellent commentary on "Drum-Taps." He emphasizes Whitman's remarkable modulation of the sound imagery, suggesting the emotional changes in poet and nation as the tragedy of war closed in.[145] Asselineau touches on this same idea and then moves on to discuss the changes in poetic style demanded by the subject matter of war, thereby expressing an interest sounded more than once in this study. In "Drum-Taps" Asselineau sees a new war poetry in which the celebration of heroes is lost in concern for the sufferings of ordinary men.[146]

The subtle modulation of style and imagery which carries us from the early excitement of war through increasingly sobering experiences until we arrive at the very side of the wounded and dying is accompanied by a gradual conversion of the exuberant poet-prophet, who can tally the banner "haughty and resolute," into the all but mute wound-dresser found at the center of "Drum-Taps"—by a gradual conversion of one who proudly proclaims the Christ in himself into the chastened sufferer who murmurs over the yellow-white face of a fallen comrade "I think this face is the face of the Christ himself,/ Dead and divine and brother of all, and here again he lies." The central experience of "Drum-Taps" is that of a new and profound and selfless love; the central attitude, a Christ-like humility.

It is not by accident that "Drum-Taps" stands at the center of *Leaves of Grass*. In a footnote to the preface, 1876 (V, 198), Whitman says, "the whole book, indeed, revolves around that four years' war, which, as I was in the midst of it, becomes, in 'Drum-Taps,' pivotal to the rest entire." Those four years were the proving ground of the poet and the nation. Both were found ready, and that the trials end in triumph for them is

[145] Miller, *A Critical Guide to Leaves of Grass*, pp. 219–225.
[146] Asselineau, *The Evolution of Walt Whitman: The Creation of a Personality*, pp. 157–268.

attested beyond doubt in the beauty and resolution of the Lincoln poems.

Long, too long America,
Traveling roads all even and peaceful you learn'd
    from joys and prosperity only,
But now, ah now, to learn from crises of anguish,
    advancing, grappling with direst fate and
    recoiling not,
And now to conceive and show to the world what your
    children en-masse really are,
(For who except myself has yet conceiv'd what your
    children en-masse really are?) [147]

Myers says of this central experience:

If Whitman had been merely the poet of political democracy, of social betterment, and of optimistic humanitarianism, he would have condemned war and pitied its victims as unequal in their fate to citizens of peace, but as the poet of spiritual democracy, he is the poet of war as well as peace, for neither war nor peace can disturb the eternal law of the world. . . . Suffering and grief touched him immeasurably, yet he never doubted that the object of his pity had shared the common lot. Envy he apparently did not experience. . . . He had laid down the principles of spiritual democracy and adopted an attitude toward evil and death consistent with them before the outbreak of hostilities. . . . The Civil War did not lend profundity and vision to a plastic mind. . . . It found its poet ready. . . . Four years of conflict gave strength to Whitman's conviction, not depth to his insight. [148]

Looking into the more personal aspects of "Drum-Taps," Stovall adds, "In the generous service of those who had no means of making an equal return he discovered in himself at

[147] "Long, Too Long America," II, 77.
[148] Myers, "Whitman's Consistency," pp. 247–253.

last a love which transcended even the love of comrades because it was the love of man."[149] In "Drum-Taps" man and nation are shaken down to spiritual depths—the experience is the recognition from which America arises more heroic, more unified, more spiritual than ever before, and through which the poet finds voice for his fullest, richest utterances, which come in the climactic poems "Memories of President Lincoln." Shapiro puts it this way, "Whitman was stricken by the war, but he was re-created by it. . . . The war returned to him the particularity of death, and it produced in him not bitterness but love. He triumphed over it. He saw beyond history and beyond America. But what he saw was with the American vision."[150]

MEMORIES OF PRESIDENT LINCOLN (4 POEMS)

In the Lincoln poems Whitman found the perfect medium for the most spiritual expression of his three great themes: love, death, and democracy. For him the passing of Lincoln, so late the victor, became a significant symbol. "The death of President Lincoln, for instance, fitly, historically closes, in the civilization of feudalism, many old influences—drops on them, suddenly, a vast, gloomy, as it were, separating curtain."[151] "Memories of President Lincoln" is a tribute to the great American individual, tried in the service of democracy and not found wanting—a tribute to a new American heroism called forth by the war. In life, Lincoln, "gentle, plain, just and resolute," had struggled and won. And now in his sudden passing Whitman saw spiritual triumph as life and death seemed reconciled in love.

> Prais'd be the fathomless universe,
> For life and joy, and for objects and knowledge
>   curious,

---

[149] Stovall, "Main Drifts in Whitman's Poetry," pp. 12–13.
[150] Karl Shapiro, "The First White Aboriginal," *Walt Whitman Review* 5 (September 1959), 51.
[151] "Preface, 1876," *Collect*, V, 198 (footnote).

And for love, sweet love—but praise! praise! praise!
For the sure-enwinding arms of cool-enfolding death.[152]

Here is spiritual triumph for the poet also as he joyously hymns the flight of "the sweetest, wisest soul of all [his] days and lands." It is singularly fitting that this first great consummation, "When Lilacs Last in the Dooryard Bloom'd," indicative of things to come, should take the form of an elegy. It continues the theme of "Out of the Cradle Endlessly Rocking," giving a more mature and elevated interpretation of death, born of the poet's war experience. Nowhere in literature is there a more striking example of thematic structure of musical fluidity and loveliness than in the progression of the death theme from "Out of the Cradle Endlessly Rocking" to the climactic restatement (reorchestrated from bird, moon, shadows, sea to bird, star, lilac, dusky pine) in "When Lilacs Last in the Dooryard Bloom'd" and fading into soft echoes in "Whispers of Heavenly Death." This threefold thematic development in all its sensitivity, beauty, and power recalls Whitman's own pronouncement in a way which he probably never fully realized, "In the future of these States must arise poets immenser far, and make great poems of death. The poems of life are great, but there must be the poems of the purport of life, not only in itself, but beyond itself."[153]

"When Lilacs Last in the Dooryard Bloom'd" is a tribute to Lincoln as a great and immortal spirit. The three short lyrics that follow are tributes to him first as head of state, second as commander in chief, and finally as a man.

By Blue Ontario's Shore

"By Blue Ontario's Shore" marks a bold shift from the personal to the national theme. Again the exuberant poet-prophet steps forward, but more mature and more profoundly identified with his nation and its destiny than before. All is involve-

---

[152] "When Lilacs Last in the Dooryard Bloom'd," II, 101.
[153] "Democratic Vistas," *Collect*, V, 141.

ment, and the poet-prophet seems less isolated and self-contained. The Christ-symbol recurs, but with less sharpness of outline and greater gentleness of expression. The allusions are to the Christ of compassion and social concern, fully identified with others. The nation has stood the test, and her poet sounds a stirring but responsible carol of victory, and the "great Idea" of the carol is the idea of perfect and free individuals. The call of the carol is for bards, native and grand, to hold these individuals together. Just as "A Broadway Pageant" proclaims the greatness of American materials, so "By Blue Ontario's Shore" proclaims the greatness of American personalities, separate and en masse, tempered by war, eager for profounder challenges, and responsive to great native voices. The progression toward the spiritual proclamation of "Thou Mother with Thy Equal Brood" is obvious.

Autumn Rivulets (38 poems)

"Autumn Rivulets" speaks hopefully for the future of postwar America in much the same way that "Birds of Passage" speaks for pioneer America. The change is from a consciousness of receding frontiers and materialistic development to an awakening social consciousness.

> Yet we walk upheld, free, the whole earth over,
>   journeying up and down till we make our ineffaceable
>   mark upon time and the diverse eras,
> Till we saturate time and eras, that the men and
>   women of races, ages to come, may prove brethren
>   and lovers as we are.

It is significant that this eloquent statement of the poet's concept of his own function and destiny is found in the poem "To Him That Was Crucified"—a poem to Christ which begins:

> My Spirit to yours dear brother,

Do not mind because many sounding your name do
    not understand you,
I do not sound your name, but I understand you . . .[154]

In "To a Pupil" there is a passage which tends to justify the
earlier poems of self in the light of the growing social and
spiritual consciousness of these later poems:

Is reform needed? is it through you?
The greater the reform needed, the greater the
    Personality you need to accomplish it.
You! do you not see how it would serve you to have
    eyes, blood, complexion, clear and sweet?
Do you not see how it would serve to have such a
    body and soul that when you enter the crowd an
    atmosphere of desire and command enters with you,
    and everyone is impress'd with your personality?[155]

This particular passage recalls the observation that "Whitman
never attacked a convention merely for the sake of reform: he
attacked only those conventions which stood in the way of
his vision of reality."[156] It is appropriate that the Christ-idea
emerge in a striking way in "Autumn Rivulets." Over and over
again the poet expresses his love for and acceptance of all individuals, especially the broken and fallen—the prostitute, the
prisoner, the felon on trial. The spirituality of the section is
expressed in terms of compassion and hope. Horizons previously darkened by war now brighten. The national theme is
voiced in "The Return of the Heroes":

Exult O lands! victorious lands!
Not there your victory on those red shuddering fields,
But here and hence your victory.

Melt, melt away ye armies—disperse ye blue-clad
    soldiers,

[154] "To Him That Was Crucified," II, 159.
[155] "To a Pupil," II, 165.
[156] See page 37.

> Resolve ye back again, give up for good your
>   deadly arms,
> Other the arms the fields henceforth for you, or
>   South or North,
> With saner wars, sweet wars, life-giving wars.[157]

The return of the heroes to the lush harvests of the future, spiritual harvests, tallies the flow of autumn rivulets.

> As consequent from store of summer rains,
> Or wayward rivulets in autumn flowing,
> Or many a herb-lined brook's reticulations,
> Or subterranean sea-rills making for the sea,
> Songs of continued years I sing.
>
> .   .   .   .
>
> In you whoe'er you are my book perusing,
> In I myself, in all the world, these currents flowing,
> All, all toward the mystic ocean tending.[158]

The imagery of the final poem suggests a culmination of what was begun in "Children of Adam" as a "newer garden of creation" is announced.

> A newer garden of creation, no primal solitude,
> Dense, joyous, modern, populous millions, cities
>   and farms,
> With iron interlaced, composite, tied, many in one,
>
> .   .   .   .
>
> The crown and teeming paradise, so far, of time's
>   accumulations,
> To justify the past.[159]

This new paradise has much in common with Milton's "Paradise within . . . happier far"—though Whitman would resist the term "within."

---

[157] "The Return of the Heroes," II, 132.
[158] "As Consequent, Etc.," II, 127.
[159] "The Prairie States," II, 177.

SPIRITUAL SONGS (5 POEMS)

The next five poems constitute an unnamed group (beginning with "Proud Music of the Storm" and ending with "To Think of Time"). For convenience they will be referred to in this study as "Spiritual Songs." These poems complement the unnamed group of eleven songs following "Calamus," which we have designated "Songs of Democracy." Just as "Songs of Democracy" record the great materialistic advance following "Calamus," so do these five poems record the great spiritual advance following "Autumn Rivulets." This tends to clinch for me the twofold development of both the nation and the poet —primarily physical up to "Drum-Taps," primarily spiritual thereafter. The spiritual laws and growth parallel the physical. This suggests the development of Christ, who first increased in wisdom and stature and then in favor with God and man.

Like "Salut au Monde!" the first poem in "Songs of Democracy," "Proud Music of the Storm" is transitional in function as well as introductory. It looks before and after. In retrospect it reaffirms the early love for things material, but views that love as the avenue to things spiritual. In its own words it announces:

> . . . a new rhythmus fitted for . . .
> Poems bridging the way from Life to Death, vaguely
>   wafted in night air, uncaught, unwritten,
> Which let us go forth in the bold day and write.[160]

It is fitting that this progression is couched in the imagery of music.

In "Democratic Vistas" Whitman declares:

> As fuel to flame, and flame to the heavens, so must wealth, science, materialism—even this democracy of which we make so much—unerringly feed the highest mind, the soul. . . . Thus, and thus only, does a human being, his spirit, ascend above, and justify objective nature, which probably nothing in itself, is in-

---

[160] "Proud Music of the Storm," II, 185.

credibly and divinely serviceable, indispensable, real, here. . . .
Then may we attain to a poetry worth the immortal soul of man,
and which, while absorbing materials, and, in their own sense,
the shows of nature, will, above all, have, both directly and indirectly, a freeing, fluidizing, expanding, *religious* character,
exulting with science, fructifying the moral elements, and stimulating aspirations, and meditations on the unknown.[161]

These five spiritual songs are the poetic realization of these
ideas. Just how important they are in bringing *Leaves of Grass*
to fruition is suggested by Whitman himself when he says, "so
I have reserved that poem 'Passage to India' with its cluster,
to finish and explain much that, without them, would not be
explain'd, and to take leave, and escape for good, from all
that has preceded them. (Then probably 'Passage to India,'
and its cluster, are but freer and fuller expression to what,
from the first, and so on throughout, more or less lurks in my
writings, underneath every page, every line, everywhere.)"[162]

"Passage to India" commemorates the completion of the
Suez Canal, the transatlantic cable, and the transcontinental
railroad, thus giving implications as to the national development while providing the perfect symbolism for the theme of
"Proud Music of the Storm"—a bridging from life to death,
from the material to the spiritual. It carries the concept of such
poems as "Song of the Open Road" into the spiritual world.
The westward progress of mankind, the cycle, is completing
itself. The body and mind of mankind return to the place of
their origin, the East; even so, the soul through death returns
to its origin, God. It is in this sense that the two complemen-
tary, in fact, identical themes which dominate *Leaves of Grass*
are love and death.

In an attempt to define the unique *religious spirit* of *Leaves
of Grass*, Whitman's unusual and profound fusion of the ancient and the modern, the cosmic and the personal has been

---

[161] *Democratic Vistas, Collect*, V, 137–138.
[162] "Preface, 1876," *Collect*, V, 193 (footnote).

noted. Nowhere is this more eloquently realized than in this remarkable poem. Having dwelt long in the modern world, traversing its vast new nation, Whitman uses the westward circling to bring back, here at the last, the remote and ancient origins of his religious thought and feeling. As he himself puts it in the poem, here is the inevitable return to the myths and fables of the primitive world, to the truths of the "elder religions." Out of the return springs a renewal of cosmic vision, first of the "vast Rondure, swimming in space" and then of human origins, and suddenly, as his thought successfully "spans" all time and space and its meaning, there comes the great prophetic vision of the ultimate and complete fusion of ancient and modern, cosmic and personal:

Yet soul be sure the first intent remains, and
    shall be carried out,
Perhaps even now the time has arrived.

After the seas are all cross'd, (as they seem
    already cross'd,)
After the great captains and engineers have accomplish'd
    their work,

.   .   .   .

Finally shall come the poet worthy that name,
The true son of God shall come singing his songs.

.   .   .   .

Then not your deeds only O voyagers, O scientists and
    inventors, shall be justified,
All these hearts as of fretted children shall be sooth'd,
All affection shall be fully responded to, the
    secret shall be told,
All these separations and gaps shall be taken up and
    hook'd and link'd together,
The whole earth, this cold, impassive, voiceless earth,
    shall be completely justified
Trinitas divine shall be gloriously accomplish'd and
    compacted by the true son of God, the poet,

(He shall indeed pass the straits and conquer the mountains,
He shall double the cape of Good Hope to some purpose,)
Nature and Man shall be disjoin'd and diffused no more,
The true son of God shall absolutely fuse them.[163]

No passage in *Leaves of Grass* is more peculiarly Whitman's
own than this great spiritual utterance. To miss its subtle and
unique fusion of themes is to miss one of the truly grand
moments in *Leaves*. From this satisfying vantage point, the
transcendental world opens to the poet-prophet; the soul takes
flight, passing ecstatically through time and space until all is
joyously transcendent, and God is seen as:

Nameless, the fibre and the breath,
Light of the light, shedding forth universes, thou centre
    of them,
Thou mightier centre of the true, the good, the loving,
Thou moral, spiritual fountain—affection's source—
    thou reservoir,

.   .   .   .

Thou pulse—thou motive of the stars, suns, systems,
That, circling, move in order, safe, harmonious,
Athwart the shapeless vastnesses of space,
How should I think, how breathe a single breath, how
    speak, if, out of myself,
I could not launch, to those, superior universes?

Swiftly I shrivel at the thought of God,
At Nature and its wonders, Time and Space and Death,
But that I, turning, call to thee O soul, thou actual Me,
And lo, thou gently masterest the orbs,
Thou matest Time, smilest content at Death,
And fillest, swellest full the vastness of Space.

.   .   .   .

Reckoning ahead O soul, when thou, the time achiev'd,

.   .   .   .

[163] "Passage to India," II, 190–191.

Surrounded, copest, frontest God, yieldest, the aim
      attain'd,
As fill'd with friendship, love complete, the Elder
      Brother found,
The Younger melts in fondness in his arms.[164]

Then comes the "passage to more than India" as the poem
sweeps to a conclusion with one of Whitman's most exhilarant
pictures of death:

Passage, immediate passage! the blood burns in my veins!
Away O soul! hoist instantly the anchor!
Out the hawsers—haul out—shake out every sail!
Have we not stood here like trees in the ground
      long enough?

. . . .

Sail forth—steer for the deep waters only,
Reckless O soul, exploring, I with thee, and thou with me,
For we are bound where mariner has not yet dared to go,
And we will risk the ship, ourselves and all.[165]

Here is the great panoramic poem of the world of spirit.
Whitman himself says that it contains a "fuller" expression of
what, from the first, lurks in his writings, "underneath every
page, every line, everywhere."[166] It reminds us that only
through the intense and varied cosmic and human experience
which is the fountainhead of all of *Leaves of Grass* can the
mysterious whisperings of "Out of the Cradle Endlessly Rocking" be finally understood and accepted as the triumphant culmination and fulfillment of man's life-quest for love.

Finally, in "Passage to India" Whitman pays homage to
Columbus, in heroism second only to Lincoln, seeing this
"rondure of the world at last accomplish'd" as the fulfillment of
his dream. The poet now stands as a second Columbus—his
vision of great spiritual accomplishments tallying the material-

[164] *Ibid.*, pp. 195–196.
[165] *Ibid.*, pp. 196–197.
[166] Walt Whitman, *Leaves of Grass* (1876), II, 5.

istic vision of the fifteenth-century admiral. In the verification of the old dream the poet finds hope for the new.

> (Curious in time I stand, noting the efforts of heroes,
> Is the deferment long? bitter the slander, poverty,
>   death?
> Lies the seed unreck'd for centuries in the ground?
>   lo, to God's due occasion,
> Uprising in the night, it sprouts, blooms,
> And fills the earth with use and beauty.) [167]

In "Prayer of Columbus" the identification of poet with ancient visionary is complete.

If "Out of the Cradle Endlessly Rocking" records the baptism of the poet, then "Prayer of Columbus" is his Gethsemane. The Christ-idea is inherent throughout the poem. The faithful ministry is completed; the anguished reaffirmation of faith ends in surrender:

> My terminus near,
> The clouds already closing in upon me,
> The voyage balk'd, the course disputed, lost,
> I yield my ship to Thee.

The surrender is not vain:

> And these things I see suddenly, what mean they?
> As if some miracle, some hand divine unseal'd my eyes,
> Shadowy, vast shapes smile through the air and sky,
> And on the distant waves sail countless ships,
> And anthems in new tongues I hear saluting me. [168]

The strife is over. The reassuring vision of "The Sleepers" and the bold testimony of "To Think of Time" are utterances of triumphant spirituality.

As the concluding poems of the group, "The Sleepers" and "To Think of Time" function in a manner parallel to the con-

---

[167] "Passage to India," II, 193.
[168] "Prayer of Columbus," II, 200.

cluding poems of "Songs of Democracy." Just as "A Song for Occupations" introduces the theme of equality into its group, so "The Sleepers," in mystical terms, introduces the theme into the spiritual poems. Sleep is the great leveler; night, the heavenly unifier making the imperfect seem whole. "To Think of Time" is at once bold, climactic, and prophetic, as is "A Song of the Rolling Earth." In these great spiritual chants the soul transcends both space and time.

WHISPERS OF HEAVENLY DEATH (18 POEMS)

The eighteen poems entitled "Whispers of Heavenly Death" might be considered the "Sea-Drift" poems of the spiritual world; they are personal in contrast to "Passage to India," just as "Sea-Drift" contrasts to "Birds of Passage." In this section we find Whitman's most complete absorption with the life-and-death theme. The majority of the poems are given to beautiful and earnest expressions of his faith in death as the only complete reality—the final fulfillment of life. As an example of the sensitive lyrics on the subject, "Whispers of Heavenly Death," the poem from which the section takes its name, is probably the most notable. For earnest utterance none is more convincing than the last:

> Pensive and faltering,
> The words *the Dead* I write,
> For living are the Dead,
> (Haply the only living, only real,
> And I the apparition, I the spectre).[169]

"The Last Invocation" becomes one of the most striking poems of the section when we remember all that has gone before. In a few quiet words of retrospection and understanding, Whitman achieves a passage of sincerity which, more than any other in *Leaves of Grass*, bespeaks his successful reconciliation of flesh and spirit:

[169] "Pensive and Faltering," II, 234.

With the key of softness unlock the locks—with a
   whisper,
Set ope the doors, O Soul.

Tenderly—be not impatient,
(Strong is your hold O mortal flesh,
Strong is your hold O love).[170]

The other significant theme in "Whispers of Heavenly
Death" is that of the nature of the universal God. The key poem
is "Chanting the Square Deific." Using the idea of thesis, antithesis, and synthesis, Whitman attempts an interpretation of
God expressed in terms of the geometrical figure of speech
contained in the title. Probably the unique phase of his concept is his acceptance of those forces of evil which orthodoxy
denies. Rejecting at once the exclusive "goodness" of the orthodox and the exclusive "evil" of the extreme unorthodox, he
announces a new wholeness, a universality of Godhead, ex-
tending the concept of the Trinity to include a fourth person,
Satan. As we have said, death is the "passage to more than
India"; and the identification of self with this universal God
is the meaning of that passage.

Thou Mother with Thy Equal Brood

"Thou Mother with Thy Equal Brood" returns to the national theme and proves the most exalted of the three prophetic poems. The title itself suggests that what is called for
in "By Blue Ontario's Shore" has been partly accomplished.
Spiritually it transcends the two earlier poems as America becomes the hope of all mankind, gathering into herself the richness of the past and projecting into the future her grand idea
of spiritual democracy.

Sail, sail thy best, ship of Democracy,
Of value is thy freight, 'tis not the Present only,
The Past is also stored in thee,

170 "The Last Invocation," II, 233.

.   .   .   .

Earth's *résumé* entire floats on thy keel O ship,
   is steadied by thy spars,
With thee Time voyages in trust, the antecedent
   nations sink or swim with thee.

.   .   .   .

Venerable priestly Asia sails this day with thee,
And royal feudal Europe sails with thee.[171]

Accompanying the spiritualization which takes place in the
poem is the broadening of the national theme to an international one. The poet foresees his nation's call to world leadership;
its destiny becomes the world's destiny. The poem ends:

Thou mental, moral orb—thou New, indeed new,
   Spiritual World!
The Present holds thee not—for such vast growth
   as thine,
For such unparallel'd flight as thine, such brood
   as thine,
The FUTURE only holds thee and can hold thee.[172]

In his notes to "Poetry To-Day in America" Whitman gives us
a prose passage relevant here:

And as only that individual becomes truly great who understands
well that, while complete in himself in a certain sense, he is but
a part of the divine, eternal scheme, and whose special life and
laws are adjusted to move in harmonious relations with the general laws of Nature, and especially with the moral law, the deepest and highest of all, and the last vitality of man or state—so the
United States may only become the greatest and the most continuous, by understanding well their harmonious relations with
entire humanity and history, and all their laws and progress,
sublimed with the creative thought of a Deity, through all time,
past, present, and future. Thus will they expand to the ampli-

[171] "Thou Mother with Thy Equal Brood," II, 237–238.
[172] *Ibid.*, p. 242.

tude of their destiny, and become illustrations and culminating parts of the cosmos, and of civilization.[173]

FROM NOON TO STARRY NIGHT (22 POEMS)

"From Noon to Starry Night" dwells upon and particularizes the themes of "Thou Mother with Thy Equal Brood." It seems almost a quiet reminiscence of the earlier poems of the materials and the panorama of American life, a reminiscence touched with new meanings and insights. The key poem of the group is "The Mystic Trumpeter." In its anticipation of the great composite democratic individuality can be seen the culmination of the theme begun in "Calamus." Romig says, "But underlying the passionate love of man for man, that electric emotion of comradeship, and transcending it, was that mystic merging of perfected personalities into the ideal democratic aggregate."[174] This "mystic merging" is pondered in these poems.

SONGS OF PARTING (17 POEMS)

"Songs of Parting" form a fittingly tranquil conclusion to the volume. They continue the reminiscence of "From Noon to Starry Night," viewing all, to use Whitman's phrase, "with reference to consummations." Parting is "finalè to the shore" —departure upon the sea. The images now speak for themselves.

The conclusion of "As the Time Draws Nigh," the first poem of the group, sounds the main themes:

O book, O chants! must all then amount to but this?
Must we barely arrive at this beginning of us?—
    and yet it is enough, O soul;
O soul, we have positively appear'd—that is enough.[175]

The themes are four: first, the poet's own confrontation with

---

[173] "Poetry To-Day in America," *Collect*, V, 226–227 (footnote).
[174] Edna D. Romig, "The Paradox of Walt Whitman," *University of Colorado Studies* 15 (June 1926), 116.
[175] "As the Time Draws Nigh," II, 271.

death; second, his loving memory of and identification with all
the dead, especially the dead of the war; third, his confidence
in the nation's ability to fulfill her great promise; and finally,
his triumphant belief in the immortality of the soul.

To conclude, I announce what comes after me.

. . . .

When America does what was promis'd,
When through these States walk a hundred millions
    of superb persons,
When the rest part away for superb persons and
    contribute to them,
When breeds of the most perfect mothers denote America,
Then to me and mine our due fruition.

. . . .

My songs cease, I abandon them,
From behind the screen where I hid I advance personally
    solely to you.
Camerado, this is no book,
Who touches this touches a man . . .
[suggestive of Christ and Thomas]

. . . .

Remember my words, I may again return,
I love you, I depart from materials.
I am as one disembodied, triumphant, dead.[176]

Very much as Christ departed the poet departs. He is gone
from the material world. And we are left with the feeling that
the future of the individual, the nation, and humanity depends
upon his reception or rejection. Even as Christ's gospel, Whitman's gospel is grand, and yet needs be intimate and personal
if real at all.

Whitman says of his poems, "If you see them in their place
in the book, you know why I wrote them." Every poem becomes
more expressive and significant when seen in its relation to the

[176] "So Long," II, 286–287, 289–290.

whole. The greatest single evidence of the unified spirit of *Leaves of Grass* is the tremendous cumulative effect of the extended work. This is achieved by the unifying figure of the Christ-like poet-prophet and his unique relationship to his reader and nation; by the simultaneous and harmonious unfolding of poet and nation; by the thematic development of recurring symbols applied at once to the personal and national themes; by the careful grouping of the lyrics and the establishment of relationships within groups and between them; by the parallel structure of the two major movements, the first leading up to "Drum-Taps" and the second pushing on beyond; and by the subtle echoes in the second movement, harking back to all that has gone before.

> In cabin'd ships at sea,
> The boundless blue on every side expanding,
> With whistling winds and music of the waves, the large
>   imperious waves,
>
> .   .   .   .
>
> By sailors young and old haply will I, a reminiscence of
>   the land be read,
> In full rapport at last.
>
> *Here are our thoughts, voyagers' thoughts.*
> *Here not the land, firm land, alone appears,* may then
>   by them be said,
> *The sky o'erarches here, we feel the undulating deck*
>   *beneath our feet,*
> *We feel the long pulsation, ebb and flow of endless*
>   *motion,*
>
> .   .   .   .
>
> *The boundless vista and the horizon far and dim are here,*
> *And this is ocean's poem.*[177]

The last poems are enriched by the first. The first find their final justification in the last. The departing champion of death gives us pause, for he was first the lover of life.

[177] "In Cabin'd Ships at Sea," I, 3.

CHAPTER V

The Evolution of
Leaves of Grass

The devices which Whitman uses in uniting the lyrics of 1881 into a single poetic achievement of epic proportions have been analyzed in detail. It has been maintained that in the 1881 edition the individual lyrics finally assume their proper position and function in the over-all design of the work. As has been seen, this view is supported by Whitman's own testimony.

The immediate concern of this chapter is a study of the various editions of *Leaves of Grass* leading up to the 1881 edition, in an attempt to understand the process whereby it finally arrived. Each edition of the work published during Whitman's lifetime (1855, 1856, 1860, 1867, 1872, 1876, and 1881) has been considered individually, special attention being given to the new poems added, to any changes in the order or groupings of the poems, and to any major revisions within the poems themselves—in other words, to those details which may throw some light on the growth of the work. The purpose is to ascertain, if possible, just how early Whitman became aware of the final design of his work and just how that awareness came about. Was the structural pattern of the 1881 *Leaves* the result of an early, preconceived plan in the mind of the poet, or did it gradually evolve and unfold itself finally to be recognized by him as the end toward which he had been moving more or less unconsciously from the start?

Miller, in his comparatively brief discussion of the evolution of the structure of *Leaves of Grass*, follows an entirely different approach from that taken here. He looks to developments in the poet's life. In addition he bases his interpretation more on Whitman's prefaces and prose explanations than he does on the poetry itself.[1] This is quite understandable and appropriate because his consideration of the evolution is decidedly functional and his purposes in no way demand a consistent focus upon the book itself, involving a detailed review of each edition.

Asselineau gives more attention to the evolution of *Leaves* than anyone else. Although his second volume has the subtitle "The Creation of a Book," he makes no attempt at a systematic examination of the various editions, including most of his pertinent remarks regarding the editions in his discussion of the evolution of Whitman the man. A brief glance at the table of contents of volume two indicates a diffuseness of method and a twofold structure, involving first a consideration of themes and then a consideration of style, which are quite foreign to the technique used in this study. A third contrast is Asselineau's method of focusing upon the man rather than the book. This can be seen in his desire to present each edition of *Leaves of Grass* as a triumph over some personal crisis. This

[1] James E. Miller, Jr., *A Critical Guide to Leaves of Grass*, pp. 175–185.

strained attempt at establishing a pattern and the unexpected and frequent emergence of Whitman's very active "anomaly" detract from an otherwise admirable work.[2]

The purpose here can best be served by continuing to focus upon *Leaves* itself. And in proceeding from edition to edition of *Leaves*, it has seemed advisable to use consistently the title given each poem in the 1881 edition, rather than resort to the variant titles of the early editions—titles which are not always familiar. Thus, for purposes of clarity and ease, the first untitled poem in 1855 ("A Poem of Walt Whitman, an American" in 1856, "Walt Whitman" in 1860, etc.) is referred to from the very start as "Song of Myself." This system is especially practical here, as we are concerned with the arrangement of the poems of each edition in relation to that of 1881. (The various titles used in the early editions are conveniently listed in the variorum readings in Holloway's "Inclusive Edition," under the titles used in this study.[3]) Instances in which the 1881 poem is either a mere fragment of the original poem or a greatly supplemented version have been carefully indicated. The new poems appearing in each edition, listed at the beginning of the discussion of each, are given beneath the group titles under which they appear in 1881. Again, the purpose is to facilitate comparisons of the various editions. A STERN WARNING IS TIMELY HERE. The use of such titles and groupings can be very misleading in making all the editions look much more alike than they really are. If this warning is kept in mind, the procedure followed here seems to be the least of a number of possible evils.

THE 1855 EDITION

The arrangement of the twelve untitled poems of 1855 is as follows:

1. Song of Myself

---

[2] Roger Asselineau, *The Evolution of Walt Whitman: The Creation of a Book*, pp. 253–260.

[3] Emory Holloway, ed., *Leaves of Grass*, pp. 541–709.

As indicated above, only the first section of "Song of the Answerer" appears in the 1855 edition. The last poem, "Great Are the Myths," was dropped after 1876. Although some revisions were made in the other ten poems between 1855 and 1881, their tone and purport remain unchanged. It is significant that in 1855 the twelve lyrics appear without titles, suggesting a singleness of purpose and development throughout the volume. While the position that the twelve are carefully woven into one long poem is hardly tenable, some purpose may be served by turning for a moment to a consideration of the relationships of the poems to one another.

The most important thing to be noted about the 1855 *Leaves* is that its first poem, which makes up over half of the entire volume, is "Song of Myself"—the rhapsodic utterance which has continued to stand as the nuclear poem of the entire work and has remained the most original of all of Whitman's lyrics. The primary function of this poem (in 1881 as well as 1855) was that of revealing the nature and the dedication of the central personality of the volume, the poet-prophet, Walt Whitman. That the poet saw a vital connection between the first and the second poems is indicated by the opening lines of the latter, lines which were discarded later when the poem was relocated. The transition is as follows:

Come closer to me,
Push close my lovers and take the best I possess,

Yield closer and closer and give me the best you possess.

This is unfinished business with me . . . how is it
    with you?
I was chilled with the cold types and cylinders and
    wet paper between us.
I pass so poorly with paper and types . . . I must
    pass with the contact of bodies and souls.

I do not thank you for liking me as I am, and
    liking the touch of me . . . I know that it is
    good for you to do so.[4]

These lines are a fitting transition from the great poem of
the ego to one of Whitman's most effective poetic statements
of the essential dignity and equality of all human souls, no
matter how exalted or humble their station in society. It is significant that these transitional lines state very briefly the essence of the "Children of Adam" and "Calamus" poems, the
two groupings which later take their place between "Song of
Myself" and the "Songs of Democracy" of which "A Song for
Occupations" becomes an important part. The relationship between "A Song for Occupations" and "To Think of Time" is
not as clearly indicated; there is, however, an obvious progression. The intense social consciousness of the first is accompanied by an exaltation of man here and now; it is his
present, with its occupations and materials, that matters.

Will you seek afar off? You surely come back at last,
In things best known to you finding also the sweetest
    and strongest and lovingest,
Happiness not in another place, but this place . . .
    not for another hour, but this hour.[5]

But with Whitman more needs to be said; the present must be

---

[4] Walter Whitman, *Leaves of Grass* (1855), p. 57. (The various editions of
Leaves of Grass supervised by Whitman are referred to hereafter by date
only.)
[5] *1855*, pp. 63–64.

identified with the eternal. Such a theme requires a new poetic mood—hence a new poem in which social consciousness gives way to mysticism.

> To think of time ... to think through the
>   retrospection,
> To think of today ... and the ages continued
>   henceforward.
>
> .   .   .   .
>
> Have you feared the future would be nothing to you?
>
> Is today nothing? Is the beginningless past nothing?
> If the future is nothing they are just as surely nothing.[6]

That the earlier poem lurks behind every line is clearly indicated in the refrain of the first half of "To Think of Time," "Others taking great interest in them ... and we taking small interest in them."[7] Note one variant of this in particular:

> The markets, the government, the working man's
>   wages ... to think what account they are
>   through our nights and days;
> To think that other workingmen will make just as
>   great account of them ... yet we make little
>   or no account.[8]

Here is a poem of intense spiritual struggle. The ultimate triumph is the triumph of the mystic.

> I swear I think there is nothing but immortality!
> That the exquisite scheme is for it, and the nebulous
>   float is for it, and the cohering is for it,
> And all preparation is for it ... and identity is
>   for it ... and life and death are for it.[9]

The mysticism of "To Think of Time" is carried over into and

---

[6] *1855*, p. 65.
[7] *1855*, p. 66.
[8] *1855*, p. 67.
[9] *1855*, p. 70.

sustained throughout "The Sleepers." Here the poet transcends space as well as time; escaping the limits of the body, he becomes one with all human experience. As was suggsested in Chaper IV, the theme of equality developed in "A Song for Occupations" is restated in more spiritual terms.

Everyone that sleeps is beautiful . . . Peace is
    always beautiful,
The myth of heaven indicates peace and night.

The myth of heaven indicates the soul;
The soul is always beautiful . . .[10]

Standing in contrast to these two mystical poems is "I Sing the Body Electric." It is a personalized restatement of the materialism inherent in "A Song for Occupations." Its presence after "The Sleepers" and "To Think of Time" may be accounted for in such lines as these:

If life and the soul are sacred the human body is
    sacred;
And the glory and sweet of a man is the token of
    manhood untainted,
And in man or woman a clean, strong, firm-fibred
    body is beautiful as the most beautiful face.[11]

A number of pertinent relationships between "I Sing the Body Electric" and "Faces" can be detected. One stands out. In "Faces" the theme of the former is democratized as the exaltation of the human being is extended beyond persons of physical beauty and strength to the deformed, the ugly, as well. Whitman refuses to be shaken by such.

Features of my equals, would you trick me with your
    creased and cadaverous march?
Well then you cannot trick me.

. . . .

[10] *1855*, p. 75.
[11] *1855*, p. 82.

I see 'neath the rims of your haggard and mean disguises.
Splay and twist as you like . . . poke with the
    tangling fores of fishes or rats,
You'll be unmuzzled . . . you certainly will.[12]

"Song of the Answerer" (Section 1) states the place and
function of the true poet among his fellows. It proclaims his
universality and democracy, his capacity for appreciating and
interpreting for all men alike.

His welcome is universal . . . the flow of beauty
    is not more welcome or universal than he is,
The person he favors by day or sleeps with at
    night is blessed.[13]

An echo of the two preceding poems rings through one of the
last stanzas:

The gentleman of perfect blood acknowledges his
    perfect blood,
The insulter, the prostitute, the angry person,
    the beggar, see themselves in the ways of him
    . . . he strangely transmutes them,
They are not vile any more . . . they hardly know
    themselves, they are so grown.[14]

From this point on it is difficult to account for the particular
arrangement of the poems; it is well to remember, however,
that this brings us to page eighty-seven of the ninety-five–page
volume. "Europe" and "A Boston Ballad" are obviously companion pieces. They have a place in the volume as they foreshadow a theme to be fully developed later—the theme of
democratic America as the fulfillment of all past sacrifices for
freedom and equality. In speaking of Europe's war dead, the
poet says:

[12] *1855*, pp. 83–84.
[13] *1855*, p. 86.
[14] *1855*, p. 87.

> These corpses of young men, . . . cold and motionless
>   as they seem . . . live elsewhere with unslaughter'd
>   vitality.
>
> .   .   .   .
>
> Not a grave of the murdered for freedom but grows
>   seed for freedom . . . in its turn to bear seed,
> Which the winds carry afar and re-sow, and the rains
>   and the snows nourish.[15]

"A Boston Ballad," although satiric, makes it clear that the winds blow toward America.

"There Was a Child Went Forth" and "Who Learns My Lesson Complete?" also fall naturally together. Their late appearance in the volume (in 1881 they appear late and in the same group) brings with it a confident and comparatively serene restatement of the paradoxical themes of materialism and spiritualism seen in "A Song for Occupations" and "To Think of Time." They set the tone for the final poem—for the affirmation of faith that concludes the volume.

> Great is life . . . and real and mystical . . .
>   Wherever and whoever,
> Great is death . . . Sure as life holds all parts
>   together, death holds all parts together;
> Sure as the stars return again after they merge in
>   the light, death is great as life.[16]

Although the 1855 edition contains only twelve poems, it has been generally accepted as a brilliant beginning for an unknown poet. It seems inescapable that from the very start Whitman viewed *Leaves of Grass* as a single poetic composition and that as early as 1855 he had some conception of the form and sweeping proportions the work was eventually to assume. The absence of titles for the individual poems of 1855 and the manner in which they are tied together with transitional pas-

---

[15] *1855*, p. 88.
[16] *1855*, p. 95.

sages or pertinent allusions is striking evidence of a unified concept and purpose for the whole. That Whitman had some conception of scope not foreign to what *Leaves of Grass* actually became is evinced in the fact that the twelve poems give a broad statement of the characteristic Whitmanian progression from the material to the spiritual, from the songs of the body to the songs of the soul. We have clearly indicated the course of this progression in our discussion of the relationships of the twelve poems to one another. It is obvious that these relationships foreshadow many of those of 1881.

It is an important fact (unique in literary history) that the first poem in 1855 is as much the nuclear poem of the 1881 *Leaves* as it was of its own edition and that at the last it stands as the greatest single achievement of the poet's career. The fact that "Song of Myself" is usually looked upon as something more than an introduction to *Leaves* as a whole—as something approximating a miniature of it—suggests that a careful look at it may help in arriving at some notion of just how far the poet had progressed in 1855 in grasping the true significance of what he was about. If it is something of a miniature, it confirms the conclusion that as early as 1855 Whitman viewed *Leaves* as a single work made up of individual lyrics and that he had some concept of the potential scope of the body-soul progression. Even more important, the appearance of "Song of Myself" in 1855 is proof of the fact that from the start Whitman planned his volume around a central personality, his own, and that it was his primary aim to depict, as a compelling example for all mankind, the evolution of that personality from sensual egoist to loving comrade, to emancipated soul. That this example was conceived of as fundamentally Christlike from the start can be seen in the Christ-symbol which dominates all of "Song of Myself." These elements, giving stamp to the final *Leaves of Grass*, are all inherent in the miniature poem.

It would seem, then, that as early as 1855 Whitman had a fairly clear notion of what he wished to accomplish. His amazing flexibility, his patience and confidence in letting the work take its own course and develop piece by piece, without becoming apprehensive and doubtful to the extent of abandoning or altering his practice of the organic theory, are evidence of just how firmly the over-all concept had laid hold of his imagination and his hopes. In the face of critical attack and misapprehension, he must have been aware of the grossly unbalanced nature of the volumes of 1856 and 1860 in particular, of their inadequacy in presenting the full purport of his thought and feeling; but he was not diverted, because he knew his heading was true. Whitman's happy faith, even in the face of grievous odds, that the poet of the body would in time become the true poet of the soul is no small part of his greatness and genius, no small factor in his ultimate and unique success.

The *Leaves* of 1855 was the first literary manifestation of the teeming brain and heart of the new Whitman. A spiritual and intellectual germ that could produce such an initial blossoming needs be of an intensity and vitality worthy of a final fruition of the proportion of the 1881 *Leaves of Grass*. It could hardly have been less. The creative mind of Emerson seems to have appreciated this. The task ahead of Whitman after 1855 was the tremendous and tedious one of clarifying, enriching, and expanding his poetic account of the full significance of the vision behind that first edition.

THE 1856 EDITION

New Poems (20)

> *Children of Adam* (2)
> 1. A Woman Waits for Me
> 2. Spontaneous Me
>
> *Songs of Democracy* (6)
> 3. Salut au Monde!
> 4. Song of the Broad-Axe
> 5. Crossing Brooklyn Ferry
> 6. Song of the Open Road

7. Song of the Answerer (Section 2)
8. A Song of the Rolling Earth

Birds of Passage (1)
9. To You

Sea-Drift (1)
10. On the Beach at Night Alone

11. By Blue Ontario's Shore

Autumn Rivulets (5)
12. Unfolded Out of the Folds
13. This Compost
14. Song of Prudence
15. To a Foil'd European Revolutionaire
16. Miracles

Whispers of Heavenly Death (1)
17. Assurances

From Noon to Starry Night (1)
18. Excelsior

Not in 1881 (2)
19. A Poem of Remembrances for a Girl or a Boy
of These States
20. Respondez

As we turn to the twenty new poems appearing in the 1856 edition, it seems advisable to consider them in groups rather than individually. The major development to be noted is the complete dominance of important poems which are sociological, which exalt the material and physical progress of America and individual Americans, and which are imbued with the optimistic spirit of growth and expansion. They include "Salut au Monde!" "Song of the Broad-Axe," "By Blue Ontario's Shore" (drawn largely from the 1855 preface and revised extensively later), "Crossing Brooklyn Ferry," "Song of the Open Road," and "A Song of the Rolling Earth." This group of poems (scattered throughout the volume) is a more significant portion of the new contributions than the six-twenty ratio suggests, for they are all long poems and taken together occupy more than two-thirds of the total space given to new poetry. There is a second group primarily sociological, but less materialistic. Two of the poems are reminiscent of the first group, but their tone is one of defense or justification rather than unqualified praise. They are "Song of Prudence" (drawn in part from the 1855 preface) and "Miracles." The remaining lyrics share the serious, rather somber tone of these two, but are concerned not so much with materials as with questionings of this life and the capacity of the human spirit to rise above them. They are "To You," "On the Beach at Night Alone," "Assurances," "To a Foil'd European Revolutionaire," "A Poem of Remembrances for a Girl or a Boy of These States" (dropped after 1860), and "Respondez" (dropped after 1876 except for two short sections finally incorporated under the titles "Transpositions" and "Reversals"). Finally, "Spontaneous Me" and "A Woman Waits for Me" are poems of the body and sex, similar to the earlier "I Sing the Body Electric." "Excelsior" and "Song of the Answerer" (Section 2) are poems of the dreams and accomplishments of the ideal poet. "Unfolded Out of the Folds" and "This Compost" are difficult to classify.

The edition begins with "Song of Myself" and finds a spiritual culmination in "To Think of Time." The general movement within this framework is from the physical and material toward the spiritual; but the course is not clearly charted. It is possible that Whitman was influenced in his arrangement by considerations of variety of style and mood. More significant is the fact that *Leaves* of 1856 is hopelessly unbalanced when compared with the 1855 or 1881 editions—a point to be discussed later.

The revisions in the twelve poems brought forward from the edition of the previous year are for the most part minor and routine. The one exception is the addition of a conclusion of several pages to "I Sing the Body Electric," stressing the

dependence of the soul upon the body and modifying somewhat
the tone and emphasis of the poem.[17]

In 1856, then, a major secondary theme of *Leaves of Grass*
has obviously claimed the imagination of the poet—the material and social development of the New World. As Asselineau
suggests, Whitman's interest shifted from the individual to
national themes.[18] Unmistakable evidence of this is the appearance of six of the eleven poems which eventually make up the
untitled groups which in this study have been called "Songs of
Democracy" and "By Blue Ontario's Shore." This is the most
significant development of the 1855 edition. The indispensable
role of material and social America in the ultimate redemption
of all mankind and in preparing the way for, inspiring, and sus-
taining the new poet-prophet is an 1881 concept that did not
clearly emerge in the 1856 edition as a whole, although it is
latent in "Song of Myself." The real significance here is not so
much the actual appearance of the seven important poems themselves as it is the early emergence of a consciousness of the
development of a national character and its relation to the development of the representative American, the modern man. The
poet could hardly have realized in 1856 just how these two elements were destined to move forward simultaneously as *Leaves
of Grass* developed, touching almost every lyric, functioning
either side by side or alternately as a flexible, but continuous,
unifying device. There is good evidence that Whitman was not
fully conscious of this for some time to come. Nevertheless, the
two elements were already writing themselves into the poems
and needed only to be educed for this particular function at the
appointed time.

More than two-thirds of the new poetry of 1856, then, is
given over to the development of a very particular area of the
poet's interest. The poetic possibilities of that area are very
nearly exhausted, while other areas are neglected. This tend-

[17] *1856*, pp. 177–179.
[18] Roger Asselineau, *The Evolution of Walt Whitman: The Creation of a
Personality*, pp. 85–86.

ency is worth noting here, for it is indicative of the method Whitman seems to have used in gradually clarifying, enriching, and expanding the faint sketching of 1885. As a result, *Leaves of Grass* is thrown out of balance and does not again approximate anything like the balance of 1855 until nearing completion. Whitman's likely awareness of this fact may in large part account for the absence of any noticeable effort toward maintaining an over-all structural pattern between 1855 and 1872. Lack of balance between his various themes, moods, and poetic styles would have become increasingly obvious had order been prematurely sought after. That he had some misgivings on this score is suggested by the fact that in addition to poems on the particular interest at hand, Whitman includes a few poems typical of the other phases of his poetic vision. These variants (and they are found among the new poems of every edition), support the idea that the grand design was always there, though in no sense static. It was a living and growing presence, essentially organic in its development.

THE 1860 EDITION
New Poems (122)

Inscriptions (12)
1. To a Historian
2. Poets to Come
3. On Journeys through the States
4. Me Imperturbe
5. I Hear America Singing
6. What Place Is Besieged?
7. To a Certain Cantatrice
8. To the States
9. To Foreign Lands
10. To You
11. Beginners
12. Savantism

Introductions (1)
13. Starting from Paumanok

Children of Adam (11)

14. To the Garden the World
15. From Pent-up Aching Rivers
16. O Hour to Joy and Madness
17. We Two, How Long We Were Fool'd
18. Native Moments
19. Once I Pass'd through a Populous City
20. Facing West from California's Shores
21. Ages and Ages Returning at Intervals
22. O Hymen! O Hymenee!
23. I Am He That Aches with Love
24. As Adam Early in the Morning

Calamus (38)

25. In Paths Untrodden
26. Scented Herbage of My Breast
27. Whoever You Are Holding Me Now in Hand
28. These I Singing in Spring
29. For You O Democracy
30. Not Heaving from My Ribb'd Breast Only
31. Of the Terrible Doubt of Appearances
32. Recorders Ages Hence
33. When I Heard at the Close of Day
34. Are You the New Person Drawn toward Me?
35. Roots and Leaves Themselves Alone
36. Not Heat Flames Up and Consumes
37. Trickle Drops
38. City of Orgies
39. Behold This Swarthy Face
40. I Saw in Louisiana a Live-Oak Growing
41. To a Stranger
42. This Moment Yearning and Thoughtful
43. I Hear It Was Charged against Me
44. The Prairie-Grass Dividing
45. We Two Boys Together Clinging
46. When I Peruse the Conquer'd Fame

NOTE: In 1860 "What Place Is Besieged?" and "What Ship Puzzled at Sea" are one poem; "Vocalism" and "The World Below the Brine" are each treated as two poems. This makes the actual total of new poems as presented in the edition 123.

The most significant new poems of the 1860 edition are those grouped under the titles "Children of Adam" and "Calamus." These two sections of *Leaves of Grass* were virtually completed between 1856 and 1860. The first group is made up of poems of the body and sex; the second, of poems of friendship, closely associated with the first in intense sensuality of imagery. A total of forty-seven poems scattered throughout the volume (here grouped under "Inscriptions," "Songs of Democracy," "Birds of Passage," "By the Roadside," "Autumn Rivulets," and "From Noon to Starry Night"), concerned primarily with social and national themes, are a continuation of the type of poem which dominated the 1856 edition. They are less personal and earthy than "Children of Adam" and "Calamus." On the other hand, they lack the spirituality characteristic of the fifteen songs here grouped under "Sea-Drift," "Whispers of Heavenly Death," and "Songs of Parting." Each of the ten poems which are discarded later (of little concern here) fits into one of these categories. "Starting from Paumanok" stands alone in function and importance.

As in the case of the edition of 1856, the 1860 edition is unbalanced. Nevertheless, there are several developments regarding arrangement which should be noted. First, "Starting from Paumanok" appears as an introduction to the volume as a whole and to "Song of Myself" in particular. Second, for the first time Whitman gathers poems into groups which are given appropriate titles. Two of these groups are particularly important because they are permanent, "Children of Adam" ("Enfans d'Adam") and "Calamus." The arrangement of the poems within each group is destined to be modified only slightly; the pattern within each is set.

Two factors may be significant in relation to the development of Whitman as an artist. They are a definite trend toward shorter, more intense poems, and the appearance of his first great aesthetic poem "Out of the Cradle Endlessly Rocking." The few revisions made are similar to the routine ones effected in the 1856 edition.

The years between 1856 and 1860 were fruitful years. The 122 poems that came into being are indicative of a number of important developments in Whitman's plan for *Leaves of Grass*. It has already been suggested in the discussion of the 1856 edition that the tremendous part the development of the New World was to play in *Leaves* itself was not fully recognized by Whitman in 1855. His thoughts on the New World and its society were vital to the poetry of that edition, but they were not a part of it; rather, they found expression in the long preface. The transfer of many of these prefatory ideas (phrase by phrase at times) to "By Blue Ontario's Shore" and "Song of

Prudence" and the emergence of the six major poems of 1856 mark the first real development of the theme as a part of the poetry itself. This development is continued in forty-seven comparatively short lyrics of 1860. Between 1856 and 1860 most of Whitman's attention seems to have been given to the relation of this new secondary theme to the primary one "I sing myself." That the fundamental relationship was partially resolved is clearly indicated by the appearance of "Starting from Paumanok." This poem becomes introductory to both "Song of Myself" and *Leaves of Grass* as a whole and has as its chief function the introduction of the poet as a development and integral part of the New World which he is to identify and interpret for mankind. "Solitary, singing in the West, I strike up for a New World." "I will report all heroism from an American point of view."[19] No poem in *Leaves of Grass* throws more light upon Whitman's unique method of evolving and suggesting relationships. Bowers, in his introduction to *Whitman's Manuscripts*, uses "Starting from Paumanok" as a key to what was going on between 1856 and 1860.[20]

It was during these years that Whitman seized firm hold on the idea that the full social and spiritual impact of the development of the great individual of "Song of Myself" could be conveyed dynamically only if that individual were placed in a society—given a time and a place—a country. "Starting from Paumanok" gives real body to a concept that was little more than suggested by the 1856 title "A Poem of Walt Whitman: An American." It is interesting that with the appearance of this new introductory poem "An American" is dropped. In the light of the earlier discussion of the "Analysis of the Structure of *Leaves of Grass*" it is worth noting that Whitman's clearest poetic statement of the religious purport of his volume comes in the poem which first identifies the poet-prophet with a country. This theme is inherent in "Song of Myself" from the start, but

---

[19] *1881*, pp. 19, 21.
[20] Fredson Bowers, ed., *Walt Whitman's Manuscripts: Leaves of Grass* (1860), pp. lii, lix–lxi.

it had not been introduced into *Leaves* as a whole before. In "Starting from Paumanok" Whitman is lucid:

> I too, following many and followed by many, inaugurate
>   a religion, I descend into the arena,
> (It may be I am destin'd to utter the loudest cries
>   there, the winner's pealing shouts,
> Who knows? they may rise from me yet, and soar
>   above every thing.)
>
> Each is not for its own sake,
> I say the whole earth and all the stars in the sky are
>   for religion's sake.
>
> I say no man has ever yet been half devout enough,
> None has ever yet adored or worshipped half enough,
> None has begun to think how divine he himself is,
>   and how certain the future is.
>
> I say the real and permanent grandeur of these
>   States must be their religion,
> Otherwise there is no real and permanent grandeur.[21]
>
> .   .   .   .
>
> O I see the following poems are indeed to drop in the
>   earth the germs of a greater Religion.[22]

"Starting from Paumanok" is the key poem to what was happening between 1856 and 1860 in another respect. It helps account for the emergence of "Children of Adam" and "Calamus" (the two major contributions of the 1860 edition) at this particular time, and with them the practice of grouping poems. As has been suggested, Whitman was preoccupied with the development of a true relationship between his primary and secondary themes ("I sing myself" and "I strike up for a New World")—with a poetic expression of the true basis of the relationship of the individual to society and nation. The first

---

[21] *1881*, p. 22.
[22] *1881*, p. 23. Revised later to read "Know you, solely to drop in the earth the germs of a greater religion,/ The following chants each for its kind I sing."

step in establishing this relationship, as we have seen, is found in "Children of Adam." The following lines from "Starting from Paumanok" are suggestive of this group of poems:

> As I have walked in Alabama my morning walk,
> I have seen where the she-bird the mocking-bird
>   sat on her nest in the briers hatching her brood.
>
> I have seen the he-bird also,
> I have paused to hear him near at hand inflating his throat and
>   joyfully singing.
>
> And while I paused it came to me that what he
>   really sang for was not there only,
> Nor for his mate nor himself only, nor all sent
>   back by the echoes,
> But subtle, clandestine, away beyond,
> A charge transmitted and gift occult for those
>   being born.
>
> Democracy! near at hand to you a throat is now
>   inflating itself and joyfully singing.
> Ma femme! for the brood beyond us and of us,
> For those who belong here and those to come,
> I exultant to be ready for them will now shake
>   out carols stronger and haughtier than ever
>   yet have been heard upon earth.
>
> . . . .
>
> I will effuse egotism and show it underlying all,
>   and I will be the bard of personality,
> And I will show of male and female that either is
>   but the equal of the other,
> And sexual organs and acts! do you concentrate in
>   me, for I am determined to tell you with courageous
>   clear voice to prove you illustrious . . .[23]

One passing observation: One can hardly read "Out of the Cradle Endlessly Rocking," a second important poem of 1860

[23] *1881*, p. 24.

destined to play a major role in pointing up the thematic development of *Leaves*, without remembering this joyous he-bird singing for his living, fertile mate. This morning bird of life and love and the evening bird of love and death, both of Alabama, were obviously one in the mind of Whitman. The songs of neither were "all sent back by the echoes."

The second step in establishing this relationship of individual and nation is found in "Calamus." The following earlier lines from "Starting from Paumanok" are suggestive of this group of poems:

> I will sing the song of companionship,
> I will show what alone must finally compact these,
> I believe these are to found their own ideal of
>   manly love, indicating it in me,
> I will therefore let flame from me the burning fires
>   that were threatening to consume me,
> I will lift what has too long kept down those
>   smouldering fires,
> I will give them complete abandonment,
> I will write the evangel-poem of comrades and
>   of love,
> (For who but I should understand love, with all
>   its sorrow and joy?
> And who but I should be the poet of comrades?) [24]

"Starting from Paumanok" supports the view that "Children of Adam" and "Calamus" are the early results of an attempt to express the real physical and emotional bases of the spiritual bonds between individual and nation—of spiritual democracy, if you will. The tremendous advance that has been accomplished between 1856 and 1860 is evident in the manner in which Whitman brings his themes together:

> What do you seek so pensive and silent?
> What do you need camerado?
> Dear son do you think it is love?

[24] *1881*, p. 21.

Listen, dear son—listen, America, daughter or son!
It is a painful thing to love a man or woman to
    excess—and yet it satisfies—it is great;

But there is something else very great—it makes
    the whole coincide;
It, magnificent, beyond materials, with continuous
    hands, sweeps and provides for all.

.   .   .   .

My comrade!
For you, to share with me, two greatnesses—and a
    third one, rising inclusive and more resplendent,
The greatness of Love and Democracy—and the greatness
    of Religion.[25]

True, "I Sing the Body Electric" is an early appearance of the "Children of Adam" idea; however, its relation to the whole is hardly the clear relationship established by the subsequent group. Then, of course, there is no similar early poem expressing the "Calamus" idea. It emerges between 1856 and 1860 as the real answer of the poet to the problem of the relationship of the individual and the state. If Whitman was to be true to his philosophy of the interdependence of the physical and the spiritual, "Children of Adam" and "Calamus" had to be. It is quite relevant to this study that these poems are the first to receive a permanent group title, signifying on Whitman's part a sense of oneness and completeness for this particular phase of his work. Whether "Starting from Paumanok" was written before or after these groups were completed would not alter the significance of the relationships pointed out here.

These considerations, plus considerations of actual proportion, justify the statement that "Children of Adam" and "Calamus" are the major contributions of 1860. There are in addition, however, fifteen poems of a spiritual nature, fore-

[25] *1881*, p. 23. Frederik Schyberg, *Walt Whitman*, pp. 142–144, 153–155. Here is a good example of similar conclusions but sharply contrasting approaches.

shadowing later developments. That Whitman was keenly aware of them is seen in those passages in "Starting from Paumanok" which go beyond the major concern of the relationship of poet and nation and take into account the yet unformed groupings of which the fifteen poems are to become a part.

> And I will show that whatever happens to anybody,
>   it may be turn'd to beautiful results—and I
>   will show that nothing can happen more beautiful
>   than death;
> And I will thread a thread through my poems that
>   time and events are compact,
> And that all the things of the universe are perfect
>   miracles, each as profound as any.
>
> I will not make poems with reference to parts;
> But I will make leaves, poems, poemets, songs,
>   says, thoughts, with reference to ensemble:
> And I will not sing with reference to a day, but
>   with reference to all days;
> And I will not make a poem, nor the least part of
>   a poem, but has reference to the Soul;
> (Because, having looked at the objects of the
>   universe, I find there is no one, nor any particle
>   of one, but has reference to the Soul.) [26]

"Out of the Cradle Endlessly Rocking," one poem of the fifteen, is particularly important, for it is a pivotal poem for all of *Leaves of Grass*. Pearce sees in it a progression from "poetry of diffusion to poetry of integration."[27] It is highly significant that this poem was composed at a time when Whitman had completed (with a few minor exceptions) the first phase of *Leaves of Grass*. As already noted, the two introductory poems, "Children of Adam," "Calamus," nine of the eleven poems

---

[26] *1881*, pp. 24–25.
[27] Roy Harvey Pearce, ed., *Leaves of Grass: Facsimile of the 1860 Text*, p. xxxix.

which are here called "Songs of Democracy," and all but one major poem of "Birds of Passage" have taken form. In its opening theme of physical and passionate love, "Out of the Cradle Endlessly Rocking" looks back to these poems and, in its closing theme of spiritual love and death, looks forward, preparing us for poems to come. The actual positions of these poems in the over-all work of 1860 (a matter with which Whitman, it seems, was little concerned at the time) do not substantiate all these observations, but their closeness in time of composition and the accompanying emergence of "Starting from Paumanok" do. "Out of the Cradle Endlessly Rocking" is destined to shift position in *Leaves of Grass* for a number of editions to come; nevertheless, at the end, when the sections to which it is harbinger are complete and the poet is clearly concerned with poem order and its relation to the chronological development of poet and nation, this poem comes to rest at a point paralleling its approximate time of composition.

In each new edition of *Leaves* there are scattered poems which state briefly the themes that have claimed the poet's imagination during the preparation of that particular volume. At the last most of these poems were gathered together in "Inscriptions" and assigned an appropriate role in that introduction to the entire work. The themes covered by the twelve scattered throughout the 1860 volume substantiate what has been said: that these songs grow out of America and her poet and identify both, that they must show man at ease in nature, and that they are to be finally justified by the songs that grow out of them.

One final word before moving on to 1867. "Song of Myself" has been spoken of as a miniature of *Leaves of Grass*. The poems that accompany it in the 1855 edition suggest that the poet contains more to be let out. He lets it out, piece by piece, over a period of five years—observing, pondering, slowly establishing relationships. By 1860 things are falling rapidly into place, titled groups emerge for the first time and a milestone is achieved in the grand design announced in "Starting from

Paumanok." In this poem the course is clearly charted for all of *Leaves of Grass* and the "starting" upon it is undertaken with exuberant good spirit. Whitman takes heart from the assurance that inherent in his five years of composition was a unity which, with time and cultivation, asserted itself. He is confirmed in his methods, now proven to his satisfaction, and he looks to the task ahead with new confidence and enthusiasm. For the first time he dares write into *Leaves of Grass* the projection of a plan for an achievement of which his remarkable "Song of Myself" is but a miniature. In "Starting from Paumanok" is foothold "tenon'd and mortis'd in granite." It must have friended him often in the dark and cloudy days of hesitation and anxiety.

THE 1867 EDITION
New Poems (75)

Inscriptions (5)
1. The Ship Starting
2. Shut Not Your Doors
3. One's-Self I Sing
4. When I Read the Book
5. Beginning My Studies

Children of Adam (2)
6. Out of the Rolling Ocean the Crowd
7. I Heard You Solemn-Sweet Pipes of the Organ

Birds of Passage (1)
8. Pioneers! O Pioneers!

9. A Broadway Pageant

Sea-Drift (2)
10. Tears
11. Aboard at a Ship's Helm

By the Roadside (6)
12. When I Heard the Learn'd Astronomer

13. O Me! O Life!
14. A Farm Picture
15. A Child's Amaze
16. Mother and Babe
17. The Runner

Drum-Taps (34)

18. First O Songs for a Prelude
19. From Paumanok Starting I Fly Like a Bird
20. Rise O Days from Your Fathomless Depths
21. City of Ships
22. Cavalry Crossing a Ford
23. Bivouac on a Mountain Side
24. An Army Corps on the March
25. By the Bivouac's Fitful Flame
26. Come Up from the Fields Father
27. Vigil Strange I Kept on the Field One Night
28. A March in the Ranks Hard-prest, and the
    Road Unknown
29. A Sight in Camp in the Daybreak Gray and Dim
30. As Toilsome I Wander'd Virginia's Woods
31. Year That Trembled and Reel'd Beneath Me
32. The Wound-Dresser
33. Long, Too Long America
34. Give Me the Splendid Silent Sun
35. Dirge for Two Veterans
36. I Saw Old General at Bay
37. The Artilleryman's Vision
38. Not Youth Pertains to Me
39. Race of Veterans
40. World Take Good Notice
41. O Tan-faced Prairie-Boy
42. Look Down Fair Moon
43. Reconciliation
44. How Solemn as One by One
45. As I Lay with My Head in Your Lap Camerado

46. To a Certain Civilian
47. Lo, Victress on the Peaks
48. Spirit Whose Work Is Done
49. Turn O Libertad
50. To the Leaven'd Soil They Trod
51. Beat! Beat! Drums!

Memories of President Lincoln (3)

52. When Lilacs Last in the Dooryard Bloom'd
53. O Captain! My Captain!
54. Hushed Be the Camps To-Day

Autumn Rivulets (4)

55. Old Ireland
56. Others May Praise What They Like
57. The Torch
58. The City Dead-House

Whispers of Heavenly Death (2)

59. Chanting the Square Deific
60. Quicksand Years

From Noon to Starry Night (4)

61. Ah Poverties, Wincings, and Sulky Retreats
62. Weave In, My Hardy Life
63. Old War-Dreams
64. Thick-sprinkled Bunting

Songs of Parting (4)

65. Years of the Modern
66. Ashes of Soldiers
67. Pensive on Her Dead Gazing
68. Camps of Green

Not in 1881 (7)

69. Stronger Lessons
70. Leaflets
71. Drum-Taps

72. Bathed in War's Perfume
73. Solid, Ironical, Rolling Orb
74. Not My Enemies Ever Invade Me
75. This Day, O Soul

The seventy-five new poems of the 1867 edition are dominated by "Drum-Taps" and its companion Lincoln poems. Of
the poems outside that grouping, twenty-nine (those grouped
under "Sea-Drift," "By the Roadside," "Autumn Rivulets,"
"Whispers of Heavenly Death," "From Noon to Starry Night,"
"Songs of Parting," and "Not in 1881") are clearly associated
with "Drum-Taps" in subject matter and tone. Though they
are not all about the war specifically, they show a marked departure from the optimism, exuberance, and sensuality characteristic of the majority of the earlier poems and an increasing
tendency toward spiritual reflection in resolving conflicts and
questionings. Of the eight lyrics destined to take their place
among the earlier poems of the volume, only one "I Heard You
Solemn-Sweet Pipes of the Organ" is sensual in the old way;
and only two "Pioneers! O Pioneers!" and "A Broadway
Pageant" are exuberant in the old way.

The 1867 edition is the most important edition so far in
connection with our study of the order of the poems. The
presence of a single poem "Inscriptions" foreshadows the important grouping eventually developed under that title. "Drum-
Taps" and "Songs of Parting" demonstrate a continuation of
the poet's interest in the arrangement of individual lyrics into
unified groups. Even more important is the shift of "Children
of Adam" and "Calamus." Here for the first time it becomes
clear that Whitman is reinforcing the relationships between his
groups by care in arrangement. Except for the development of
"Inscriptions" into a group and a few minor adjustments, the
first hundred and fifty pages of the 1881 *Leaves* have taken
shape. The pattern is established: "Inscriptions," "Starting
from Paumanok," "Song of Myself," "Children of Adam,"
"Calamus," and "Salut au Monde!" "Drum-Taps" and "Songs

of Parting" are to undergo considerable internal modification, but they have found positions in relation to one another and to the first 150 pages, which they are to retain. "By Blue Ontario's Shore," one of the prophetic poems regarding national development, is shifted to a position following "Drum-Taps."

The new concern for arrangement which Whitman reveals in preparing the 1867 edition is accompanied by thoughtful attention to revision within individual poems. Many of these revisions are pertinent to this study. First, there is a new effort toward compression and intensity of expression. Excellent examples of this can be seen in major revisions in "For You O Democracy,"[28] "A Song for Occupations,"[29] "On the Beach at Night Alone,"[30] "Laws for Creations,"[31] "To a Historian,"[32] and "So Long!"[33] Second, there is a decided tendency toward toning down the sensuality and shock-expressions in the poems outside of "Children of Adam" and "Calamus." Such changes can be seen in "As the Time Draws Nigh,"[34] "Out of the Cradle Endlessly Rocking,"[35] "As I Ebb'd with the Ocean of Life,"[36] and in sections of "Song of Myself,"[37] "Song of the Broad-Axe,"[38] and "A Song for Occupations."[39] Third, there are additions to poems written before the war which take into account that significant event either by direct reference to it or by vivid pictures drawn from it. It is interesting to note that these additions are found only in those poems destined to follow "Drum-Taps" and in "Starting from Paumanok," and "Song of Myself," the great introductory poems which are designed to fore-

[28] *1860*, pp. 349–351; *1867*, pp. 125–126.
[29] *1860*, pp. 143–158; *1867*, pp. 239–248.
[30] *1860*, pp. 229–231; *1867*, p. 315.
[31] *1860*, pp. 185–186; *1867*, p. 317.
[32] *1860*, p. 181; *1867*, p. 31.
[33] *1860*, pp. 451–456; *1867*, pp. 33–36.
[34] *1860*, pp. 449–450; *1867*, p. 27.
[35] *1860*, p. 269; *1867*, p. 199.
[36] *1860*, p. 197; *1867*, p. 332.
[37] *1860*, pp. 40–41; *1867*, pp. 38–39.
[38] *1860*, p. 139; *1867*, p. 180.
[39] *1860*, p. 158; *1867*, p. 244.

shadow all of *Leaves of Grass*.[40] There are a few other evidences of growing concern for the national life occasioned by the anxieties of war; these can be seen in "Song of the Broad-Axe,"[41] where major revisions make it a poem of the "shape of the nation," and in "With Antecedents," where the sense of national turmoil receives new emphasis.[42] Fourth, there are extensive changes in "By Blue Ontario's Shore." Here is the first clear-cut evidence of an awareness of an evolving pattern precise enough to require that a relocated poem undergo major revision. When "By Blue Ontario's Shore" is shifted from a position comparatively early in the volume to one following "Drum-Taps," the entire poem is revised to take into consideration the war and its effect on both poet and nation.[43] Accompanying these changes are modifications in tone and emphasis resulting in a more reflective and controlled expression.[44] The concluding section with the refrain "the war is over" is an addition of major importance.[45]

These observations indicate that between 1861 and 1867 Whitman's major literary interest was in recording the war experience of himself and the nation in "Drum-Taps" and in honoring the great personality emerging from that war, Lincoln. Significant for us here is the fact that accompanying this interest was a new concern for matters of tone and organization throughout *Leaves of Grass*; a new consciousness of an evolving pattern can be detected in revisions taking into account the development of the nation and poet and in the relocation of poems in relation to those groups which have taken on a definite quality and function (i.e., "Children of Adam," "Calamus," "Drum-Taps," and "Songs of Parting").

---

[40] *1867*, pp. 7, 26, 90.

[41] *1860*, pp. 140–142; *1867*, pp. 180–182.

[42] *1860*, pp. 174–176; *1867*, pp. 182–184.

[43] *1867*, pp. 3, 9, 12, 18 (Sequel to *Drum-Taps*).

[44] *1860*, p. 109; *1867*, p. 4 (Sequel to *Drum-Taps*). *1860*, p. 118; *1867*, p. 14 (Sequel to *Drum-Taps*).

[45] *1867*, pp. 20–21 (Sequel to *Drum-Taps*).

It has been suggested that up to the 1867 edition the piece-by-piece development of *Leaves* took its character from two main ideas, that of the grand individual ("Song of Myself," 1855) and that of the nation ("Songs of Democracy" and "By Blue Ontario's Shore," 1856) and from the attempt to present the true relationship of the two ("Children of Adam" and "Calamus," 1860). "Out of the Cradle Endlessly Rocking" (1860) anticipates the songs of the soul and death, ultimately realized in the "Passage to India" poems of 1872. These poems were delayed; war intervened, an event whose full impact Whitman could not have anticipated, an event opening new, undreamed-of poetic vistas. And the event came at the right moment for the poet—at that moment when he was contemplating poems which, according to his own testimony, he felt unprepared to write, true poems of the soul. Thus the pensive, at times faltering, poems of "Drum-Taps" become the central poems of *Leaves*. When Whitman repeatedly claimed this, he must have had in mind their central position in the actual process of poetic vision and composition as well as in the final arrangement of *Leaves* itself. This group is singularly vital in any study of the development of an over-all plan for *Leaves of Grass* for two reasons: it was the revelation which ultimately caused Whitman to see that his two proposed volumes, the first of "poems of the body," the second of "poems of the soul," should be one; and it made him see in a new light a country that was no more static and detached than the poet at its center, the development of the one paralleling in many ways the development of the other. The first of these points must await discussion until the approach to the 1876 edition. The second is of immediate concern, for it finds confirmation in what happens to "By Blue Ontario's Shore." When that poem was moved to a position immediately after "Drum-Taps," it was supplemented with passages indicating a new oneness of the poet and the nation emerged from the war. There are two notable additions demonstrating this:

As I sat alone, by blue Ontario's shore,
As I mused of these mighty days and of peace return'd,
    and the dead that return no more,
A Phantom, gigantic, superb, with stern visage,
    accost'd me;
Chant me a poem, it said, of the range of the high
    Soul of Poets,
And chant me, before you go, the Song of the throes
    of Democracy.

(Democracy—the destined conqueror—yet treacherous
    lip-smiles everywhere,
And Death and infidelity at every step.) [46]

. . . .

For the great Idea!
For that we live my brethren—that is the mission
    of poets.

With their poems of stern defiance, ever ready,
With songs of the rapid arming, and the march,
And the flag of peace quickfolded, and the song,
    instead, of the flag we know,
The flag of the youths and veterans—flaunting flag,
Warlike flag of the great Idea.

(Angry cloth I saw there leaping!
I stand again in the leaden rain, your flapping
    folds saluting;
I sing you over all, flying, beckoning through the
    fight—O the hard-contested fight!

. . . .

Now the corpses tumble curl'd upon the ground,
Cold, cold in death, for precious life of you,
Angry cloth I saw there leaping.) [47]

---

[46] *1867*, p. 3 (Sequel to *Drum-Taps*).
[47] *1867*, p. 12 (Sequel to *Drum-Taps*).

It is this common experience of war, from which both poet
and nation emerge more powerful and dedicated than ever,
that seems to have suggested the concept of a simultaneous
development of the two. The interplay of the personal and
national themes in "Drum-Taps" itself and in "By Blue Ontario's Shore" is immediate evidence of this; however, it was
not until the last years before 1881 when the poet was giving
practically all of his attention to the final arrangement of *Leaves
of Grass* that this new concept became apparent throughout.

The new spirituality with which both poet and nation arise
from the muck of war is beautifully demonstrated in "When
Lilacs Last in the Dooryard Bloom'd." By restating the theme
of "Out of the Cradle Endlessly Rocking" in a new and more
confident manner, Whitman indicates the effect of the war on
poet and nation. For the first time we get that absence of questioning and that triumphant spirituality so characteristic of the
songs to follow. An examination of the editions of 1872 and
1876 shows that this poem was separated from "Drum-Taps" to
become a part of the "Passage to India" annex. The tug of
"Drum-Taps" on one side and the tug of "Passage to India"
on the other are symbolic of the situation pointing up for Whitman the fact that the intervening, unforeseen circumstances of
his war experience produced in "Drum-Taps" that unmistakable bridge between the poems of the body and the poems of
the soul which afforded easy passage from the one to the other;
the extremes of *Leaves of Grass* in finding their juncture have
justified the poet's persistent faith in the interdependence of
the material and the spiritual. "Drum-Taps" records a recognition experience the results of which, as the source of new ideas
for the organization of *Leaves of Grass* as a whole, were not
fully realized until 1881. That these results were already on the
way is suggested in two new poems, "As I Ponder'd in Silence"
and "To Thee Old Cause." The second concludes:

> Thou orb of many orbs!
> Thou seething principle! Thou well-kept, latent
>   germ! Thou centre!

Around the idea of thee the strange sad war revolving.
With all its angry and vehement play of causes,
(With yet unknown results to come, for thrice a
    thousand years,)
These recitatives for thee—my Book and the War are one,
Merged in this spirit I and mine—as the contest
    hinged on thee,
As a wheel on its axis turns, this Book unwitting
    to itself,
Around the Idea of thee.[48]

THE 1872 EDITION

New Poems (33)

Inscriptions (5)

1. As I Ponder'd in Silence
2. In Cabin'd Ships at Sea
3. For Him I Sing
4. To Thee Old Cause
5. Still Though the One I Sing

Calamus (1)

6. The Base of All Metaphysics

Sea-Drift (1)

7. On the Beach at Night

By the Roadside (2)

8. Gods
9. Gliding o'er All

Drum-Taps (3)

10. Adieu to a Soldier
11. Delicate Cluster
12. Ethiopia Saluting the Colors

Memories of President Lincoln (1)

13. This Dust Was Once the Man

[48] *1872*, pp. 11–12.

Autumn Rivulets (5)

14. The Return of the Heroes
15. The Singer in the Prison
16. Warble for Lilac-Time
17. Sparkles from the Wheel
18. Outlines for a Tomb

Spiritual Songs (2)

19. Passage to India
20. Proud Music of the Storm

Whispers of Heavenly Death (7)

21. Whispers of Heavenly Death
22. Darest Thou Now O Soul
23. Of Him I Love Day and Night
24. A Noiseless Patient Spider
25. The Last Invocation
26. As I Watch'd the Ploughman Ploughing
27. Pensive and Faltering

Songs of Parting (6)

28. Now Finalè to the Shore
29. As They Draw to a Close
30. The Untold Want
31. Portals
32. These Carols
33. Joy, Shipmate, Joy!

The thirty-three new poems of 1872 fall for the most part into two main categories: ten poems (listed under "Inscriptions," "Calamus," "Drum-Taps," and "Memories of President Lincoln") written in the light of the war and postwar experience to fill in gaps or attain new emphasis in groupings already established, and fifteen poems of a new, triumphant spirituality, resulting from the revelation recorded in "Passage to India." (These are listed under "Spiritual Songs," "Whispers of Heavenly Death," and "Songs of Parting.") These latter poems are the real contribution of the edition, for they are all marked by a spirituality which is beyond all questioning, all sense of strife, and are in that respect different from those that have gone before. The remaining eight poems join the hundred or so already published which are biding their time in a sort of spiritual and poetic limbo until a proper place is established for them.

A study of the order of the poems of 1872 shows a further advance in grouping. The four Lincoln poems are brought together, although they are given no group title; the nucleus of "Sea-Drift" is formed (under the title "Sea-Shore Memories"); the major poems of "Whispers of Heavenly Death" are brought together under that title. Finally, the group "Songs of Insurrection," though broken up later, is further evidence of the concern with organization. A glance at the over-all pattern reveals one particular circumstance of significance—"Drum-Taps" has definitely found its place in the center of the volume. In addition, with the exceptions of "The Sleepers," "There Was a Child Went Forth," "Pioneers! O Pioneers!" "A Song of Joys," and "Sea-Drift," all the major poems and all the groups already formed have found their appropriate positions either fore or aft of "Drum-Taps."

The key to a number of important changes within the poems is found in a passage added to "By Blue Ontario's Shore," "As a wheel turns on its axle, so I find my chants turning finally on the war."[49] It is this new awareness of the significance of the war that causes revisions and additions in "As I Walk These Broad Majestic Days,"[50] "To a Foil'd European Revolutionaire,"[51] "Ashes of Soldiers,"[52] and "Shut Not Your Doors" (the particular addition referred to in this poem is dropped later when the poem is relocated among "Inscriptions").[53] Whitman has come to view the war experience recorded in

[49] *1872*, p. 327.
[50] *1872*, p. 338.
[51] *1872*, pp. 364–365.
[52] *1872*, p. 24 (*Passage to India*).
[53] *1872*, pp. 117–118 (*Passage to India*).

"Drum-Taps" as the central experience in the history of the
nation, in *Leaves of Grass*, and in his own life. Here is a new
revelation through which the poet begins to see more clearly
a principle of unity in all that he has written and to achieve
new spiritual heights in his poetry as he focuses his attention
upon the post–"Drum-Taps" elements of *Leaves of Grass*.

Among these elements are found those poems of the spirit
and death which were anticipated prematurely in "Out of the
Cradle Endlessly Rocking." "Passage to India," from which
the annex of spiritual songs gets its title, is the key to these
fifteen new poems. It marks another major advance in the evolution of *Leaves of Grass*. As Whitman comes to revere the ties
between the development of the nation and his own development, a national event becomes a symbol of the destiny of both
nation and poet. In the completion of the Suez Canal, of the
transcontinental railroad, and of the transatlantic cable, Whitman sees God's plan:

> The earth to be spann'd, connected by network,
> The people to become brothers and sisters,
> The races, neighbors, to marry and be given in marriage,
> The oceans to be cross'd, the distant brought near,
> The lands to be welded together.
>
> (A Worship new, I sing;
> You captains, voyagers, explorers, yours!
> You engineers! you architects, machinists, yours!
> You, not for trade or transportation only,
> But in God's name, and for thy sake, O soul.) [54]

The first part of the poem focuses attention on the role of
America as the culmination of the divine purpose.

> Again Vasco de Gama sails forth;
> Again the knowledge gain'd, the mariner's compass,
> Lands found, and nations born—thou born, America,
>   (a hemisphere unborn,)

[54] *1872*, p. 6 (*Passage to India*).

For purpose vast, man's long probation fill'd,
Thou, rondure of the world, at last accomplish'd.[55]

The second portion of the poem focuses upon the role of
the poet. Here unfolded before him is the verification of the
dream of a dead visionary, and through it he seizes upon the
hope that his greater vision—the vision of the true significance
of the act that Columbus dreamed of—will also in time be
verified.

O soul repressless, I with thee and thou with me,
Thy circumnavigation of the world begin;
Of man, the voyage of his mind's return,
To reason's early paradise,
Back, back to wisdom's birth, to innocent intuitions,
Again with fair Creation.[56]

Thus from the bosom of America there sprang her second
Columbus, projecting the yet unfulfilled significance of all that
the first had dreamed. At last Whitman has given full expression to the poet-nation relationship; later critical remarks
indicate that at the time of this expression his mind was cleared
for defining in new ways relationships long since latent in
Leaves of Grass as a whole. In fact, he says this in the poem
itself:

With inscrutable purpose—some hidden, prophetic
    intention;
Now, first, it seems, my thought begins to span
    thee.[57]

And at this point he demonstrates the nature of this revelation
in terms reminiscent of his "Children of Adam" and the Christ-
symbol of "Song of Myself." Adam and Eve and their myriad
progeny, feverish children, shall find solace in the true Son of
God who shall come singing his songs.[58] It is obvious that the

[55] *1872*, p. 8 (*Passage to India*).
[56] *1872*, p. 12 (*Passage to India*).
[57] *1872*, p. 8 (*Passage to India*).
[58] *1872*, pp. 8–9 (*Passage to India*).

revelation of "Passage to India" relates to *Leaves of Grass* as a whole, as well as to the spiritual songs that follow it. Thus another great poem joins the company of "Starting from Paumanok," "Out of the Cradle Endlessly Rocking," "Drum-Taps," "When Lilacs Last in the Dooryard Bloom'd," and "By Blue Ontario's Shore" as a milestone in the evolution of the final structure and significance of *Leaves of Grass*.

THE 1876 EDITION (2 VOLS.)
New Poems (29)

> *Inscriptions* (1)
> 1. Eidólons
>
> *Songs of Democracy* (2)
> 2. Song of the Exposition
> 3. Song of the Redwood-Tree
>
> *Birds of Passage* (1)
> 4. Song of the Universal
>
> *Sea-Drift* (2)
> 5. After the Sea-Ship
> 6. Song for All Seas, All Ships
>
> *Drum-Taps* (1)
> 7. Virginia—the West
>
> *Autumn Rivulets* (7)
> 8. Two Rivulets
> 9. Or From That Sea of Time
>   (passages from 8 and 9 later included in "As Consequent, Etc.")
> 10. Out from Behind This Mask
> 11. The Ox-Tamer
> 12. Wandering at Morn
> 13. An Old Man's Thought of School
> 14. With All Thy Gifts
> 15. O Star of France

Spiritual Songs (1)
16. Prayer of Columbus

17. Thou Mother with Thy Equal Brood

From Noon to Starry Night (4)
18. Spain
19. To a Locomotive in Winter
20. The Mystic Trumpeter
21. By Broad Potomac's Shore

Songs of Parting (1)
22. My Legacy

Not in 1881 (7)
23. As in a Swoon
24. The Beauty of the Ship
25. When the Full-Grown Poet Came
26. After an Interval
27. From My Last Years
28. In Former Songs
29. One Song, America, Before I Go

"Thou Mother with thy Equal Brood" is the most characteristic poem of the twenty-five new ones appearing in Volume II (*Two Rivulets*) of the 1876 edition. It combines the two themes dominating the majority of the poems. The first is reflection upon the nature and purpose of the true poet of the modern world, and the second, prophecy of the ultimate realization of freedom and brotherhood in America. Both themes are developed also in "Song of the Exposition" and "Wandering at Morn." Attention is focused upon the poet in "Out from Behind This Mask," "Song of the Universal," "By Broad Potomac's Shore," "Prayer of Columbus," "My Legacy," "Two Rivulets," "From My Last Years," and "In Former Songs." The element of prophecy dominates "The Mystic Trumpeter," "Spain," "O Star of France," "Song of the Redwood-Tree," "Or From That Sea of Time," "One Song, America, Before I Go," and in a

special sense "An Old Man's Thought of School." Of the remaining seven poems "Eidólons," one of Whitman's most effective expressions of his concept of the interdependence of
matter and spirit, body and soul, is by far the most important.
"After the Sea-Ship," "The Ox-Tamer," and "To a Locomotive in Winter" are beautiful examples of concrete picture-
poems such as those encountered frequently in "Drum-Taps."
"Song for All Seas, All Ships," "With All Thy Gifts," and
"Virginia—the West" are difficult to classify. Finally, the new
poems which are included in Volume I *Leaves of Grass* ("As in
a Swoon," "The Beauty of the Ship," "When the Full-Grown
Poet Came," and "After an Interval") do not concern us particularly because it is obvious that they were inserted as space
fillers. They were discarded in 1881.

Turning to the matter of arrangement, we find that Volume
I of the 1876 edition is little more than a reprint of the 1872
edition minus the "Passage to India" annex. The pagination is
unchanged, unaffected by the insertion of the four new poems.
"Passage to India" becomes the concluding section of Volume
II. It is also a reprint of 1872, pagination unchanged. Falling
between these two and comprising the first and larger portion of
Volume II are the twenty-five new poems already discussed.
They appear under the group titles "Two Rivulets," "Centennial Songs—1876," and "As a Strong Bird on Pinions Free"
and are accompanied by two prose prefaces, footnotes, and
two independent prose tracts, "Democratic Vistas" and "Memoranda during the War." This interruption of the poetry with
prose passages is unique in the history of Whitman publication,
as is the separation of his poems into two volumes. Suffice it to
say here that Whitman makes it clear in the preface to "Two
Rivulets" that he considers the two volumes as one.[59]

The order of the poems of 1876, then, is in essence that of
1872, with this important exception: "Passage to India" is preceded by twenty-five poems which look backward to the gradual
development of the poet and the nation, give expression to a

[59] *1876*, II, 9.

state of comparative maturity and enlightenment not easily attained, and look forward to the prophetic and spiritual utterances of the concluding poems of *Leaves of Grass*. It is significant that in both function and location these poems are harbin-
gers of the two final groupings, "Autumn Rivulets" and "From
Noon to Starry Night."

More important to this study than the actual poetry of 1876
is a consideration of the two-volume plan and of some pertinent
passages from its prose preface. As indicated earlier, at times
during the development of *Leaves of Grass* Whitman enter-
tained the idea of two volumes, one containing "poems of the
body" and one "poems of the soul." There is evidence that this
idea began to fade after the emergence of "Drum-Taps," when
new concepts of relationships began to form. Even if this were
not true, it is hardly possible to take the edition of 1876 as a
healthy, enthusiastic attempt to carry out the two-volume plan.
If Volume II were seen as the fulfillment of the original concept of the "poems of the soul," how can one explain the presence of such groups as "Two Rivulets," "Centennial Songs,"
and "As a Strong Bird on Pinions Free," to say nothing of
"Democratic Vistas"? In 1875–1876 Whitman was an ill man
and fancied himself at the very brink of death. The 1876 edition
was a desperate attempt at one last publication. In view of
what had been happening after "Drum-Taps" Whitman could
hardly have been pleased with the hodgepodge nature of Volume
II. It may be that he no longer relished the idea of two volumes at all, but found himself in a position where time seemed
to be running out and rushed his edition through. His preface
to *Two Rivulets* is a brave attempt to justify the arrangement of
the work; however, to the perceptive reader it is filled with
plaintive undertones.

At the eleventh hour, under grave illness, I gather up the pieces
of Prose and Poetry left over since publishing, a while since, my
first and main Volume, LEAVES OF GRASS—pieces here, some new,
some old—nearly all of them (sombre as many are, making this

almost Death's book) composed in bygone atmospheres of perfect
health—and, preceded by the freshest collection, the little Two
RIVULETS, and by this rambling Prefatory gossip, now send them
out, embodied in the present Melange, partly as my contribution
and outpouring to celebrate, in some sort, the feature of the time,
the first Centennial of our New World Nationality—and then as
chyle and nutriment to that moral, Indissoluble Union, equally
representing All, and the mother of many coming Centennials.

And e'en for flush and proof of our America—for reminder, just
as much, or more, in moods of towering pride and joy, I keep
my special chants of Death and Immortality to Stamp the coloring-
finish of all, present and past. For terminus and temperer to all,
they were originally written; and that shall be their office at the
last.[60]

This first statement is brave, but, as the preface wanders on, it
is compromised. Whitman begins to "protest too much" as he
attempts to justify the disjointed mixture of themes and of
poetry and prose to follow. The attempt ends in this unexpected
statement which, it seems to me, throws true light on his
dilemma:

The varieties and phases, (doubtless often paradoxical, contradictory,) of the two Volumes, of LEAVES, and of these RIVULETS,
are ultimately to be considered as One in structure, and as mu-
tually explanatory of each other—. . . Of the former Book, more
vehement, and perhaps pursuing a central idea with greater closeness—join'd with the present One, extremely varied in theme—
I can only briefly reiterate here, that all my pieces, alternated
through Both, are only of use and value, if any, as such an inter-
penetrating, composite, inseparable Unity.[61]

Finally, in a footnote, Whitman says:

It was originally my intention, after chanting in LEAVES OF
GRASS the songs of the Body and Existence, to then compose a fur-

60 *1876*, II, 5–6.
61 *1876*, II, 9–10.

ther, equally needed Volume, based on these convictions of per-
petuity and conservation which, enveloping all precedents, make
the unseen Soul govern absolutely at last. . . .

But the full construction of such a work (even if I lay the
foundation, or give impetus to it) is beyond my powers, and must
remain for some bard in the future. . . .

Meanwhile, not entirely to give the go-by to my original plan,
and far more to avoid a mark'd hiatus in it, than to entirely fulfil
it, I end my books with thoughts, or radiations from thoughts, on
Death, Immortality, and a free entrance into the Spiritual world.[62]

These remarks seem to imply that the two-volume plan
originally in mind had been abandoned. The story of what took
place between 1876 and 1881, when the poet had more time
than he dreamed of, suggests that this abandonment was occasioned by something more than the press of time. Be that as
it may, this preface of 1876 is filled with passages showing how
much considerations of the over-all structure of *Leaves* were
weighing on the poet's mind. It is here that he comments on the
importance of "Passage to India" in giving fuller expression
to what, from the first, lurks in his writings, "underneath every
page, every line, everywhere."[63] He comments at length on the
war theme and the four years' war around which his book revolves—" 'Drum-Taps' being pivotal to the rest entire." He sees
in his poetry a running commentary dealing at once with the
rapid growth of the great individual and the United States of
the nineteenth century, a chronology finding its climax in the
death of President Lincoln.[64] He concludes, "Out of the Hundred Years just ending, (1776–1876,) with their genesis of
inevitable wilful events, and new introductions, and many un-
precedented things of war and peace, . . . and especially out of
the immediately preceding Twenty-Five Years, . . . with all their
rapid changes, . . . my Poems too have found genesis."[65]

[62] *1876*, II, 6–7.
[63] *1876*, II, 5 (footnote).
[64] *1876*, II, 9–10.
[65] *1876*, II, 14.

This is the frame of mind in which we leave Whitman in 1876. It is not surprising to discover in 1881 that the intervening years have been given not so much to new composition as to a reevaluation and rearrangement of the old. Prefaces are gone. *Leaves of Grass* now speaks for itself with a new eloquence all its own. One look at the 1881 edition leaves little doubt that here is the final form wished for in the 1876 preface. The pertinent passages in that preface were not so much a justification of that edition as an expression of the poet's regret that an appropriate organization had not yet been achieved.

THE 1881 EDITION

New Poems (19)

> *Inscriptions* (1)
> 1. Thou Reader
>
> 2. Youth, Day, Old Age and Night
>
>> *Sea-Drift* (2)
> 3. To the Man-of-War-Bird
> 4. Patroling Barnegat
>
>> *By the Roadside* (3)
> 5. The Dalliance of the Eagles
> 6. Roaming in Thought
> 7. Hast Never Come to Thee an Hour
>
>> *Autumn Rivulets* (3)
> 8. Italian Music in Dakota
> 9. My Picture-Gallery
> 10. The Prairie States
>
> 11. A Paumanok Picture
>
>> *From Noon to Starry Night* (6)
> 12. Thou Orb Aloft Full-Dazzling
> 13. A Riddle Song
> 14. From Far Dakota's Cañons
> 15. What Best I See in Thee

16. Spirit That Form'd This Scene
17. A Clear Midnight

Songs of Parting (2)
18. As at Thy Portals Also Death
19. The Sobbing of the Bells

NOTE: "Youth, Day, Old Age and Night" and "A Paumanok Picture" are two of four space fillers in the 1881 edition.

The new poems of 1881 can be divided broadly into three groups. The first, consisting of very short, isolated pictures, includes "To the Man-of-War-Bird," "Patroling Barnegat," "The Dalliance of the Eagles," and "A Paumanok Picture." The second, consisting of brief, isolated thoughts on a variety of subjects, includes "Thou Reader," "Youth, Day, Old Age and Night," "Roaming in Thought," "Hast Never Come to Thee an Hour," "Italian Music in Dakota," "My Picture-Gallery," "The Prairie States," "What Best I See in Thee," "Spirit That Form'd This Scene," "A Clear Midnight," "As at Thy Portals Also Death," and "The Sobbing of the Bells." These short poems, it seems, were composed for the most part to fill out newly developed groups; in fact, nine of the sixteen find places among groupings which took shape between 1876 and 1881. The third group is composed of longer poems, "Thou Orb Aloft Full-Dazzling," "A Riddle Song," and "From Far Dakota's Cañons," all three of which become key lyrics in "From Noon to Starry Night." The first was apparently created as the introductory poem for the cluster. As such it points up the relationship of the grouping to the rest of *Leaves* and sounds the phrases from which its group title is drawn.

The changes in arrangement taking place between 1876 and 1881 were the most important in the entire development of the volume. To begin with, four new groups came into being, "Birds of Passage," "By the Roadside," "Autumn Rivulets," and "From Noon to Starry Night." "Birds of Passage" was made up for the most part of poems coming after "Drum-Taps"

in the 1876 edition. Only two of the poems were in the approximate position of the present group; they were "With
Antecedents" and "Year of Meteors." "By the Roadside" was
a completely new group made up of poems formerly scattered
throughout the volume; prior to its appearance in 1881 there
was no nuclear cluster and no way to anticipate its coming.
The beginnings of "Autumn Rivulets" are more obvious. The
name is a modification of the title "Two Rivulets," and the
first two poems of that annex were united to become the introductory poem of the group. In addition, six of the poems from
"Two Rivulets" found a place within it. These poems were
joined by thirteen lyrics which had already been grouped together late in the "Passage to India" annex and five poems already situated in the approximate location taken by the new
group. Three of the poems were new, and the remaining ten
were scattered throughout the 1876 edition. Turning to "From
Noon to Starry Night," we find that six of its key poems were
composed between 1876 and 1881. The rest of the poems were
scattered in 1876, all except two being located immediately
after "Drum-Taps" or among the concluding poems of the
"Passage to India" annex.

These four new groups were just one phase of Whitman's
final reorganization. Of comparable importance was the expansion of many of those groups already in existence. "Inscriptions" was increased from nine to twenty-four poems. One of
these additional fifteen poems, "Thou Reader," was new; the
remainder were either outside any titled grouping or from
temporary groups which were broken up ("Songs of Insurrection," "The Answerer," and "Now Finalè to the Shore"). Of
the four poems added to "Sea-Drift," two were new and two
were taken from discontinued groupings ("Centennial Songs"
and "Two Rivulets"). Of the eleven poems added to "Drum-
Taps," five were taken from "Bathed in War's Perfume" and
three from "Marches Now the War Is Over"; three were poems
that had not been grouped previously. Five poems from the
"Passage to India" annex were added to "Whispers of Heaven-

ly Death." "When I Heard the Learn'd Astronomer" and "To Rich Givers" were removed from "Songs of Parting" and eleven poems were added. The latter were drawn mainly from the broken groups "Now Finalè to the Shore" and "Ashes of Soldiers." Thus all of the short, so-called limbo poems finally found their places within the permanent, titled groups, and all of the minor clusters of a temporary nature were broken up and their poems distributed among larger groups.

It now remains to look at the order of the groups and the major poems which were left to function individually. "Inscriptions," "Starting from Paumanok," "Song of Myself," "Children of Adam," and "Calamus" fall into their permanent positions without further rearrangement. Since all the poems of secondary importance had been gathered into clusters, the following major poems were left (in the order given) between "Calamus" and "Drum-Taps": "Salut au Monde!" "Our Old Feuillage," "Song of the Broad-Axe," "Song of the Open Road," "Crossing Brooklyn Ferry," "Song of the Answerer," "A Song for Occupations," "The Sleepers," "A Song of the Rolling Earth," and "A Broadway Pageant." Following "Drum-Taps" (in Volume I) was "By Blue Ontario's Shore." Moving to Volume II, we find the ungrouped major poems left in the following order: "Prayer of Columbus," "Song of the Exposition," "Song of the Redwood-Tree," "Thou Mother with Thy Equal Brood," "Passage to India," "Proud Music of the Storm," "A Song of Joys," and "To Think of Time." Only three major shifts were made. "The Sleepers" was moved over to join "To Think of Time" among the spiritual songs, and "Song of the Exposition" and "Song of the Redwood-Tree" were shifted forward to join the earlier "Songs of Democracy." The final relationships established among these poems have already been analyzed in Chapter IV. The second major shift involves "A Broadway Pageant," "By Blue Ontario's Shore," and "Thou Mother with Thy Equal Brood," the three prophetic poems Whitman evidently wanted to stand apart from the rest. The first two were left in the approximate positions of 1876,

"A Broadway Pageant" being set off from "Songs of Democracy" by "Birds of Passage." "Thou Mother with Thy
Equal Brood" was moved to a late position in the volume just
before "From Noon to Starry Night," the group with which it
has most in common. Finally, "Youth, Day, Old Age and
Night," "Reversals," "Transpositions," and "A Paumanok
Picture," the four short poems left standing alone, were inserted where needed as space fillers. Turning from individual
poems to clusters, we find only two major shifts. The most important is the relocation of "Sea-Drift" from the "Passage to
India" annex to a pre–"Drum-Taps" position. The second is
the shift of "Songs of Parting" to the end of *Leaves,* where it
replaces the "Now Finalè to the Shore" of 1876, absorbing
most of the poems from that earlier grouping. The newly
organized "Autumn Rivulets" and "From Noon to Starry
Night" take positions approximating those of their nuclear
poems.

Nearly all the revisions within the poems of 1881 seem to
be the result of a consideration of the over-all pattern of *Leaves
of Grass* and of the new locations and functions assigned to
the poems concerned. Exceptions are the three minor additions
to "Song of Myself" which seem to have been added merely as
echoes of the new title. They are "I sing myself," "not a person
or object missing, absorbing to myself and for this song," and
"of these one and all I weave the song of myself."[66] In "Shut
Not Your Doors," a poem moved from the "Passage to India"
annex to "Inscriptions," an ending involving an intensely
spiritual theme was discarded and the poem rendered purely
introductory in nature.[67] "Salut au Monde!" retained its position following "Calamus"; however, its function as the first
poem reaching beyond America to all mankind was empha-
sized by a careful weeding out of all American scenes and other
passages of little relevance to its international theme.[68] The

[66] *1881,* pp. 29, 38, 42.
[67] *1881,* p. 17.
[68] *1876,* I, 146, 148, 149, 150, 152, 153, 156, 157; *1881,* pp. 114–123.

change from "Toward all" to "Toward you all, in America's name" points up the new emphasis achieved by the revisions.[69] A transitional passage was added at the beginning of "Song of the Exposition,"[70] and another discarded at the beginning of "A Song for Occupations" because of their new locations.[71] "Song of the Banner at Daybreak" was moved from its post– "Drum-Taps" position to become a part of "Drum-Taps" itself. All passages referring to the fact that the war was over were carefully deleted.[72] "By Blue Ontario's Shore" became clearly a poem of postwar optimism as somewhat bitter passages concerning the old poetic forms and function were dropped.[73] "Two Rivulets" and "Or From That Sea of Time" were revised when combined to form "As Consequent, Etc." the poem that introduces "Autumn Rivulets," giving the group its name.[74] "The Sleepers," upon joining the late songs of the spirit, was relieved of two discordant passages, the sensual passage beginning "O hot-cheek'd and blushing" and the dark passage beginning "Now Lucifer was not dead."[75] Finally, "Thou Mother with Thy Equal Brood" was given a new introductory section emphasizing its prophetic nature.[76]

A final interpretation of these changes of 1881 should begin with a backward glance at Whitman's actual accomplishments up to that time in setting his poems in order. Briefly, he had already formed the following permanent groups of poems and arranged them in the order given: "Inscriptions," "Children of Adam," "Calamus," "Drum-Taps," "Songs of Parting," "Memories of President Lincoln," "Whispers of Heavenly Death," and "Sea-Drift." As we have seen, only two of these groups were shifted drastically in 1881. "Songs of Parting" was moved to the end of the volume. As soon as "Passage to India" was

---

[69] *1876*, I, 157; *1881*, p. 120.
[70] *1881*, p. 157.
[71] *1876*, I, 209; *1881*, p. 169.
[72] *1876*, I, 352, 355; *1881*, pp. 223–227.
[73] *1876*, I, 311, 327; *1881*, pp. 264–275.
[74] *1881*, pp. 277–278.
[75] *1876*, I, 222–223, 226.
[76] *1881*, pp. 346–347.

brought into the body of *Leaves of Grass*, this shift was inevitable. At the time of relocation it absorbed the similar group
"Now Finalè to the Shore," which had ended the "Passage to
India" annex. These two groups were obviously serving a similar purpose. Whitman's unwillingness to separate "Songs of
Parting" from the early poems (Volume I) of 1876 (a separation which would have seemed natural if he had been given
wholeheartedly to the original idea of two volumes) suggests
his growing sense of the oneness of all that he had to say—a
concept which eventually triumphed.

It will be recalled that the poem which is the key to "Sea-
Drift," "Out of the Cradle Endlessly Rocking," came early in
the composition of *Leaves*. Its shift to the "Passage to India"
annex, in 1876, along with the Lincoln poems, was probably
based on consideration of subject matter. That Whitman was
aware of chronology even then, however, is suggested by the
temporary title given the group, "Sea-Shore Memories." As
we have seen, the poems and prose of 1867, 1872, and 1876
show that Whitman was becoming increasingly conscious of the
fact that he was recording the development of both nation and
poet—the pattern of which was being determined by unforeseen, momentous events of the nineteenth century. His creation
of "Birds of Passage" and the restoration of "Out of the
Cradle Endlessly Rocking" to an early position are indicative
of what was happening in the reorganization of *Leaves of Grass*
between 1876 and 1881. "Birds of Passage" records the final
stages of America's pioneer days and of the poet's youthful
growth. In "Sea-Drift" the nation has reached the West Coast;
with frontiers lost, it turns in upon itself and is soon to face up
to internal strife and adjustment. The poet is faced with a
similar experience. The sobering inquietudes of both poet and
nation are vital in preparing them for the stern realities of
war. Whitman had found time to crystallize the ideas that had
been shaping, but they were still a little confused in 1876.

The broad outlines of 1881 had already emerged in the
groups recording the early development of poet and nation,

the group depicting the major crises of poet and nation, and the final groups depicting the new, revitalized poet and nation rising triumphantly above these crises. Two bridges, or transitional periods, essential from both a realistic and an artistic point of view, were needed. One was needed between the exuberant story of material and social development and success of "Song of Myself," "Children of Adam," "Calamus," "Songs of Democracy," and "Birds of Passage" and the dark, critical experiences of "Drum-Taps." That need was hardly fulfilled by the brief inquietudes of "Sea-Drift." Scattered poems of doubt and turmoil were collected under "By the Roadside" to perform this function. A second was needed after "Drum-Taps" to depict clearly the renewed vitality of the poet and the nation, as a whole new phase of development was initiated, moving both poet and nation toward spiritual attainments previously undreamed of. Scattered poems of renewed vision and good faith were brought together under the titles "Autumn Rivulets" and "From Noon to Starry Night" to perform this function. Prior to 1881 the main experiences of *Leaves of Grass* had found adequate expression. The final attention of the poet was directed toward those periods of transition which were less vital, but still essential to an accurate re-creation of the development of poet and nation—the dark prewar years, the hopeful years of reconstruction and readjustment for a richer, more perfect peace. It is remarkable that so little final composition was needed to round off a work of such proportions; the essential material was at hand awaiting the proper assignment. A detailed analysis of the final results of 1881 is given in "A Structural Analysis of *Leaves of Grass*."

This chapter has been primarily concerned with the development of *Leaves of Grass* itself. Some interest has been professed in the development of Whitman as an artist. This has been a quite secondary and, in a sense, negative interest. It has seemed advisable to keep the matter in mind lest some revisions and rearrangements which were the result of the developing artistry of the poet be mistaken for evidence of the development of his plan or pattern. Independent of this concern, however, one idea has presented itself repeatedly, which in a general way bears upon any study of the development of *Leaves of Grass*. It is that Whitman displays a mastery of contrasting poetic styles and moods which has not been fully appreciated. The tendency has been to settle upon one of these styles or moods as peculiarly Whitmanian and to lament any deviation from it.

Today most critics agree that the appearance of such superior poems as "Song of Myself," "To Think of Time," and "There Was a Child Went Forth," in the first edition, is evidence of Whitman's maturity as an artist as early as 1855. Too many nineteenth-century critics tended to associate what they considered the particular excellence of "Drum-Taps" and subsequent poems with a major advance in Whitman's basic artistry. Such a view fails to take into account the fact that the progression from the poetic style and form of such poems as "Song of Myself," "I Sing the Body Electric," "Scented Herbage of My Breast," or "Salut au Monde!" (all of which are exquisite poems in their way), to the more compressed, phrase-conscious style of "Bivouac on a Mountain Side," "Old Ireland," or "To a Locomotive in Winter" may not be so much a matter of advance in artistic competence as a matter of the practice of Emerson's idea of "meter-making thoughts." The subjects or events and the emotional experiences rising from them demand different poetic forms. "By Blue Ontario's Shore" is a greater poem after "Drum-Taps" than it was originally. However, the view that the difference is the result of new skill at the time of revision does not take into account the whole story. The new themes growing out of war experience were the true enrichment, bringing with them qualities reminiscent of "Drum-Taps."

An inevitable reaction to this tendency to disparage the early poems has dominated much of the Whitman scholarship of the last decade. We have already commented on recent expressions of preference for early editions, expressions too often accompanied by an unfortunate tendency to disparage the late poems. Chase, for example, goes so far as to declare "Passage to India" the work of a speechmaker rather than a poet and later on states that the war was "Whitman's salvation as a man, but his doom as a poet."[77]

Such views on the part of nineteenth-century critics on the one hand and of such critics as Chase on the other grow out of an oversimplification of the whole matter of style in *Leaves of Grass*. In reality such poems as "Passage to India" and "Thou Mother with Thy Equal Brood" are excellent examples of a combination of the best of the early and late styles where the rich thematic variety admits of it. Whitman shows little inclination to discard or revise either the early or the late poems as if he considered either one or the other inferior from an artistic point of view. At the last he claimed the early poems of materials and the late poems of spirit with equal confidence. As inevitable phases in the development and fruition of healthy human personality and society, one is as essential to the truth as the other. One of Whitman's objections to the New Testament treatment of Christ may have been the fact that the account of his development, vital to every earnest disciple, is largely neglected. He for the most part emerges full-grown, mature, flawlessly spiritual, to accomplish, in three short years, his final mission.

The difference between such groups as "Calamus," "Songs of Democracy," "Drum-Taps," and "Passage to India" is more the result of the development of the subjects than the detached development or disintegration of artistry of expression on Whitman's part. This is, of course, a statement to be qualified; no one would deny that Whitman, like all artists, learned and improved with practice and ebbed from time to time under the stresses of experience and age. Nevertheless, it is a final attempt to suggest that there is still something to be said about the great variety of poetic form and style in *Leaves of Grass*— about the ways in which this variety encourages the careful

[77] Richard Chase, *Walt Whitman Reconsidered*, p. 137.

reader to inquire into the thematic development of the volume.

Both Asselineau and Kuhn have written convincingly of the consistency of Whitman's poetic career and his poetic techniques.[78] The source of this consistency, the gentle, steadying force that kept his heading true, was his dedication to the organic theory of art. *Leaves of Grass* itself is the final vindication of that theory as Whitman championed it. In 1855 the poet gave expression to the scope of his intentions—"faint clews and indirections" as to the enormous stirrings within him. But he did not force the processes of composition. In subsequent editions we find him true to his organic theory, and we see that—free from any rigid, preconceived notions of how his poetic vision would be realized—the growth of *Leaves of Grass* was truly organic. It evolved gradually, the poet not always conscious of the ultimate significance of the component parts as they emerged. To sustain such a free, unobstructed flow of creativity involves humility, bravery, and, above all, dedication.

Striking evidence of the validity of Whitman's theory and practice is the fact that as the "main drifts" established themselves and the processes of shifting and revising subsided, there emerged the final meaningful arrangement which in essence follows the chronology of composition. The major movements of poems were those essential to the expansion of the germ of 1855 without loss of its shape and the basic relationships of its component parts; they are to the imaginative observer fascinating in the way in which they suggest actual "growth." Apart from these movements, shifts are the results of minor matters of transition or addition. The exceptions falling into this category are just frequent enough to accommodate those human variants and inadequacies which always compromise any absolute theory. It may be worthwhile, in con-

---

[78] Asselineau, *The Evolution of Walt Whitman: The Creation of a Book*, pp. 256–257; John G. Kuhn, "Whitman's Artistry: 'Then Reproduce All in My Own Forms,'" *Walt Whitman Review* 8 (September 1962), 51–63.

clusion, to look for a moment at these departures from the order of composition as they appear in the 1881 arrangement.

Because of their introductory function, the poems of "Inscriptions" and "Starting from Paumanok" lie outside our interest here. According to actual date, "Children of Adam" and "Calamus" follow "Songs of Democracy." However, this is hardly a departure from the concept of organic growth or a compromise of its basic logic, since they are an integral part of the progression beginning with "Song of Myself" and ending with "Songs of Democracy." They were created for the purpose of pointing up the transition from the one to the other. In a sense the entire unit (beginning with "Song of Myself" and ending with "Songs of Democracy") was still in the process of growth until "Children of Adam" and "Calamus" clarified this relationship.

More striking is the shift of the late poems, "Song of the Exposition" and "Song of the Redwood-Tree," to positions well in advance of "Drum-Taps." The close association in theme and tone between these poems and the "Songs of Democracy" accounts for this. The concerns of war interrupted the optimistic national character of exuberant development and expansion. With the restoration of peace Whitman saw the country, in the early days of reconstruction, consciously attempting recovery with a vigor reminiscent of pioneer days. It is logical that similar poems would reassert themselves. When Whitman began to visualize clearly the twofold development of *Leaves of Grass*, primarily physical prior to "Drum-Taps" and primarily spiritual thereafter, he had reason to shift these poems to the earlier position. In the final version of *Leaves* the logic of their advent is vindicated. The particular aspects they depict are represented in "Autumn Rivulets," where they are kept appropriately subordinate to more spiritual concepts. Similar conclusions can be drawn regarding "Song of the Universal." "Pioneers! O Pioneers!" presents a more difficult problem. Its new location is apparently the result of the new systematic presentation of the parallel development of nation and poet.

Since the key to "Sea-Drift" is in "Out of the Cradle Endlessly Rocking," it is proper that the group fall into the position dictated by that particular poem. A few of these poems were written late and are characteristic of the final poems of spirituality. Their shift to an early position may have been part of a plan whereby the two sections of *Leaves* would be pulled together and the one shown to be inherent in the other. This same purpose may account for the final departure from the order of composition—the shift of "The Sleepers" and "To Think of Time" to the "Passage to India" group. We have already discussed the appearance of these spiritual poems in 1855 as an early indication of what Whitman hoped finally to accomplish. Though spiritual, the poems in their elements of sensuality and questioning are really closer to the early poems than they are to the later ones and would have actually been more at home among them than some of the relocated "Sea-Drift" poems. Nevertheless, they were germinal to these late poems and their concluding messages are certainly worthy of the final spirituality. Coming late, as they do in 1881, they stand as a sort of reminiscence of the early elements of *Leaves*, again drawing the two parts together and suggesting their interdependence. This is quite clear in "To Think of Time" where the act of spiritual triumph grows out of a reaffirmation of the reality and virtue of materials. These few deviations from the actual order of composition, then, either were necessary to accommodate the expansion of the germ of 1855 or were the result of expedient and comparatively minor adjustments counteracting the human variants and inadequacies inevitable in actual practice.

Whitman wanted *Leaves of Grass* to be organic; he wanted to "grow" it as nature grows things; believing in the "sanity" of nature, his teacher, he believed that there was a logic in her ways. Asselineau says that he allowed "his book to grow within his mind little by little with an organic and almost vegetable growth."[79] The striking correlation between the chronology of composition and the final arrangement of 1881 suggests that there *was* a *logic* of growth.

In concluding that *Leaves of Grass* itself is the final vindication of Whitman's organic theory of poetry, this study comes full circle. We began with a consideration of the way in which Whitman's concept of the poet-prophet grew out of his belief in the organic theory and his concept of the role of nature as teacher, which is central to his commitment to such a theory. Certainly one of the striking dimensions of his poetic vision is his exalted, mystical view of the poetic process itself, that process upon which he saw *Leaves of Grass* as a profound comment. As the oak tree unfolds out of the folds of the acorn, so Whitman's *Leaves* of 1881 unfolded out of the folds of 1855.

Whitman is not unlike Milton in his demonstration of faith and fortitude in preparing for and awaiting the ripening of powers sufficient to his poetic vision. His intentions were epic, and like Milton he felt within himself the potential which would with time and cultivation bring him "afoot with [his] vision." With genius comes obligation, the debt to be paid, the duty to be performed, and above all the lesson of preparation and patience:

> Immense have been the preparations for me,
> Faithful and friendly the arms that have help'd me.
>
> Cycles ferried my cradle, rowing and rowing like
>   cheerful boatmen,
> For room to me stars kept aside in their own rings,
> They sent influences to look after what was to hold me.
>
> Before I was born out of my mother generations
>   guided me,
> My embryo has never been torpid, nothing could
>   overlay it.

[79] Asselineau, *The Evolution of Walt Whitman: The Creation of a Personality*, p. 11.

For it the nebula cohered to an orb,
The long slow strata piled to rest it on,
Vast vegetables gave it sustenance,
Monstrous sauroids transported it in their mouths
    and deposited it with care.

All forces have been steadily employ'd to complete
    and delight me,
Now on this spot I stand with my robust soul.[80]

[80] "Song of Myself," I, 98–99.

APPENDIX

Passages of Religious Significance in Whitman's Works

Unless otherwise indicated all references are to *The Complete Writings of Walt Whitman,* edited by Richard Maurice Bucke, Thomas B. Harned, and Horace L. Traubel. More than one reference may occur on a given page.

ON CHRIST

Prose: This list includes only direct references to Christ (quotations, allusions, or expressions of Christ-like ideas not included).

IV, 68, 324; V, 77, 118, 136 n., 276; VI, 255, 262, 263, 267; VII, 112; VIII, 249; IX, 59, 63, 100, 104, 112, 122, 147, 149, 169, 211, 213, 214, 215; X, 17, 40, 51.

Emory Holloway, ed., *The Uncollected Poetry and Prose of Walt Whitman,* I, 40, 94, 221, 222; II, 17, 82, 83, 92.

Clifton Joseph Furness, ed., *Walt Whitman's Workshop,* pp. 41, 57.

Horace Traubel, ed., *An American Primer,* pp. 18–19.

Cleveland Rodgers and John Black, eds., *The Gathering of the Forces,* I, 67, 102, 113, 144, 173; II, 91, 92, 212, 215, 305.

Emory Holloway and Vernolian Schwartz, eds., *I Sit and Look Out,* pp. 60, 80.

Horace Traubel, *With Walt Whitman in Camden,* I, 98, 102–103; III, 192, 208, 257, 582; IV, 8, 9, 362–363, 480–481.

Leaves of Grass: This list includes not only direct references to Christ, but also allusions and expressions of the Christ-idea.

I, 16, 18, 21, 23, 25, 27, 28, 29, 32, 35, 37, 38, 41, 43, 44, 48, 52,

54, 55, 57, 58, 59, 60, 61, 62, 63, 66, 72, 78, 80, 81, 87, 88, 89,
90, 91, 94, 95, 96, 97, 98, 100, 101, 102, 103, 104, 105, 106,
107, 109, 134, 137, 138, 140, 141, 142, 144, 146, 147, 150, 151,
153, 154, 156, 157, 159, 160, 161, 162, 165, 168, 173, 175, 180,
181, 183, 184, 185, 187, 188, 189, 190, 193, 194, 195, 196, 197,
198, 200, 201, 202, 203, 204, 205, 221, 257, 259, 262, 267,
272, 275, 278, 285, 290; II, 13, 30, 35, 52, 71, 75, 88, 90, 109,
115, 116, 120, 121, 123, 143, 147, 149, 157, 159, 161, 165, 171,
191, 195, 196, 198–200, 223, 229, 231, 240, 289, 290.

On the Bible

Prose: The list includes only direct references to the word *Bible*, its
derivatives, and equivalents (Old and New Testaments, Hebrew
scripture, etc.).

III, 48, 55, 66; IV, 87, 212, 307, 323; V, 96 n., 105, 117, 118,
136 n., 141, 199 n., 224, 228, 238, 269, 276, 292; VI, 102, 104,
105, 107, 108, 109, 112, 113, 137, 222, 242, 243, 259 n., 260,
270, 274, 276, 284, 296; VII, 6, 23, 66, 112; IX, 6, 69, 70, 92,
96, 97, 98, 100, 105, 149, 169, 179, 185, 191, 210, 227; X, 9,
13, 16.

The Uncollected Poetry and Prose of Walt Whitman, Holloway, ed.,
I, 102, 103, 111, 127; II, 17, 61, 315.

Walt Whitman's Workshop, Furness, ed., pp. 67, 154.

An American Primer, Traubel, ed., p. 19.

The Gathering of the Forces, Rodgers and Black, eds., II, 269.

I Sit and Look Out, Holloway and Schwartz, eds., pp. 80–82.

With Walt Whitman in Camden, Traubel, I, 454; II, 314; III, 167,
470; IV, 86.

Leaves of Grass: This list includes only direct references to the word
Bible, its derivatives, and equivalents (Old and New Testaments,
Hebrew scripture, etc.).

I, 63, 95, 165, 262, 294; II, 187, 193, 240, 263.

On Religion

Prose: This list includes only direct references to the word *religion*
and its derivatives; passages which by implication are of religious
significance are not, of course, covered here.

III, 48, 52, 59; IV, 68, 185, 212, 213, 293, 294; V, 43, 44, 54,

56, 62, 63, 65, 66, 80, 91, 93, 95, 96, 99, 104, 105, 123, 125,
132, 134 n., 136 n., 140, 141, 149, 161, 188, 189, 190, 191,
194 n., 196, 201, 202, 225 n., 232, 293; VI, 105, 117, 151, 183,
205, 223, 228, 242, 257, 259 n., 260, 264, 268, 270, 271, 287;
VII, 6, 68, 69, 112; IX, 29, 40, 55, 70, 105, 115, 118, 135, 157,
168, 170, 173, 183, 184, 192, 193, 194, 207, 209, 211; X, 20,
49, 56.

The Uncollected Poetry and Prose of Walt Whitman, Holloway, ed.,
I, 39, 104, 134; II, 17, 84, 85.

Walt Whitman's Workshop, Furness, ed., pp. 39, 42, 44, 50, 128.

An American Primer, Traubel, ed., p. 26.

The Gathering of the Forces, Rodgers and Black, eds., pp. 294–295.

I Sit and Look Out, Holloway and Schwartz, eds., pp. 75–76, 77.

With Walt Whitman in Camden, Traubel, I, 10, 109, 163; II, 36–
37, 64, 563; IV, 220.

Leaves of Grass: This list includes only direct references to the
word *religion* and its derivatives; passages which by implication
are of religious significance are not, of course, covered here.
I, 21, 22, 23, 30, 53, 94, 117, 165, 181, 188, 205, 238, 262, 273,
274, 293; II, 118, 187, 192.

BIBLIOGRAPHY

BOOKS BY WHITMAN

Collected Writings (in Order of Publication)

Leaves of Grass. Brooklyn, New York, 1855.
————. Brooklyn, New York, 1856.
————. Boston, 1860.
————. New York, 1867.
————. Washington, D.C., 1872.
————. 2 vols. Camden, New Jersey, 1876.
————. Boston, 1881.
The Complete Writings of Walt Whitman. Edited by Richard Maurice Bucke, Thomas B. Harned, and Horace L. Traubel. 10 vols. New York: Knickerbocker Press, 1902.
Walt Whitman: Representative Selections. Edited by Floyd Stovall. New York: American Book Co., 1934.
The Complete Works of Walt Whitman. With an Introduction by Malcolm Cowley. 2 vols. New York: Pellegrini and Cudahy, 1948.
Leaves of Grass. Inclusive Edition. Edited by Emory Holloway. New York: Doubleday, 1948.
Walt Whitman's Poems. Edited by Gay Wilson Allen and Charles T. Davis. New York: New York University Press, 1955.

Uncollected Writings (in Order of Publication)

An American Primer. Edited by Horace Traubel. Boston: Small, Maynard, 1904.
The Letters of Anne Gilchrist and Walt Whitman. Edited by Thomas B. Harned. New York: Doubleday, Page, 1918.

The Gathering of the Forces. Edited by Cleveland Rodgers and John Black. New York and London: Putnam, 1920.

Walt Whitman's Workshop. Edited by C. J. Furness. Cambridge: Harvard University Press, 1928.

A Child's Reminiscence. Edited by Thomas O. Mabbott and Rollo G. Silver. Seattle: University of Washington Book Store, 1930.

I Sit and Look Out. Edited by Emory Holloway and Vernolian Schwartz. New York: Columbia University Press, 1932.

The Uncollected Poetry and Prose of Walt Whitman. Edited by Emory Holloway. New York: Peter Smith, 1932.

Walt Whitman and the Civil War. Edited by Charles I. Glicksberg. Philadelphia: University of Pennsylvania Press, 1933.

Walt Whitman's Backward Glances. Edited by Sculley Bradley and John A. Stevenson. Philadelphia: University of Pennsylvania Press, 1947.

Faint Clews and Indirections: Manuscripts of Walt Whitman and His Family. Edited by Clarence Gohdes and Rollo G. Silver. Durham: Duke University Press, 1949.

Walt Whitman of the New York Aurora. Edited by J. J. Rubin and C. H. Brown. State College, Pa.: The Bald Eagle Press, 1950.

Whitman's Manuscripts: Leaves of Grass (1860). Edited by Fredson Bowers. Chicago: University of Chicago Press, 1955.

Walt Whitman's Leaves of Grass: The First (1855) Edition. Edited by Malcolm Cowley. New York: Viking, 1959.

Walt Whitman: An 1855–56 Notebook. Toward the Second Edition of Leaves of Grass. Edited by H. W. Blodgett. Carbondale: Southern Illinois University Press, 1959.

Leaves of Grass: Facsimile of the 1860 Text. Edited by Roy Harvey Pearce. Ithaca: Cornell University Press, 1961.

Walt Whitman: The Correspondence. Edited by Edwin Haviland Miller. 2 vols. New York: New York University Press, 1961.

Walt Whitman: The Early Poems and the Fiction. Edited by Thomas L. Brasher. New York: New York University Press, 1963.

Walt Whitman: Prose Works 1892. Edited by Floyd Stovall. 2 vols. New York: New York University Press, 1963, 1964.

Works about Whitman
Books

Allen, Gay Wilson. *American Prosody.* New York: American Book Co., 1935.

————. *The Solitary Singer: A Critical Biography of Walt Whitman.* New York: Macmillan Co., 1955.

————. *Walt Whitman: Man, Poet, and Legend.* Carbondale: Southern Illinois University Press, 1961.

————. *Walt Whitman Handbook.* Chicago: Packard and Company, 1946.

Arvin, Newton. *Whitman.* New York: Macmillan Co., 1938.

Asselineau, Roger. *The Evolution of Walt Whitman: The Creation of a Book.* Cambridge: Harvard University Press, Belknap Press, 1962.

————. *The Evolution of Walt Whitman: The Creation of a Personality.* Cambridge: Harvard University Press, Belknap Press, 1960.

Bailey, John. *Walt Whitman.* London: Macmillan & Co., 1926.

Barrus, Clara. *Whitman and Burroughs: Comrades.* Boston: Houghton Mifflin, 1931.

Barton, William E. *Abraham Lincoln and Walt Whitman.* Indianapolis: Bobbs-Merrill, 1928.

Bazalgette, Leon. *Walt Whitman, the Man and His Work.* Translated by Ellen Fitzgerald. Garden City, N.Y.: Doubleday, 1920.

Binns, Henry Bryan. *A Life of Walt Whitman.* London: Methuen, 1905.

Blodgett, Harold. *Walt Whitman in England.* Ithaca: Cornell University Press, 1934.

Born, Helena. *Whitman's Ideal Democracy.* Boston: Everett Press, 1902.

Briggs, Arthur E. *Walt Whitman, Thinker and Artist.* New York: Philosophical Library, 1952.

Brooks, Van Wyck. *America's Coming of Age.* New York: B. W. Huebsch, 1915.

————. *The Times of Melville and Whitman.* New York: Dutton, 1947.

Bucke, Richard Maurice. *Walt Whitman.* Philadelphia: D. McKay, 1883.

Burroughs, John. *Notes on Walt Whitman, as Poet and Person.* New York, 1871.

————. *Whitman: A Study.* Boston, 1896.

Canby, Henry Seidel. *Walt Whitman: An American.* New York: Literary Classics, 1943.

Carlyle, Thomas. *The Works of Thomas Carlyle.* The Centenary Edition. 30 vols. New York: Scribner, 1896–1901.

Carpenter, Edward. *Days with Walt Whitman.* London: George Allen, 1904.

Carpenter, F. I., ed. *Ralph Waldo Emerson.* New York: American Book Co., 1934.

Carpenter, George Rice. *Walt Whitman: With Some Notes of His Life and Works.* New York: Macmillan Co., 1909.

Chapman, John Jay. *Emerson and Other Essays.* New York: Moffat, Yard, 1909.

Chase, Richard. *Walt Whitman Reconsidered.* New York: Sloane, 1955.

Clark, Leadie M. *Walt Whitman's Concept of the American Common Man.* New York: Philosophical Library, 1955.

Clarke, William. *Walt Whitman.* London, 1892.

Coleridge, Samuel Taylor. *The Literary Remains of Samuel Taylor Coleridge.* Edited by Henry Nelson Coleridge. 4 vols. London, 1836.

Coyle, William. *The Poet and the President.* New York: Odyssey Press, 1962.

Deutsch, Babette. *Walt Whitman, Builder for America.* New York: Julian Messner, 1941.

Donaldson, Thomas. *Walt Whitman the Man.* New York, 1896.

Dowden, Edward. *Studies in Literature: 1789–1877.* London, 1892.

Eby, Edwin H. *A Concordance of Walt Whitman's "Leaves of Grass" and Selected Prose Writings.* Seattle: University of Washington Press, 1949–1955.

Eliade, Mircea. *The Sacred and the Profane.* Translated by W. R. Trask. New York: Harcourt, Brace, 1959.

Elliott, Charles N. *Walt Whitman, as Man, Poet and Friend.* Boston: Badger, 1915.

Emerson, Ralph Waldo. *The Complete Works of Ralph Waldo Emerson.* The Centenary Edition. 12 vols. Boston, 1903–1904.

Faner, Robert D. *Walt Whitman and Opera.* Philadelphia: University of Pennsylvania Press, 1951.

Fausset, Hugh l'Anson. *Walt Whitman, Poet of Democracy.* New Haven: Yale University Press, 1942.

Foerster, Norman. *American Criticism*. Boston: Houghton Mifflin, 1928.

Frey, Ellen Frances. *Catalogue of the Whitman Collection in the Duke University Library . . . Trent Collection*. Durham: Duke University Library, 1945.

Guthrie, William Norman. *Modern Poet-Prophets*. Cincinnati, 1899.

Hayes, Will. *Walt Whitman: The Prophet of the New Era*. London: C. W. Daniel, 1921.

Higginson, Thomas Wentworth. *Contemporaries*. Boston and New York, 1899.

Hindus, Milton, ed. *Leaves of Grass One Hundred Years After*. Stanford: Stanford University Press, 1955.

Holloway, Emory. *Free and Lonesome Heart: The Secret of Walt Whitman*. New York: Vantage Press, 1960.

————. *Whitman: An Interpretation in Narrative*. New York: Knopf, 1924.

Kennedy, W. S. *The Fight of a Book for the World*. West Yarmouth, Mass.: Stonecroft Press, 1926.

————. *Reminiscences of Walt Whitman*. London, 1896.

Lawrence, D. H. *Studies in Classic American Literature*. New York: Boni, 1923.

Long, Haniel. *Walt Whitman and the Springs of Courage*. Santa Fe: Writer's Editions, 1938.

Masters, Edgar Lee. *Whitman*. New York: Scribner, 1937.

Mathews, Godfrey W. *Walt Whitman*. Liverpool: "Daily Post" Printers, Wood Street, 1921.

Matthiessen, F. O. *American Renaissance*. London: Oxford University Press, 1940.

Metzger, C. R. *Thoreau and Whitman: A Study in Their Esthetics*. Seattle: University of Washington Press, 1961.

Miller, James E., Jr. *A Critical Guide to "Leaves of Grass."* Chicago: University of Chicago Press, 1957.

————. *Walt Whitman*. New York: Twayne Publishers, 1962.

————, Karl Shapiro, and Bernice Slote. *Start with the Sun*. Lincoln: University of Nebraska Press, 1960.

More, Paul Elmer. *Shelburne Essays*. Fourth Series. New York and London: Putnam, 1907.

Mumford, L. Quincy, ed. *Walt Whitman: Man, Poet, Philosopher: Three Lectures*. Washington, D.C.: Library of Congress, 1955.

Mumford, Lewis. *The Golden Day*. New York: Liveright, 1926.

Murry, J. Middleton. *Unprofessional Essays*. London: Cape, 1956.

Myers, Henry A. *Tragedy: A View of Life*. Ithaca: Cornell University Press, 1956.

Noyes, Carleton. *An Approach to Walt Whitman*. Boston: Houghton Mifflin, 1910.

O'Connor, William Douglas. *The Good Gray Poet: A Vindication*. New York, 1866.

Parrington, Vernon Louis. *Main Currents in American Thought*. New York: Harcourt, Brace, 1927.

Pearce, Roy Harvey. *The Continuity of American Poetry*. Princeton: Princeton University Press, 1961.

Perry, Bliss. *Walt Whitman*. American Men of Letters Series. Boston and New York: Houghton Mifflin, 1906.

Poe, Edgar Allan. *The Complete Poems and Stories of Edgar Allan Poe with Selections from His Critical Writings*. Edited by Arthur Hobson Quinn and Edward H. O'Neill. 2 vols. New York: Knopf, 1946.

Rivers, W. C. *Walt Whitman's Anomaly*. London: George Allen, 1913.

Santayana, George. *Interpretations of Poetry and Religion*. London: Adam and Charles Black, 1900.

Sawyer, Roland D. *Walt Whitman: The Prophet-Poet*. Boston: Gorham Press, 1913.

Schyberg, Frederik. *Walt Whitman*. Translated by Evie Allison Allen. New York: Columbia University Press, 1951.

Selincourt, Basil de. *Walt Whitman: A Critical Study*. London: Martin Secker, 1914.

Shaw, George Bernard. *The Collected Works of Bernard Shaw*. The Ayot St. Lawrence Edition. 30 vols. London: Constable, 1930–1932.

Shephard, Esther. *Walt Whitman's Pose*. New York: Harcourt, Brace, 1936.

Spiller, Robert E. *Cycle of American Literature*. New York: Macmillan Co., 1955.

Stedman, Edmund D. *Poets of America*. Boston and New York, 1897.

Stevenson, Robert Louis. *The Essay on Walt Whitman by Robert Louis Stevenson—with a Little Journey to the Home of Whitman by Elbert Hubbard.* London: Roycroft 1900.

Stovall, Floyd. *American Idealism.* Norman: University of Oklahoma Press, 1943.

———, ed. *The Development of American Literary Criticism.* Chapel Hill: University of North Carolina Press, 1955.

Swinburne, Algernon Charles. *Under the Microscope.* London, 1872.

———. *William Blake.* London, 1868.

Symonds, John Addington. *Walt Whitman: A Study.* London, 1893.

Thomson, James. *Walt Whitman: The Man and the Poet.* London: Dobell, 1910.

Traubel, Horace. *With Walt Whitman in Camden.* First Volume, Boston: Small, Maynard, 1906; Second Volume, New York: Appleton, 1908; Third Volume, New York: Mitchell Kennerly, 1914; Fourth Volume, Philadelphia: University of Pennsylvania Press, 1953.

———, ed. *Camden's Compliment to Walt Whitman.* Philadelphia, 1889.

———, Richard Maurice Bucke, and Thomas B. Harned, eds. *In Re Walt Whitman.* Philadelphia, 1893.

Triggs, Oscar L. *Browning and Whitman: A Study in Democracy.* London, 1893.

Trowbridge, John Townsend. *My Own Story: With Recollections of Noted Persons.* Boston: Houghton Mifflin, 1903.

Wallace, J. W. *Walt Whitman and the World Crisis.* Manchester, England: The National Labor Press, 1920.

Willard, Charles B. *Whitman's American Fame.* Providence: Brown University, 1950.

Winwar, Frances. *American Giant: Walt Whitman and His Times.* New York: Harper, 1941.

Articles

Adams, Richard P. "Whitman: A Brief Revaluation." *Tulane Studies in English* 5 (1955), 111–149.

———. "Whitman's 'Lilacs' and the Traditional Pastoral Elegy." *PMLA* 72 (1957), 479–487.

Allen, Gay Wilson. "Biblical Echoes in Whitman's Works." *AL* 6 (November 1934), 302–315.

————. "Walt Whitman—Nationalist or Proletarian." *English Journal* 26 (January 1937), 48–52.

————. "Walt Whitman's 'Long Journey' Motif." *JEGP* 38 (January 1939), 76–95.

Amacher, R. E. "Walt Whitman's 'Passage to India.' " *Explicator* 9 (December 1950), Item 2.

Beatty, R. C. "Whitman's Political Thoughts." *South Atlantic Quarterly* 46 (January 1947), 72–83.

Beck, M. "Walt Whitman's Intuition of Reality." *Ethics* 53 (October 1942), 14–24.

Bradford, Gamaliel. "Portraits of American Authors: II. Walt Whitman." *Bookman* 42 (December 1915), 533–548.

Bradley, Sculley. "The Fundamental Metrical Principle in Whitman's Poetry." *AL* 10 (January 1939), 437–459.

————. "The Problem of a Variorum Edition of *Leaves of Grass*." *English Institute Annual, 1941*, pp. 129–157. New York: Columbia University Press, 1942.

Brown, Clarence A. "Walt Whitman and 'The New Poetry.' " *AL* 33 (March 1961), 33–45.

Campbell, Killis. "The Evolution of Whitman as Artist." *AL* 6 (November 1934), 254–263.

Carpenter, F. I. "Walt Whitman's Eidolon." *College English* 3 (March 1942), 534–545.

Coffman, S. K., Jr. "Form and Meaning in Whitman's 'Passage to India.' " *PMLA* 70 (June 1955), 337–349.

Cooke, Alice L. "A Note on Whitman's Symbolism in 'Song of Myself.' " *MLN* 65 (April 1950), 228–232.

Cowley, Malcolm. "Walt Whitman: The Miracle." *New Republic*, March 18, 1946, 385–388.

————. "Walt Whitman: The Philosopher." *New Republic*, September 29, 1947, 29–31.

————. "Walt Whitman: The Poet." *New Republic*, October 20, 1947, 27–30.

Daiches, David. "Walt Whitman As Innovator." In *The Young Rebel in American Literature*, ed. Carl Bode, pp. 25–48. London: Heinemann, 1959.

Erskine, John. "Note on Whitman's Prosody." *SP* 20 (July 1923), 336–344.

Falk, R. P. "Walt Whitman and German Thought." *JEGP* 40 (July 1941), 315–330.

Feinberg, Charles E. "A Whitman Collector Destroys a Whitman Myth." *Papers of the Bibliographical Society of America* 52 (1958), 73–92.

Glicksberg, C. I. "Walt Whitman in 1862." *AL* 6 (November 1934), 264–282.

Gohdes, Clarence. "A Note on Whitman's Use of the Bible as a Model." *MLQ* 2 (March 1941), 105–108.

———. "Whitman and Emerson." *Sewanee Review* 37 (January 1929), 79–93.

Griffith, C. "Sex and Death: The Significance of Whitman's Calamus Themes." *PQ* 39 (January 1960), 18–38.

Hayes, Will. "Birth of a Bible." *Texas Review* 8 (October 1922), 21–31.

Hollis, C. Carroll. "Names in 'Leaves of Grass.' " *Names* 5 (1957), 129–156.

———. "Whitman and the American Idiom." *Quarterly Journal of Speech* 43 (1957), 408–420.

Holloway, Emory. "Whitman as Critic of America." *SP* 20 (July 1923), 345–369.

———. "Whitman's Message for Today." *American Mercury* 62 (February 1946), 202–206.

Howard, Leon. "For a Critique of Whitman's Transcendentalism." *MLN* 47 (February 1932), 79–85.

Hume, R. A. "Walt Whitman and the Peace." *College English* 6 (March 1945), 313–319.

Jarrell, Randall. "Walt Whitman: He Had His Nerve." *Kenyon Review* 14 (Winter 1952), 63–71.

Jones, Joseph. "Whitman's 'When Lilacs Last in the Dooryard Bloom'd.' " *Explicator* 10 (April 1951), Item 42.

Krause, Sydney J. "Whitman, Music and 'Proud Music of the Storm.' " *PMLA* 72 (1957), 705–721.

Kuhn, John G. "Whitman's Artistry: 'Then Reproduce All in My Own Forms.' " *Walt Whitman Review* 8 (September 1962), 51–63.

Lewis, R. W. B. "The Danger of Innocence: Adam as Hero in American Literature." *Yale Review* 39 (1950), 473–490.

Lorch, Fred W. "Thoreau and the Organic Principle of Poetry." *PMLA* 53 (March 1938), 286–302.

Lovell, John, Jr. "Appreciating Whitman: 'Passage to India.'" *MLQ* 21 (June 1960), 131–141.

Lowell, Amy. "Walt Whitman and the New Poetry." *Yale Review* 16 (1926–1927), 502–519.

Mann, Klaus. "The Present Greatness of Walt Whitman." *Decision* 1 (April 1941), 14–30.

Marks, Alfred H. "Walt Whitman's Triadic Imagery." *AL* 23 (March 1951), 99–126.

Mathews, J. C. "Walt Whitman's Reading of Dante." *University of Texas Studies* no. 3926 (1939), 172–179.

Moore, J. B. "The Master of Whitman." *SP* 23 (January 1926), 77–89.

Myers, H. A. "Whitman's Conception of the Spiritual Democracy, 1855–56." *AL* 6 (November 1934), 239–253.

———. "Whitman's Consistency." *AL* 8 (November 1936), 243–257.

Newman, H. "Walt Whitman." *American Scholar* 2 (May 1933), 261–268.

Nuhn, Ferner. "'Leaves of Grass' Viewed as an Epic." *Arizona Quarterly* 7 (Winter 1951), 324–338.

O'Higgins, Harvey. "Alias Walt Whitman." *Harper's Magazine*, May 1929, 698–707.

Paine, Gregory. "The Literary Relations of Whitman and Carlyle, with Especial Reference to Their Contrasting Views of Democracy." *SP* 36 (July 1939), 550–563.

Pulos, C. E. "Whitman and Epictetus: The Stoical Element in *Leaves of Grass*." JEGP 55 (January 1956), 75–84.

Randel, William. "Walt Whitman and American Myths." *South Atlantic Quarterly* 59 (Winter 1960), 103–113.

Romig, Edna D. "The Paradox of Walt Whitman." *University of Colorado Studies* 15 (1926), 95–132.

Rountree, T. J. "Whitman's Indirect Expression and Its Application to 'Song of Myself.'" *PMLA* 73 (December 1958), 549–555.

Schumann, D. W. "Enumerative Style and Its Significance in Whitman, Rilke, and Werfel." *MLQ* 3 (1942), 171–204.

Scott, Fred Newton. "A Note on Walt Whitman's Prosody." *JEGP* 7 (April 1908), 134–153.

Shapiro, Karl. "The First White Aboriginal." *Walt Whitman Review* 5 (September 1959), 43–52.

Sixbey, G. L. " 'Chanting the Square Deific'—A Study in Whitman's Religion." *AL* 9 (May 1937), 171–195.

Smith, F. M. "Whitman's Debt to Carlyle's *Sartor Resartus*." *MLQ* 3 (March 1942), 51–65.

———. "Whitman's Poet-Prophet and Carlyle's Hero." *PMLA* 55 (December 1940), 1146–1164.

Stauffer, Ruth. "Walt Whitman's 'Passage to India.' " *Explicator* 10 (April 1951), Item 50.

Story, Irving C. "The Growth of *Leaves of Grass:* A Proposal for a Variorum Edition." *Pacific University Bulletin* 37 (February 1941), 1–11.

———. "The Structural Pattern of *Leaves of Grass*." *Pacific University Bulletin* 38 (January 1942), 1–12.

Stovall, Floyd. "Main Drifts in Whitman's Poetry." *AL* 4 (March 1932), 3–21.

———. "Walt Whitman: The Man and the Myth." *South Atlantic Quarterly* 54, no. 4 (October 1955), 538–551.

———. "Walt Whitman and the American Tradition." *Virginia Quarterly Review* 31 (1955), 540–557.

Strauch, C. F. "The Structure of Walt Whitman's 'Song of Myself.' " *English Journal* 27 (September 1938), 597–607.

Sutcliffe, Emerson Grant. "Emerson's Theory of Literary Expression." *University of Illinois Studies in Language and Literature* 8 (1923), 9–143.

Swayne, Mattie. "Structural Unity in *Leaves of Grass*." Ph.D. dissertation. The University of Texas, 1938.

———. "Whitman's Catalogue Rhetoric." *University of Texas Studies* no. 4126 (1941), 162–178.

Thorp, Willard. "Walt Whitman." In *Eight American Authors*, ed. Floyd Stovall, pp. 271–318. New York: Modern Language Association, 1956.

Tolles, F. B. "A Quaker Reaction to *Leaves of Grass*." *AL* 19 (May 1947), 170–171.

Ware, Lois. "Poetic Conventions in *Leaves of Grass*." *SP* 16 (January 1929), 47–57.

Weeks, Ruth Mary. "Phrasal Prosody." *English Journal* 10 (January 1921), 11–19.

Wiley, A. N. "Reiterative Devices in *Leaves of Grass.*" *AL* 1 (March 1929), 161–170.

Williams, M. L. "Whitman Today." *University of Kansas City Review* 14 (September 1948), 267–276.

INDEX